# William Wallace

– CHAMPION OF SCOTLAND –

# William Wallace

## – CHAMPION OF SCOTLAND –

*In all England there was not*
*As William Wallace so true a man*
*Whatever he did against their nation*
*They made him ample provokation*
*Nor to them sworn never was he*
*To Fellowship, faith or loyalty*
Andrew of Wyntoun (1419)

## Margaret Wallace

**GOBLINSHEAD**
MUSSELBURGH

# William Wallace
## – Champion of Scotland –

First Published 1999
© Margaret Bowbelski 1999

Published by GOBLINSHEAD
130B Inveresk Road
Musselburgh
EH21 7AY
Scotland
Tel: 0131 665 2894
Fax: 0131 653 6566
Email: goblinshead@sol.co.uk

British Library Cataloguing in Publication Data
A catalogue record for this book is available from the British Library.

ISBN 1 899874 19 4

Typeset by GOBLINSHEAD using Desktop Publishing
Typeset in Bembo

Dedicated to Mary MacDonald 1886-1985, Mill of Tore, Balnain, Glen Urquhart and my grandmother Margaret Wallace as both taught me to love Scotland; and my husband Roman who encouraged me to write this book.

# Contents

# Wallace's Scotland

Inverness

Urquhart Castle

Aberdeen •

SCOTLAND          Dunnottar •

• Glamis
• Dundee

Perth •          • St Andrews
Elcho • Cupar

Stirling • • Dunfermline
Gargunnock • • Falkirk
Paisley •          • Dunbar
• Elderslie  Torphichen • Edinburgh
Lamington •     • Lanark
Berwick ★ •
• Irvine     Borthwickwater • Hawick

Arran     • Ayr

ENGLAND
• Carlisle

★ although Berwick was an old Scottish
burgh it was finally taken by the English
in 1482 and has since been in England.

# Introduction

'In 1297 William Wallace lifted up his head'
*John of Fordun – Annals of Scotland*

In European history there are few patriotic leaders with more charisma and appeal than William Wallace. His chaplain and friend John Blair was reputed to have written a biography of Wallace but this has not survived. Later historians and story tellers, such as John of Fordun, Blind Harry and others, based their writings about Wallace on Blair's work and most of their narratives are available to present day historians.

Wallace was born around 1272 at Elderslie. In Victorian times when Wallace's life came under great scrutiny, Elderslie was assumed to be the parish on the outskirts of Glasgow. Now some historians believe that his birthplace was near the seaside town of Ayr in south-west Scotland. He was the second son of Sir Malcolm Wallace, a minor knight, and Margaret Crawford, daughter of Sir Reginald Crawford, the Sheriff of Ayr. There were three sons in the family and William's younger brother John was as determined a fighter against English domination as his famous brother.

The Wallace kinsmen owed their allegiance to James Stewart, the hereditary steward of the Kings of Scots. He was their liege lord and in return for their estates they gave him military support when he demanded it. Thus at the battle of Dunbar, the first battle of the Wars of Independence, the Wallace kinsmen answered the Stewart's call to fight against the English. In turn the Wallaces ordered their own followers to take up arms and follow them. This was the usual way to raise an army in medieval Europe. The earls of Scotland and England also kept their own private armies and the more powerful the earl, the more men-at-arms he supported – thus wielding greater influence in state affairs.

Medieval life was short, unpleasant and brutal. The church and religion played an important role in society. It offered sanctuary to the poor, sick and dying, and the promise of reconciliation and eternal life in Paradise. Second sons unable to inherit their fathers' estates were encouraged to dedicate their lives to God and an able man like William

Wallace could expect to progress through the church in the service of the king or an earl.

William Wallace is said to have been destined for a religious career. As a boy he attended the monastic schools at Paisley and Dundee and was conversant in both Latin and French. In early manhood he met and fell in love with Marion Braidfute, heiress of Lamington, but we know nothing of their romance and life together, although Blind Harry tells us that they had a daughter who grew to womanhood.

Scotland has been a most unfortunate nation in her choice of kings. Many died childless or while their heir was still a child. A king had to be a strong leader able to lead an army into battle. The lack of such a monarch left a country prey to its neighbours and internal strife from rival nobles. Wallace came to maturity when the Scottish King Alexander III died leaving an infant female – Margaret, Maid of Norway, his granddaughter – heir to the throne. The small queen died on her journey to Scotland from Norway and King Edward of England chose John Balliol to be the next Scottish king. While King Edward ranks among the greatest of English kings, King John was weak and ineffectual. To compound the problems between the two kingdoms, England was relatively wealthy, well organised with a population of about four million, while Scotland was a rougher country, mountainous in places and covered by thick forest, with an inhospitable climate and a scattered population of about one million.

The most important burgh in Scotland was Berwick, which traded with the Hanseatic League ports. Wool, hides and furs were exported, iron ore and metal goods imported. The sack of Berwick by the English in 1296 lasted three days and some historians have estimated the Scottish dead – men, women and children – at about thirty thousand. Berwick changed hands many times during the next two hundred years but today stands on the English side of the border.

Wallace had a rare character. He was incorruptible, able and resolute, fighting for love of his country and remaining firm when lesser men took the easy path. He turned his back on power and privilege when the temptation to acquire them must have been great.

Blind Harry in his epic poem *The Wallace* describes Marion's murder by the English Sheriff of Lanark. It is after her death that the historical chronicles of England and Scotland frequently mention Wallace's exploits at Stirling, his command of the Scottish 'Peoples' Army', and his governorship as Guardian of Scotland. He gave up the Guardianship of Scotland after his defeat at the Battle of Falkirk because of his love for th Scottish nation. He said that he would rather suffer with them than be the cause of their suffering.

In any age men like William Wallace make enemies and his greatest adversary was Edward, King of England. Edward was a great war leader and an experienced and cunning ruler who knew men's weaknesses. He commanded an English army of veterans from his numerous campaigns in France and the Low Countries. Once Edward succeeded in isolating Wallace, he pursued him relentlessly. If Wallace had been a great earl perhaps the King might have forgiven him, as Edward was not an unreasonable and cruel man for the times in which he lived. What he could not tolerate was defiance and incorruptibility from a man of more humble origins.

The English chronicles say that Wallace was betrayed by a man called Short in the summer of 1305. His journey to London took three weeks and he was tried and executed the day after his arrival. His execution was the most barbaric which medieval minds could devise. He was hanged, cut down while still alive and his genitals were cut off. He was then disembowelled and finally his torment ended by the headsman's axe.

Edward thought that Wallace's execution would end all Scottish resistance leaving him master of Scotland. He was wrong. Within six months of Wallace's death Robert the Bruce, Earl of Carrick, was proclaimed King of Scots and began his long war against England. This culminated in his famous victory at Bannockburn in 1314, which assured Scottish independence – ending three hundred years later with the Union of Scotland and England under the Stewart King James.

# William Wallace

– CHAMPION OF SCOTLAND –

# Champion
# of Scotland

Wallace retreated into the Methven woods, but this time the avenging English were able to follow his trail. They prepared themselves to hunt down the murderers and flush them out, but in the heavily wooded country they were forced to fight on foot. The Scots skirmished and fled so that the English were never sure when to expect the next strike, but during one melee Wallace received an unlucky wound. An arrow grazed his neck just below his chin. It did not find any vital organ, but the wound became increasingly painful. Many of his men fell. They were good men who had fought with him at Dunbar. To save those who remained he gave the order to scatter. That way they stood a chance. Before continuing on their way Wallace spoke to his brother, "John, if I don't return, look after Marion and the babes. She'll need a brother's care." Under cover of darkness each went their own way.

As dawn broke Wallace reached the ford by the river Earn. He smelt wood smoke and in the early light could see the English camped near the water's edge, barring his way. Their horses were tethered close by in the shelter of a large oak. "Well, you buggers. It'll take more than you to stop me," he murmured.

Crouching low and seeking cover wherever he could behind gorse or rock, he made his way to the tethered animals. He had already mounted one and released others before the English became aware of him. He dug his heels into the beast's flanks and headed for the ford. They tried to lunge for his reins, but Wallace slashed to left and right. He heard the deadly song of an arrow but it passed him by harmlessly. As he reached the river bank, a young knight rushed towards him, sword in his hand.

Wallace reined in his horse and struck the man a blow across his neck with such force that he severed head from body. The head spun into the river bumping and banging from rock to rock as Wallace fled across the ford pursued by his enemies. At Blackford his horse stumbled and fell. Wallace regained his feet but found the animal had broken its front leg.

"You'll not rise again laddie". He patted the great beast. It had carried him safely for many miles and he had no wish to leave it to the wolves. Drawing his dagger he cut the animal's throat then turned to continue on foot. He kept to a south-westerly route, dog tired, wet and cold. He had strips of dried meat in his pouch and he chewed these, but the wound in his neck was painful and he found swallowing difficult. He came to a small stream and tried to drink a little. The water was icy cold and he began to shiver uncontrollably. It was growing dark and he climbed into the shelter of some rocks, pulled his cloak around him and tried to sleep, his claymore ready by his side. It was dark when he awoke, stirred by the sound of braying hounds in the distance. In spite of the darkness he arose and continued his journey towards the Forth, but the baying from the hounds grew nearer and nearer.

In the early dawn he looked down at the Forth winding its way towards the sea. He was very wet and tired. His boots squelched with every step and his body ached from fever. He allowed himself to rest for a few moments on a fallen tree, looking across at the opposite bank that offered safety: he must make a final effort. The hounds were close and he could hear men's voices as they called to each other. The Forth was deep and wide at this point, icy cold from the winter's snows and he shuddered as he waded out from the bank. He had tied his sword, battleaxe and boots into his cloak which he strapped to his back. His chain mail he flung into the swirling waters where the English hounds could not find it. He gritted his teeth, each stroke an agony in the strong current as he reached out for freedom.

# The Wallace Kindred

The birth pains had begun early even before the strutting cockerel had proclaimed ownership of the new day. Neighbours' wives had been sent for so they could help the mother at her lying in, and the hall was bustling with women. The cradle and swaddling clothes were airing by the fire, water steamed in a cauldron and the good women could be heard encouraging the mother, as women do at such times. This would be a big child and it would take its time coming. The birthing chamber was no place for men and Sir Malcolm Wallace had been chased out into the morning mist with the promise of a fine spring day to come. There was new life everywhere.

Sir Malcolm could hear his two draught oxen moving restlessly in their stall. He walked over to them and rubbed their soft pink nostrils, speaking quietly to both. He must find something to do. The business of giving birth always disturbed him. It was so uncertain, so precarious. Still, she was in good hands. They were sensible women, well known for their midwifery skills and knowledge of ointments and potions.

His eldest son, named after him, trotted out into the yard. He saw his father and ran towards him holding out his arms to be picked up. The big man swung the boy onto his shoulders, "Well Malcolm, while your mother is busy you and I will ride." The boy always enjoyed riding with his father and half an hour later Sir Malcolm rode up the track leading from the manor to the forest, his son sitting in front of him, and two great deer hounds trotting behind.

Margaret Wallace lay back on the bolster with her new son at her breast. The women had already cleaned and wrapped him tightly in the bands of linen. The mother had been given a good bowl of broth and now lay gazing at the small red face. She kissed the soft downy cheek. He was a large healthy boy who had cried lustily at birth. The women laughed and nodded their heads.

"This one will doubtless be a fine soldier. He's a lusty fellow. Why, he's already trying to break loose from his clothes." The baby was wrestling with the tight bands that held him and, finding it impossible to break free, began to cry heartily.

The sound of hooves on the cobbles outside announced the return of the father, and Mistress Jean Haliday went outside to tell him that his wife's labour was over and that he had another fine and healthy son.

The two Malcolms, father and son, came into the hall to greet the new arrival. When the small boy caught sight of the white bundle with the tiny red face peering out, he gave a howl of rage and tried to jump onto his mother. The warmth of her body had so recently been his. Who was this interloper in his place? Jean Haliday laughed and taking him by the hand led him out into the yard and across to his mother's big storeroom. He loved this room. It smelled of the cheeses and smoked meats, which she prepared during the summer and autumn. She was well known throughout the region for her housewifery skills. No one ever went hungry under her roof. Mistress Haliday took a large wooden spoon and dipped it into a jar containing the last of the year's honey and gave it to the boy. Malcolm began to suck at the sweet sticky mess, forgetting for a time the intruder in his mother's arms. "Well, well, Malcolm, you have a playmate now," but the boy had wandered out into the yard having heard Tom's voice. He liked Tom.

Malcolm Wallace looked down at his wife and son. She was pale. Her blue eyes were heavy with fatigue, and her thick chestnut hair had been braided and a plait lay over each breast. "What do you say to naming him William, Meg?" Margaret Wallace smiled up at her husband. "It's a good strong name, as good as any." The recipient of the good, strong name had ceased to cry and now slept peacefully. Malcolm kissed his wife's broad white forehead, told her to rest and went out into the yard. The sun was beginning to climb high. It was a wonderful day, a good omen for the birth of his son.

His man, Tom Johnston, was whittling a small whistle for young Malcolm. He was a man in his middle years, big and dark. He finished the toy and blew through it. Young Malcolm clambered up onto his knees and squealed with delight at the high pitched noise. Sir Malcolm said, "Come Tom, we'll go to the mill to see how the work is progressing." The small boy was handed over to the women. He was happy with his whistle, and the two men took the path leading through the woods. The sun filtered through the young leaves, and wood violets lifted their soft blue faces to its golden rays. It was the kind of morning when even the hardest man felt relaxed and cheerful.

Malcolm Wallace was not a hard man. He was known for shrewd and thrifty management of his estates and his skill with the bow. A quiet man, it was not always easy to judge his thoughts. Those who owed him service agreed that he was a fair man, slow to anger, but one who did not bear fools and rogues with a glad heart.

The affair of Jack Short, the miller, had been discussed the whole winter by bondsmen, tenants and cotters alike. Jack Short had been the miller at Lower Elderslie for two years. Everyone knew he gave short weight and was mean in small petty things, regularly taking more than was his due for milling oats and rye. When he took advantage of the widow who lived with her drooling simple son, returning to her oats with so much grit and dust swept from the mill floor that the poor woman wondered how they would survive through the winter, then there were mutterings. Someone, nobody knew who, complained to Sir Malcolm.

Matilda, the widow, was surprised when her boy came running to her as she picked her last crop of beans. He was laughing and pointing down the track, and spittle was dribbling out of his mouth. He had never learnt how to speak making only grunting noises; like an old sow rooting for acorns, one of the village lads had said. Plainly something had excited him. Matilda rubbed her grimy hands on her coarse dress and hastened to meet her visitor whoever he was.

When she rounded the corner of her small cot there was Sir Malcolm Wallace greeting her and asking about her crops, beasts and the gleaning. Then he began to question her closely about the oats she had taken to the mill. She showed him her meal bin in which the dirty, gritty stuff was stored and he ran his fingers through it. Certainly there was little doubt that it was the sweepings that the poor woman had. "Why did you accept such stuff, Matilda?" "Ah well, Sir, he said it was my oats which were poor and if I did not take this he would give me nothing. How could I feed us, Sir, with the bad weather yet to come and no man to protect us?" Sir Malcolm said little but as she watched him ride away she felt almost happy, an emotion she had not felt since she was a child.

The miller was down by the river when Sir Malcolm arrived. He kept a net stretched near a large pool and was busy rearranging it. On the bank lay two good-sized trout. "Good day to you miller." Short had seen him coming and was already pulling himself onto the river bank. Without bothering with any further civilities, Sir Malcolm asked why the widow Matilda had been given floor sweepings instead of her rightful measure. Short reddened, but confidently said, "Sir, I gave her what was hers. If she tells you any other she lies." "I have heard what others say of you; if anyone lies, you do. This is not the first time you have given short measure, nor the first time you have lied to me."

Short looked up at his lord, saw his anger and knew he had gone too far. A crafty look came over his face, "Sir, it was a mistake. I remember now I had swept the floor and put the rubbish into a sack, but was so busy on that day that I gave the widow the wrong one. I will show you, I have her sack in the mill ready to give to her when next I pass that way."

Such a yarn would have appeased many lords. Why should they concern themselves with a widow and her daft son? Sir Malcolm, however, was a just man and stared coldly at his tenant, saying, "The rent is due; you will leave my land and I shall find myself an honest miller." The man's face flushed with horror, then anger. "Sir Malcolm, I have a wife and family." "You should have considered them before you played the robber to Matilda. You have the week to leave my estate." Without waiting for any further excuses, Sir Malcolm turned his horse and rode back to his manor.

By the following day Sir Malcolm's followers and tenants had heard about the eviction of Jack Short. Everyone agreed that it was a good riddance: no one had a good word to say for the man. All had suffered from his meanness and petty nature. It was sad for the family, but then it was always the family who suffered. When they were observed with bag and baggage heading east, no tears were shed.

The evening was cold with the first frost and all sensible people stayed by their fires, but John the Smith was out with his old furrowing sow and, as he told the Lord Stewart later, "The ol' girl was making heavy weather of it." His wife, Annie, came out to see how things were progressing, and it was she who saw the red glow from the fire. They could see the flames begin to leap, and the smell of burning was plain, even above the smell from their own fire.

John ran down the path leading to the mill, while his wife went back into the cottage to rally her eldest son. "Go quickly to Sir Malcolm and tell him that the mill is burning."

Her husband had reached the small stone bridge. The flames had a strong hold now and the thatch on the mill and the cottage were burning fiercely. There was little he could do by himself. There would be hungry families in and around Elderslie this winter for much of the oat, barley and rye harvest was in the burning mill. Jack Short had been working on it when he had been evicted. As he watched, he became aware of a movement in the shadows near some bushes. He ran towards the shrubs, but found nothing and turned back towards the fire. As the cottage roof collapsed inwards sending a shower of sparks high into the dark night sky, John the Smith, struck from behind, fell onto the cold earth.

Jack Short's wife, Elspeth, had found out early in her marriage that her husband had a mean and violent nature. She suffered blows from his fist or belt since her father had first given her to him. His violence had brought on two miscarriages, and the second of her two sons was sickly and deformed, a victim of his father's violence. Sometimes she wondered how the boy had survived such abuse. He was six years old now, pale and silent, and walking with a limp. His left leg was shorter than the other. It had been broken two winters before when his father, annoyed because the child had not moved out of his way quickly enough, had thrown him down the steps of the mill. It had taken a long time to mend, and remained shorter than the other, making the boy lame.

After Sir Malcolm told them to leave Elspeth had expected him to turn on her and the children, but he remained silent and morose. Hesitatingly she suggested that she should go to Sir Malcolm and beg him to allow them to stay, for he was known for his forbearance and kindness to the old, the sick, and to women and children. At the suggestion her husband had flared up and threatened all kinds of punishments. He knew which ones hurt and upset her the most. He leered at her and made one of his obscene gestures. Elspeth began to pack their belongings. Sir Malcolm had given them seven days to depart, but Short insisted they leave the following day, although the weather was cold. Nobody came to wish them a safe journey or offered them a small keepsake.

He had loaded the wagon with their belongings, had whipped the oxen into a lumbering pace and by midday they were well on their way, leaving the estate some miles behind. Elspeth had no idea where they were going and was surprised when he stopped the wagon and told her to light a fire. They would stop for the night. She sent the children to search for firewood and began organising shelter for her family in the lee of a rocky outcrop. Her cauldron was carefully wedged in a corner of the wagon so that it could not turn over. Helped by her eldest boy Jack, she put it onto the fire. It contained the remains of a good hare stew and the smell of the warming food soon drifted on the still air.

The miller finished eating. Wiping up the last of the gravy with a piece of bread, he gave a loud belch and strolled off: no doubt to relieve himself. He returned shortly, settled in a sheltered crevice between the rocks, and fell asleep. The woman tidied away the cooking pot, checked the grazing oxen, told the boys to play away from their sleeping father, and sat down to enjoy the welcome rest.

The only sounds came from a calling curlew, the oxen cropping the grass, and soft snores from her sleeping man. In the late afternoon Short woke up, quenched his thirst from the small barrel of ale and told his wife to wait. He would be back later, he said, as he had some work to do.

He made his way back to Elderslie Mill by a roundabout route, anxious to keep hidden from the prying eyes of his former neighbours. He arrived just after darkness had fallen, collected kindling from his wife's store and, stacking it against the dry inner walls of the cottage and the mill, started a fire. He stood, watching with satisfaction. The wattle and thatch of the cottage were well alight before he turned, intending to leave. Then in the glow from the fire he saw John the Smith running down the track.

Short had hit the smith with a rock, but not killed him. He stood for a few moments, then made up his mind and knelt down beside his victim, raising the stone in both hands. He was about to bring it down again when he heard Annie calling her husband's name, as she came towards the mill.

They saw each other at the same time. The man rose to his feet and the woman screamed, turned and began running back up the track. The race was a one-sided affair. Annie Smith was still young, but in poor health and very fat as a result of eight pregnancies in as many years. He caught up with her and brought the rock down onto her head. As she fell, he pounded her skull again.

He turned back to the inferno, intending to finish off the smith and return to his family. The cottage was a heap of red and orange cinders and burning beams. The mill, a substantial building of stone and good oak beams, was proving more resilient to the consuming fire. The thatched roof had already fallen inwards. The great oaken wheel was hissing and steaming like an angry serpent, the flames flickering around it. Short noted with satisfaction that the store was burning well. Good, he thought, let them starve.

John the Smith still lay where he had fallen. Short crept back to the Smith, stone raised above his head, as two horsemen, led by Sir Malcolm, came down the path from the manor. The flames lit up the scene and Sir Malcolm could have been in no doubt how the fire had started. He gave a shout then cut off the miller's escape into the darkness of the trees. Jack Short put up a ferocious struggle, but was pinned to the ground by Tom and Sir Malcolm.

The smith began to recover. His head was sore, and he started looking around for his attacker. His anger and indignation were as nothing compared to the grief and blind fury which descended on him when a cry of anguish was heard from the track to his smithy. His eldest daughter had ventured out in search of her mother and had stumbled on her body. John fell on the miller beating him with his fists. Wallace and his men pulled him off. "Save him for the rope," they said. The smith ran up the path to his wife's sprawling body, and cradled her head, sticky with blood, in his big arms.

The following morning Short appeared before the Lord Stewart, Sir Malcolm's lord. Twelve of his fellows found him guilty of murder and firing the property of Sir Malcolm Wallace. Nobody came forward to speak on his behalf, and he was sentenced to hang – the sentence was to be carried out immediately.

Elspeth, worried when Short did not return, harnessed the oxen and returned to Elderslie, the two boys riding happily on top of the baggage. Their father had always made them walk. When she found her former home a heap of smouldering ashes and charred beams, Elspeth turned the oxen towards Sir Malcolm's manor.

It was from Lady Margaret that she heard the news of the previous night's events and her husband's arrest. Sir Malcolm had not yet returned, and although there was little doubt in everyone's mind what the outcome would be, no one wanted to be the one to tell. The poor woman – not quite yet a widow – took her boys into a corner of the yard and sat there patiently awaiting Sir Malcolm's return. When he returned at dusk, he saw the family huddled in a corner, and beckoned them to approach.

The whole community knew that the miller was a cruel husband and father. Many had seen Elspeth's bruises, and it was Lady Margaret who had tried to set the boy's leg after his father had injured him. Nevertheless, a bad husband is better than no husband at all. Who would provide for the woman and her children? Elspeth was not a local woman and had no family with whom she could live. Wallace turned to Tom Johnston, "Tell the woman she can live by the widow

Matilda. In the morning get some of the men to build her a cot and byre, and she may glean my fields in due time. In the meantime find a place for her and her family to sleep."

It was a bad business all round. He didn't want her and her brood on his land. There would be bad blood between her and the kindred of the murdered woman as they grew older, but what could he do with the autumn already on them?

As the winter had drawn to a close Tom, on Sir Malcolm's orders, had arranged for the rebuilding of the mill and its house. The work was almost complete and a new tenant had been found: the brother-in-law of John the Smith.

I t was on a beautiful day in spring, the day of William Wallace's birth, that his father surveyed the mill. It looked good and solid. The new man was covering the wall of his house with a mixture of mud, dung and straw. It would dry well in the warm sun. He saw his lord watching and pulled off his cap.

Malcolm Wallace was right. The bad blood between the families did continue. The boy, Jack Short, inherited his father's violent and mean nature. He was not cowed by the knowledge that his father had been an arsonist and murderer. Yet he did not have the courage to fight the eldest son of the smith. Instead he contented himself with pelting their bullock with stones, and when he saw their sow and her piglets rooting in the woods unattended, managed to kill three of the piglets with his catapult and ran off with one of them. That night they ate well.

By the time he was eleven he was a bully who terrorised his younger brother, his mother, Matilda and her daft son. Lady Margaret spoke to her husband about finding the lad a suitable place away from their tenants. Now that he was so big, their responsibility for his welfare could be passed to another. He was no asset to the estate and perhaps some other lord or bondsman could make something of him. Her husband considered the youth only fit to be a man-at-arms. He was lazy and not suited to the mundane work of an estate. He promised he would speak with Lord James Stewart.

The following autumn Jack Short left to serve as a man-at-arms in Sir James' following. Even his mother and brother were pleased to see him go, but none as pleased as poor Jamie, Matilda's daft son.

When William was in his second winter, neighbours' wives were sent for once again. The new brother, called John, was not quite as big and vigorous as William, but nonetheless a tough, determined little boy who followed his elder brothers about the estate with devotion. After his birth Margaret Wallace did not recover her strength as quickly as she might. She remained in her bed with fever and was unable to attend her churching six weeks after the baby's birth as was the custom.

The Lady Gelis Stewart came herself to visit her and to give advice. She brought with her nourishing broth and a flagon of good French wine. She also left a potion which, she assured the patient, would help to break the fever. "My dear, it was given to me at Court by the personal physician to the Queen," she boasted. "He was an Englishman, my dear." Lady Gelis was fond of saying 'my dear' to people of lower rank than herself. "He learnt his skills at the French Court and assisted Her Majesty at all her deliveries. Warm the wine and put two pinches of the powder into it."

Lady Margaret gradually recovered her strength but the confinement left her sterile, and she had pain from time to time in her lower abdomen. Her three boys were strong, healthy fellows but she would have liked a little maid. Girls stayed close to their mother, but her strapping boys went out in the early morning and came back in the evening dirty, tired and hungry. They spent much of their time with Tom and the other men learning how to ride, to shoot an arrow straight and true, and to fish and hunt. They learnt the skills of men.

Malcolm, her eldest boy, was quieter than the other two lads and as he grew older he went out with his father. He had to learn how to run the estate as one day it would be his. Accompanied by his father, he would often visit Lord Stewart's castle and listen to the judgements. William and John, free from the responsibilities which fell on their older brother, remained with the estate workers and tenants, learning the skills and opinions of the ruled. Tom Johnston was a keen and skilled archer who found – like all who were to play an important role in moulding William's character – that he was quick and eager to learn. Together they hunted in the forest with the hounds at their heels.

Gilbert the miller, the new tenant, fished the river whenever he was free and William and John often went with him and his own sons to learn how to catch trout, but more than simply fishing William learnt patience.

This was the other side to William's nature. The energetic inquisitive boy was adept at book learning and had been taught to read and write by his mother. She was born Margaret Crawford, daughter to the Sheriff of Ayr, and had been taught her letters by her father's chaplain. Elderslie had a small church and the priest combined his parish duties with chaplaincy to the Wallace family. Elderslie was not an important estate, and the priest, Kenneth MacBain, was not a man of great learning or from an important family, but he was pleased to serve Sir Malcolm. He could fish and take life quietly which suited him well. From time to time he was called to assist Lady Margaret with the boys, teaching them writing and a little Latin.

Kenneth MacBain was from the north. His first tongue was Gaelic which he spoke whenever he could. Lady Margaret's serving woman Alice came from the north, and when the priest was at the manor the pair chatted in their own tongue. Alice had been with the family for many years and had helped to rear the boys. It was natural that she should speak to them in her mother tongue, and they learnt some Gaelic and its soft lilting songs and stories.

At the feast of Christmas, when William was eight winters old, his great uncle, brother to grandfather Wallace, visited them. To the young William, Uncle William appeared a giant. He was a head taller than father, with huge hands, bright blue eyes, grizzly brown hair and beard. He arrived with his two henchmen who, like himself, were of advanced years and tough appearance. They had seen many campaigns together, and the man they called Murdo had a livid scar stretching from his forehead down across his left cheek to the jaw. The wound had taken his eye, and the eyelid had puckered and closed over the empty socket. It fascinated William and his brothers.

Uncle William – who William had been named after – wore his old campaigning claymore. It was a long double-handed weapon, which the boys could not lift from the ground. The hilt was gilded and engraved with a dragon, whose glaring eye was a red stone that winked and blinked in the glow from the fire. The blade was carved with strange runic signs, and Uncle William called the weapon 'Vengeance'. At his belt on his right side swung a battleaxe and a dagger. William stared at both with an open mouth.

They had arrived the week before the Christmas feast. The winter had come early and the ground was hard with frost. Heavy snow clouds were building up from the north. As the short winter day came to an end, Uncle William rode up on his old chestnut warhorse. His red woollen cloak, held in place by a round silver brooch, enveloped the old knight and was spread over the animal's back and flanks. His two men rode small shaggy nags behind him. The three boys came out into the courtyard to greet their kinsman. As his great uncle reined in his noble mount, the young William, standing beside his father, was overcome with adoration.

It began to snow heavily, lying in drifts high against the walls of the manor. The weather remained cold with fresh falls of snow throughout the feast of Christmas. The Yule log had been dragged in, and the family sat and told stories. Margaret Wallace sang some of the old songs, and the priest and Alice sang Gaelic love songs from the north about brave and beautiful princesses and Viking warriors. Kenneth would accompany them on the harp. These gatherings were gay affairs. The long table and benches were moved, and William enjoyed watching the men dance wild circling dances with mock sword fights, fierce shouting and much stamping of feet.

Margaret Wallace and her women had decorated the great hall before the guests arrived. A wall tapestry depicting the four seasons, worked in fine wools by her mother, had been hung on the wall behind the great chair in which her husband normally sat, but now out of respect, had been offered to great uncle William. Brightly woven cushions were placed on the benches and a wolf skin lay in front of the great fireplace. She had ordered the floor to be swept clean and sweet smelling herbs had been strewn over it.

On the festival of Christ's birthday, the family and their followers walked to the small church with their bondsmen, tenants and villagers to celebrate His coming. After mass, they all returned to the manor to enjoy Sir Malcolm's hospitality. Boar, venison and capercailzie were roasting in the yard to be served with freshly baked bread, cheese, and the small honey cakes for which Lady Wallace was justly famous. She also brewed her best ale and fine mead. Everyone, from Uncle William to Matilda and her daft son, enjoyed the goodwill and festivities of the season.

On the third day of Christmas, young William was standing by the bench, near the oak door, looking at his great uncle's claymore, Vengeance, which hung on a hook just above his head. Uncle William came out from the solar where Lady Margaret was busy with her needlework. "Well lad, what do you think of my friend?" "It's a grand sword, sir. Is it true that it once belonged to a Norwegian king? Murdo says so." His uncle took the weapon from its hook and sat on the bench by the fire, with the sword resting on his knees. He turned it lovingly in his hands, and its evil red eye blinked in the glow of the fire. "It's been a good sword to me, lad, but hasn't always belonged to me."

By this time John had come over from the corner, where he had been carving a small piece of wood, and Malcolm, who had been grooming his pony, came in. All three boys stood in a crescent at their uncle's knees, gazing at the magnificent weapon. "Tell us how you came by such a wonderful sword, uncle." "God bless you, William. We'll make a soldier of you yet," laughed his great uncle. "Well, when I was young I served our Lord Stewart and the king." He scratched his beard. "Our lord followed the great King Alexander, father to our present king, on his first campaign to the Western Isles, Lorn and Argyll. It was in the spring, yes, a glorious spring in 1249. The king tried to speak reasonably and sensibly to the Norwegians. He even offered to buy from them what was rightfully ours, but to no avail, and the only course left to him was to take up the sword. We, Murdo and John were with me even then," he looked over to his two men sitting on the long bench by the wall. "We were ordered to take the area of the Firth of Lorn. We marched at dawn into that wild and remote area and met no resistance. Homesteads were deserted and we camped early with a fast deep river guarding our backs. Naturally we set watches and our pack animals were well tethered."

"They came at dawn," Uncle William's voice had taken on a conspiratorial tone, and the hall was now hushed. The only noise came from the fire and the soft snoring of the old wolfhound lying in front of it. "They were not a large group, but they took us by surprise, always dangerous. It's the element of surprise, lads. Catch the enemy when he is badly prepared. In the early light it was difficult to distinguish friend from foe. They tried to stampede the horses and they came with loud shouts. 'Vengeance', 'Blood,' 'Raven', they yelled their battle cries. I saw a huge warrior strike down Murdo, who was trying to defend the pack animals. I went after him. It was a difficult fight as he wielded this huge fellow," he tapped the sword on his knees.

"We fought by the river and he stood with his back to the flood, yet each time I cut at him he caught my weapon on his shield then hacked at me. When you are fighting hard lads, you cannot see how the battle fares around you, you just fight until your opponent lies at your feet or you sink to the ground yourself. War is a hard mistress. You must watch your enemy all the time and never lower your guard."

"My Viking forgot the rules of war. A shout went up from his leader. For a second he took his eyes from me and I seized my chance. I caught him on the neck. He staggered back and fell into the fast flowing current. The river was swollen from the spring rains. His wound was mortal and his armour heavy. I turned to defend my back from attack, but as I turned this sword was thrown with his last strength and landed point down in the turf. The battle was going our way and the enemy was withdrawing. Naturally I went after them, but when we had seen off the last, I went back to the sword and claimed it as a trophy. It served me well and has sent many brave fellows to join Our Maker."

The boys' faces shone with admiration at the old warrior's tale. William turned and gazed at Murdo and his empty eye socket, then back at his great uncle. "Uncle, why do you call the sword Vengeance?" William asked.

"God bless you, boy. A prisoner told me that these runes on the blade say: I am the vengeance of Erland Son of Arne." Lady Margaret entered from the solar and stood watching her boys. They looked so eager. They would have to decide on the future for William and John shortly. "When I am grown, I should like to own such a sword," said William.

Uncle William laughed. He enjoyed the admiration of his nephews. He had married a woman from the border country, late in life, but she had died in childbirth along with their child. William Wallace, with his two henchmen Murdo and John, had continued to live quietly on the estate near Borthwick Water which he had inherited from her. It was a remote manor in the forest of Selkirk, but Uncle Wallace appeared to live well and had a large flock of sheep whose wool he sold to a Flemish merchant in Berwick.

The following day was bright and crisp. Murdo, John and Tom, followed closely by the boys, went into the forest to hunt. In the open, the snow lay in deep drifts and sparkled in the weak sunshine, but once among the trees it was possible to walk along the forest paths. Murdo glared at the three lads as they entered the cover. "You'll be quiet if you want to catch a beast. Any prattle will carry in the silence of the wood. You'll feel my hand if you don't heed me." "Aye, Murdo," they answered in unison.

He was a fearsome sight with his one bloodshot eye. Not a man to trifle with. Tom standing behind the boys winked at John and Murdo. As they walked into the trees William looked back down the sloping path. The manor lay peacefully in folds of white snow. Smoke rose lazily into the sky. He could see a woman, probably Alice, walking across the yard to the smoke-house. When they left, she had been busy rearranging fish which were being smoked. The doves in his mother's doocot were taking advantage of the weak, winter sunshine, and William could see them sitting around enjoying the warmth.

'Swift', their old hound, whined, keen to get on with the serious business of hunting and William ran after the others with the dog at his heels.

They saw the tracks of deer and boar in the forest and trees with stripped bark, but no animal stirred. They gave up the chase and went by the moor to old Matilda's cottage, where they got four capercailzie. Matilda was at her door as they passed by. Tom greeted her and she invited them into the warmth of her hearth. The cottage was too small for so many men and boys, and the men had to bend low to enter. The peats gave a good heat, the smoke drifting lazily to the rafters. At the back of the room the earthen floor had been raised to form a platform. There was a straw filled mattress and covers, which served as Matilda and Jamie's bed.

Daft Jamie was delighted to have guests. He was fully-grown, but his mind was still that of a child. The men left their bows in the doorway and Jamie squatted on the ground caressing the quivers, his mouth hanging slackly. Matilda offered them broth, a weak watery mixture, ladled into a wooden bowl, which they passed between them. To men used to Lady Margaret's nourishing and aromatic stews, this was a poor substitute, but it was hot and the poor widow offered her hospitality with such eagerness that they could not refuse.

Swift, lying just outside and impatient to be back at his own fireside, stood up and shook himself. They left, thanking Matilda for the warming, and gave her two of the capercailzies and what remained in their mead flask. The following day would be the first day of the New Year 1281. The widow and her son would eat well on that day.

Uncle William and his companions stayed until February when the weather was somewhat milder. Lady Margaret was relieved when they began to make preparations to leave. The talk in the evenings inevitably turned to the exploits and campaigns of their youth, and her sons were plainly impressed by these yarns. Of course all boys enjoyed games of war, but Uncle William glorified warfare and praised young William's skill with the bow. She feared this would turn the boy's head. Margaret hoped William and John would follow clerical vocations, and intended to persuade her husband to send them to school as soon as was possible.

Uncle Wallace rode out on the day after Candlemas, heading for the estate of Wallace of Riccarton, head of the family, where he would stay until the spring sowing and then return to his own manor. He took with him a flagon of Lady Margaret's mead, cheese and an excellent game pie. The boys and Swift escorted the small party to the place where the road climbed up onto the moors. "You will come back soon, Uncle?" asked William. "God bless you boy, I'm getting an old man, but if He spares me we'll see each other again. Your father says he will send you to me if I cannot make the journey. Until we meet again, God be with you." He smiled at the three boys, then, giving his horse the spur, set off at a trot towards the south. Murdo scowled at them. They had not seen him smile since his arrival. John winked and nodded and they followed their master. The boys turned for home.

During the summer, Sir Malcolm visited Renfrew to take his fleeces to the merchant and to pay his own dues to his lord, Sir James Stewart. The castle was a few miles away from Elderslie. It was a beautiful summer day and the whole family and some of the household servants went with him. Lady Margaret intended to buy woollen cloth for her sons' new tunics. Alice had at last agreed to marry Tom Johnston, a widower, and she wanted to buy some fine linen cloth for her wedding dress. They took daft Jamie with them.

Matilda had died in the spring and Margaret Wallace had taken the youth into her household. Simple tasks were found for him to earn his keep: collecting firewood, cutting and stacking peat from the moor. He was good with the animals, particularly the oxen, as they were slow and gentle like himself.

The Wallace family looked a fine sight as they rode into Renfrew. The boys astride their ponies, father leading the party on his chestnut mount, Margaret Wallace riding a grey mare, and Tom bringing up the rear on a shaggy bay nag of doubtful age and temperament, Alice sitting behind him. Jamie ambled along beside them, holding the animal's bridle, for it was a particular friend of his.

It was market day and folk were walking or riding into the bustling burgh. Lady Margaret and Alice stayed in the market square while the men and boys carried on up the narrow lane which led to the great castle. The cobbled road led past the quay where the fishing vessels were tied up. They had fished during the short summer night, unloaded early and most of the catch already cleaned and gutted lay on display. Wicker baskets held crabs with their pincers waving to passers-by, and overhead gulls called soaring and diving to squabble over pieces of fish offal. William and John wanted to remain at the harbour. They knew some of the fishermen, but their father said they should come first to the castle. There would be time to talk to friends later.

The party clattered up to the main gates and entered the courtyard. Sir Malcolm and Tom were shown into the great hall and the boys were free to wander at will. On the other side of the courtyard was the smithy. Clanging and banging indicated that the smiths were hard at work and the boys stood with Jamie in the entrance watching them.

Smith to the Lord Stewart was an important position and the master smith jealously guarded the skills of his trade. He was a clever tradesman, meticulous in his work and had four apprentices and four journeymen. They carried out those tasks normally assigned to a smith, shoeing, and repairing equipment, but working for a great lord demanded the skills of an armourer. Making chain-mail and tempering the blades of his lord's weapons was work which he kept to himself. He had his old age to think of. Already he was beginning to suffer painful wrists and shoulders from years of pounding metals. He had watched his father's decline with the smith's disease and intended to make himself invaluable to his lord. He eyed Jamie and the lads standing in the doorway.

Jack Short had been ordered by the master at arms to take one of the horses to the smith for shoeing. Short had grown into a stocky, strong youth, now seventeen summers old. He was a useful foot soldier, good with the bow or sword, cunning and wily but not popular with his comrades because of his aggressive and bullying nature. He had, however, winning ways with the wenches in the kitchens and inns around Renfrew.

He recognised the Wallace brothers and Jamie. The boys saw him leading the big horse towards the Smithy and moved to one side, but Jamie absorbed in the workshop and its equipment was slow and did not move. The horse was a spirited animal, which was always nervous at shoeing and moreover had a dislike of Short. It knew where it was going and began prancing and throwing its head. As horse and handler arrived at the entrance to the smithy, Jamie was still standing looking at the work. "Get out of the way, you bleeding idiot," bellowed Short.

The horse continued prancing and sidestepping. As Short drew level with Jamie he lashed out at him with clenched fist and caught him a blow at the side of the head which sent him sprawling backwards into the smithy. Jamie caught the back of his skull on an anvil that was kept near the entrance for small rush jobs.

Short pulled the horse up and handed its bridle to a journeyman. Turning he grinned unpleasantly at the boys. Malcolm ran to Jamie's prostrate body sprawled on the earthen floor. The back of Jamie's head was thickly coated with blood. William with all the sense of injustice which a nine year old can be capable of hurled himself at Short who laughed and gave him a hefty blow. William staggered but his anger was such that he was about to fling himself at the youth again when a large hand caught the back of his jerkin. "That's enough of that boy, take your fights away from my smithy. It was an accident, sure enough. Take yon simpleton outside and throw some water over him."

William caught sight of Short's gloating grin. Short sauntered off and the three brothers dragged Jamie outside and lay him beside a water butt. He lay very still and his face was white. They ladled water over him, but he did not stir. A man-at-arms strolled over and looked down at the sad broken body. "No good, boys. He'll die, if he's not dead already." He bent down and placed his hand on the right side of the chest. "He's gone alright, you can't help him."

The boys stood unsure what to do next. How could it be? Just five minutes earlier they had been talking to him and he had been laughing, and rolling his eyes about as was his way. Now, he was silent at their feet. Tom Johnston appeared from the hall and came to their assistance.

Short had joined a group of men-at-arms cleaning equipment and watched as Tom talked to the boys, then went back into the hall. It gave Short considerable satisfaction to be the cause of Jamie's death. It was not revenge for his father's death which caused him to hate the Wallace kinsmen. He remembered his father as a bloody minded bastard, but it was something about the Wallaces and everything they did which irritated his jealous nature. Had he been a deep-thinking man, he would have known that it was their open-handedness and straight dealing which he despised, but Jack Short did not dwell on feelings or reasons.

There was no penalty to pay for the death of Jamie. Witnesses stated it was an accident and the boy had no property and no kith or kin to grieve his passing. He was taken back to Elderslie and buried in the churchyard. William thought long and hard on the injustice of Jamie's death. What harm had he ever done?

Margaret Wallace had persuaded her husband to send the boys to school at Paisley Abbey. Malcolm had gone in the autumn following Jamie's death, when he was eleven winters old, but the two younger boys were not to go for another year.

Malcolm Wallace had insisted that William and John should visit Uncle William in his manor. Lady Margaret had resisted her husband's plans. Fears for her sons' welfare were difficult to explain. Men, she had found, had little understanding of a mother's worry for her children. She did not want her boys to be soldiers, to fight and be killed. "You can't tie yon lads to you woman," he said irritably. "Malcolm will inherit after me, but William and John must make their way in the world." The arguments between husband and wife raged the whole winter until even Tom Johnston sadly shook his head. Then Mother Nature took charge – at least where John was concerned.

In cold and blustery March, John became ill. His illness began innocently enough with a cold. His nose and eyes ran and his throat hurt. His mother kept him in the house, but at night William told him of an old boar which he had been tracking and was determined to kill the following day. John so wanted to be there. "Is it really the biggest boar you have ever seen?" he whispered as they lay in bed that night." "Yes, quite the biggest," came back the reply from the darkness, "all covered in scars from many fights."

In the morning before the household was up and about William and John dressed quietly. Their mother would have been surprised for they had never been so quiet at anything before. They stole out with bows, full quivers and axes in search of the illusive animal.

When Margaret Wallace found their bed empty she blamed her husband, although he could not understand why she should. These days she held him responsible for everything that went wrong. Sir Malcolm took his old horse and went in search of his sons. He was angry. He found his wife exasperating and although the weather was cold, it was nevertheless excellent weather for sowing early barley, which he had intended to do with Tom. The shepherd had also asked him to call in to see the early lambs.

Now here he was searching the woods for his sons, who, in his opinion, had to learn to care for themselves. Still if it was true they were after a boar, they would have to be careful. Boar were dangerous when cornered. He found his boys two hours later in the forest behind the manor, victorious, for they had tracked their first kill. Father forgot his annoyance, praised their perseverance, courage and skill with the bow and the boar was carried home in triumph.

That night John began to cough. By the morning his eyes were bright with fever, his cheeks flushed, and he complained of pains in his head and chest. William remained close, looking unhappy and tense. For just over a week John fought the fever. His mother or Alice were always near him. Warmed stones were placed by the patient's feet, poultices put on his chest, and a good fire was kept burning day and night. He was given many warm drinks of milk, wine, broth and potions made from honey, herbs and spices to help his chest. The fever broke on the eighth day and Margaret Wallace, pale and dark-eyed, removed her shoes and her belt with the large bunch of keys that she always carried and lay down beside her son and went to sleep.

In the first week of April, the month of his tenth birthday, William set out with Tom and a serving man for Borthwick Water, the estate of Uncle Wallace. John was still convalescing. "Perhaps he could go another year when he was a little older," said his mother. She was in her still room preparing a herbal drink for John's cough. Naturally she had not wanted him to be ill, but since God had seen fit to spare him, she was pleased it made it easier for her to keep him close to her for a little longer. She sighed: she was becoming an old woman.

William was excited. He had never been away from home by himself before, visiting his kinsfolk Wallace and Crawford. He had always been accompanied by his parents and brothers. Of course Tom was with him and Tom was like a father. Tom and Alice were expecting their first child during May. Since Alice was no longer a young woman, Tom was to return to Elderslie as soon as he had given young William into the care of his great uncle, who was to meet them at Lanark.

It was a fine spring day. By the edges of streams and paths the pale yellow primroses smiled up at the sun. They passed many people, journeymen, tinkers, peddlers and shaggy highland cattle being driven to markets in the south. William spared a second glance for the drovers. Highlanders in their strange dress, big, fierce looking men with wild hair and beards.

William thought they strongly resembled their cattle and said so to Tom. Tom laughed but told him that his mother would not be pleased to hear such rudeness. Tom glanced again at the men and chuckled. They passed a party of entertainers, one leading a bear on a chain. In the late afternoon they were themselves overtaken by a group of men-at-arms wearing the colours of the Lord Stewart. As they trotted by, bridles and accoutrements jingling merrily, William caught sight of Jack Short among the leaders of the party.

At the end of their third day – when they were due to arrive in Lanark – the wind increased and it began raining heavily. They still had some way to go and William was tired and hungry. The wind drove the stinging rain into his face and his teeth chattered uncontrollably. Tom looked back at him and said, "It's going to be a wild night lad, it's not far now. Look you can see Lanark yonder through the trees. Keep your pony's head up. It's slippery down here."

William could see the huddle of houses and the outline of the church two or three miles down the valley. He set his eyes determinedly on his pony's nodding ears hunching his shoulders against the rain and wind. "Well, here we are boy. Let's hope your uncle has arrived ahead of us."

William raised his head allowing the folds of his cloak to fall back onto his shoulders. They had arrived at a large and prosperous manor, which was the home of Sir Hugh Braidfute, an old friend of his father. The door was open and he could smell roasted meat and wood smoke. Wonderfully warm and comfortable smells they were. A young boy about his own age took his pony's bridle. "Give them a good rubdown boy," said Tom. Sir Hugh Braidfute and Uncle William came out to greet them.

They stayed with the Braidfute family for two days, but Sir Hugh only had a small daughter and William missed the company of boys. On the morning of the third day they began their journey to Borthwick. The first night they slept in the lee of a rocky outcrop sheltered from the wind, with a good fire by their feet. It was wild country with steep crags, dense forest and boggy moorland. They were making for Peebles, and spent a night beside a mountain river which Murdo called Lynnwater.

They arrived at an arched stone bridge and on the opposite bank William could see grass covered mounds and broken stone walls covered with moss, lichen and ferns. Uncle William saw his great nephew's gaze. "Those remains were left by the Romans, lad. Clever devils they were. For a thousand years that bridge has been there." "May I go and look, sir." "Aye, lad," said Uncle William, "but first you must settle your pony, then you may do as you wish."

After leaving Peebles, the country changed and they began riding along forest tracks. Uncle told him that it was the edge of the Ettrick forest and William thought it rather dark and forbidding. "We need to keep our eyes open here, lad. This place is a refuge for rogues and outlaws." William looked about with new interest. "Why are they outlaws, uncle?" His uncle gave a shrug. "A man can be made an outlaw for all manner of things, murder, theft and misfortune. Not all outlaws are bad men, William, but life in these forests makes a man suspicious. They don't ask questions and just take what they need. They know me. I've travelled this way many times and I have many friends here. Don't you be fearful, lad!"

His uncle's estate had a fortified manor house with a moat around it. Janet, Uncle William's old serving woman came out to greet her master and his young nephew. "When you have fed and cared for your pony, William, then you may go to Janet and satisfy your own hunger," said Uncle William as he dismounted.

The manor was very old and built with huge oak beams. In the hall four stout timbers, all carved with animals and birds and blackened by smoke from the hearth, supported the roof. There was no solar nor bedchamber as in his own home, but at one end there was a carved oak screen and behind this his uncle's bed. Wolf skins hung on the walls and along one side of the chamber were trestles and boards. Uncle's carved chair was at the head, and down each side the benches for his servants and followers. When they all gathered round to eat, there were some twenty people.

The days that followed through spring and summer were busy. William helped with the sowing, shearing and harvest, fished the rivers and lochs, hunted deer, boar and wild fowl. On one of his hunting expeditions with Murdo they met two men, who greeted Murdo as a friend. After they had parted Murdo said, "Both were outlawed for theft, boy, but I have known them these three years past and they have caused me no worries." William looked back at them. They were clothed in leather and their full quivers were slung across their backs.

Janet enjoyed having the young lad to care for. She had arrived in old William Wallace's household with her mistress, his new wife then, and after her lady's death she continued to care for the master. She was a good cook and had all the housewifery skills to make a man and bairns comfortable, but she had resigned herself to a single life. When she was a young girl her father had said, "No man will marry you, my girl. Be grateful for the offer of a place serving Mary Maxwell." It seemed natural to stay with the master, hidden away on the remote manor where no one seemed to mind her crooked form and lopsided walk.

William was due to return home in the second week of September after the harvest had been brought in. Janet was busy preparing meats and preserves for the winter. In one of the storehouses smoked meats were hanging from hooks in the rafters. William sat in the open doorway gnawing at the leg of a chicken.

"Well, master William, are you looking forward to seeing your parents and brothers," asked Janet as she made room on a hook for a string of smoked sausages. "Aye, but I wish I could take all of you with me, I don't want to say goodbye." Janet turned her head away from his gaze and quickly wiped a tear from her cheek.

"Well, my dear, friends never really part you know. You and I will say farewell, but you will always be in my thoughts and when you return, for return you will, it will be as if you never left. God will look down on both of us."

William did not really understand her. His parents seemed very far away and although the priest Kenneth had told him that God saw everything, how could He be in two places so far apart.

Murdo came over leading two ponies, sacks of barley and oats hanging from both animals. "Come, William, help me take this up to Alemoor Loch. It's a gift for a friend in the forest".

The path leading from the manor was a steep scramble for ponies, man and boy. After an hour they arrived by the loch. It was very still. The clouds and trees were reflected in its surface. Near its edge, sheltered among the old Caledonian firs, was a small hut built from logs with a turf roof, difficult to see unless you were searching for such a place. As they approached the deerskin, which served as a door, was pulled aside and a man came out into the golden September sun.

They sat beside the loch. Murdo brought out bread and ale that Janet had given them and they talked about the harvest, game and local gossip. William wandered off and searched along the shore. After their walk he was very hot. He took off his clothes and swam, but the water was very cold.

When he returned to the men, John the Outlaw showed William some of his traps, which he was setting ready for the winter. In return for the sacks of flour and oats John gave them skins strung together, pine martin, otter, hare in its winter coat, and many velvety black mole skins, which Murdo slung across the back of one of the ponies. As they returned down the steep track, William asked, "What did John do that made him an outlaw." "He killed a man, lad. He had a fight with a neighbour and slew him."

Murdo looked down at William. "This is a wild place, lad. The nearest farmstead is a day's walk from us at the manor through difficult country. The forest is dense and a wise man is friends with his nearest neighbour even if he is an outlaw. Yon fellow has proved himself a good man to us. We sell his skins for him and when we have brought in the harvest we give him a little and he is grateful. In the west there are many estates and villages, William, but it's lonely hereabouts."

The day arrived for William's departure. He took with him the love of the estate followers. Janet was particularly sad. During the years spent at Borthwick performing the household duties, she had grown fond of old William Wallace. Cantankerous he was, particularly when laid low with drink, but he did not beat her and was kind in his own way.

Now this nephew of his had stolen her heart and the manor would be so quiet without his lively questions and pleadings for food as he was always hungry. Janet had stitched a cloak for William. John and Murdo between them had made a new bow with quiver and arrows. William was overjoyed with the gifts and immediately ran outside to try them out taking aim at a bird sitting in the branch of an oak. It was a difficult shot with a new bow and fortunately for the bird William's arrow fell short. The men laughed and the crow flew off squawking loudly. "Next time don't aim when you are so excited, William," said Murdo.

Two days after the feast of the Blessed Virgin Mary, in golden autumnal weather, they began their journey home. Even Janet came with them for she wanted to visit the Michaelmas fair at Peebles. Once again they camped in the lee of the old fort. The weather was holding fine and with the starlit sky for his roof, bracken and heather for his bed, and a good fire to warm his feet William thought he could hear the tramping of marching feet and the sharp orders of long dead centurions. Then he sank into the carefree sleep of youth.

They were met at Lanark by his parents and his brother John. The family had escorted Malcolm to the monastic school at Paisley and had come to await William's arrival. John had missed William. Malcolm was serious and not so inclined to laugh good-naturedly if John said or did something stupid. He was skilled with the bow, but not so skilled as William, nor so patient in passing on his knowledge to his younger brother. So John looked forward to William's arrival and hoped he would not leave him again. They spent a few days at the manor of Sir Hugh Braidfute with whom their father had business. The boys wandered around the alleys of Lanark with the sons of merchants as companions.

During Lent in the spring of the year 1283 both boys were taken to Paisley Abbey to begin their formal schooling. Malcolm had been a student for a year and adopted the attitude of an experienced and worldly elder brother, showing his proteges the school rooms, cloister, infirmary, dormitories and gardens. Yet even he lost his strutting confidence when the whole family received the holy sacrament in the great abbey at the Easter mass. The boys caught a glimpse of the Lord Stewart and his lady at the front of the abbey, which was their rightful place. The nave stretched before them: the great pillars supported the massive roof and under it the congregation, nobles, burgesses and freemen were there to give thanks for Christ's resurrection. It had a humbling effect – and in such a place it would be wrong to be too proud.

The time had come for the wild carefree William to be tamed, disciplined and tutored to turn his mental skills to learning. This was not always an easy task for his tutors. He had a questioning mind which could absorb new ideas and skills quickly, but he was restless and energetic. It was difficult, almost impossible, in the early months of his schooling for him to sit quietly at his desk while the sun shone outside. He would rather be in the forest hunting or fishing. As the months grew into a year, he began to settle, allowing himself to be disciplined by the abbey Bell, which told him when to wake, to study, to worship, to eat and to sleep.

The summer came and the three Wallace boys once again roamed the Elderslie estate assisting with the shearing and the harvest. Margaret Wallace was able to fuss around her sons. She was sad to see that the two elder boys were taller than she was herself. She did not feel old, yet here she was with such big sons. During their first family dinner she looked closely at her husband's weather-beaten face. He did not look old, perhaps a little wider above the wide leather belt he always wore, but as yet his hair was not streaked with grey.

It was a good harvest that summer and the beasts in the fields were fat and healthy. Sir Malcolm's flocks had been growing steadily over the years and he was making good money selling their wool to the cloth merchants. The country was prospering and only one black cloud hung over the kingdom: the heir to the throne was a little maid living far away in Norway. William heard his parents discussing the king, but took little interest. "The king should remarry. Why, he's a bonny man and not yet old. He can have many more sons," said Lady Margaret as they sat at their dinner. "I agree woman, but all Scotland seems to be discussing the king and his loins. Can the poor man have no privacy?"

Sir Malcolm was right. The possibility of the king remarrying and having more sons was discussed up and down the realm. The king's advisers harassed him at each and every council meeting, suggesting most of the eligible young women throughout Christendom. Alexander knew his duty. He had to, for he had been king since he was eight and under his guidance Scotland had prospered. Yet sometimes his Council continuously pointing out the needs of the kingdom roused him into outbursts of furious indignation. Why had God placed this burden, the crown of Scots, on him? Why had he not been born a common man? They were free to chose a wife and marry as and when they wished. Margaret, God rest her soul, had been sister to Edward of England. She had been chosen for him when they were both children. They had lived comfortably together, but that brother of hers had interfered at every twist and turn. Now they wanted him to form yet another union. Well, if he must marry, he would make his own choice and would not have a powerful brother-in-law to interfere in his affairs.

Eventually he agreed they should search for a suitable bride. The need for another heir to the throne, even he agreed, had become a matter of some urgency. In October 1285 the Council and the kingdom breathed a collective sigh of relief when the king remarried. For his wife he chose young and fair Yolande de Dreux. Alexander had been a widower for five years and all hoped that with such a winsome young woman in his bed there would be an heir before the year was out.

For some time Malcolm Wallace had been giving careful thought to his younger sons' future. Malcolm would inherit the manor, but the younger boys needed direction. He did not want them to drift. They both showed some talent with Latin and French, yet they could not be described as scholarly students nor were they tied to their mother's skirt. He was not sure that either boy was really suited to the monastic life. When he mentioned his fears to his wife, she flared up at him, "You're just saying this because such a life wouldn't suit you," "Nonsense Meg. I just don't think they, particularly William, will be enthusiastic about the life in a cloister." "Well my brother has a good life and it is right that we should give at least one of our children to the church," "John would make the better cleric, Will the soldier," her husband persisted rather irritably, then suddenly remembered some pressing task which demanded his attention outside.

He wandered to the barn to his oxen. He often went to the animals when he wanted to think. He found their slow steady chewing and soft brown eyes very soothing, but he was never annoyed with his wife for long. She worried so much about her boys. Further pregnancies and babies after John would have kept her busy, but as things were she had time to think, plan and worry about her brood. Well, if William and John were sent to Dunipace, to continue their education with his brother-in-law Thomas, he supposed it would do no harm. Thomas was a man who young boys could respect, and a son who trained for the priestly life could not really go wrong. With the Lord Stewart and other clerical members of the family to sponsor them perhaps the lads would gain positions of some influence.

In the autumn of 1285, William accompanied by John, set out for Dunipace. Their father escorted them, but mother remained at home to care for Uncle William who had paid them a visit in the late summer and had become unwell. William at thirteen was big and strong for his age. They were in the yard ready to depart. "Remember all I have taught you boys and William look after your brother." There were tears in her eyes which she dabbed with the edge of her coif. Tom came out from the great barn where he and the men were winnowing. "God speed you lads."

The journey to Dunipace was easier than to the manor of Borthwick Water two years earlier. There were more villages and homesteads in the area and much of the natural forest cover had been felled. They followed the Kelvin Valley for part of the way. There had been a lot of rain that summer and the river was wild and swollen. The ponies found the track difficult with mud and great pools of water everywhere. They were often forced to dismount and lead their animals. They passed many pilgrims travelling to Dunfermline as well as merchants and tinkers on their last journey before winter forced them to remain by their fires. They left the valley behind and turned north towards Dunipace.

On the fourth day the church came into view. Father and sons rode through the gates as the afternoon gave way to evening and the bell rang out for the *Angelus*. It had been a cold and blustery day with intermittent rain. They were wet and ready for their meal. Thomas had visited his brother-in-law's manor many times and he was looking forward to educating his nephews.

William and John spent three years at Dunipace. They sang with other scholars at mass, worked on the farm, assisted in the gardens and helped their uncle in the distribution of alms to the poor. There was a small infirmary and the boys were often told to collect water and carry out any other small tasks, which the brothers asked of them. It was a strict, disciplined way of life regulated by the church bells, study, religious observances and work. Thus William Wallace learnt to be a man.

The year 1286 began with gales, cold and rain. Surely the Lord must be angry with His earthly realm, but Alexander, King of Scots, was a joyful man unaffected by the weather. His bride delighted him and they were both sure she would soon have some good news for him and the kingdom.

In March the king was in Edinburgh with his Privy Council and as the afternoon wore on they indulged in some excellent French wine. As the evening passed, his advisers noticed that the king was getting restless and the worse for drink. It was already dark and the wind could be heard roaring around the castle, searching for an opening where it might enter and attack the inhabitants.

Then the king announced his intention of returning to his dear Yolande for the night. His courtiers were thrown into consternation. The queen was at Kinghorn and each secretly hoped their king would not demand that they should accompany him on his mad journey into the cold and wet night. They tried to dissuade him, telling him that the omens were bad, but he laughed and thought to himself – are they a bunch of old women fearful of a little rain?

He set out with three esquires, irritably ignoring the pleas of the ferryman at Dalmeny not to attempt the crossing and demanded to be rowed across the Forth. Safely over, he laughed at their fears, and with his young followers and two local men to guide him set off with the reckless speed of a lover for Kinghorn and Yolande.

He kept his party riding at a controlled canter with the wind billowing out his cloak, impatient with their cautious progress. "Must your king always lead the way," he yelled over his shoulder. "Sire, take care, the path leads dangerously close to the cliff along here," called one of his guides. The warning urged Alexander to spur on his horse and king and mount left the circle of light thrown out by the torches of his guides.

An owl noticed that there had been a short break in the rain and left his roost in search of food. He was successful and found a small vole forced out by the flood. The king ahead of his party did not see the owl, but his great black horse, startled by the bird, shied, reared and in the wet mud slid sideways over the cliff edge.

The news of the king's death spread rapidly throughout the kingdom. Surely the Day of Judgement was coming. His advisers, who had been present at his wedding feast in the autumn at Jedburgh, blamed the Queen. No good could possibly come from having such an evil masque at a wedding feast. They had shaken their heads sadly, "The Dance of Death," at a wedding indeed. It was bound to bring misfortune on the royal couple. The Queen cried and shut herself away in her apartment. The masque had been such a success when it had been performed in her father's castle. It was not her fault. It was the kingdom, so bleak and cold, and it never stopped raining.

The Council was in turmoil. What would become of the Realm? With the rightful heir to the throne, a babe, living in far away Norway? They must act quickly. On the 11 April four nobles, two from the north, two from the south and the bishops of Glasgow and St Andrews were made Guardians of Scotland – until the little princess Margaret could be brought to Scotland.

Old Robert Bruce sat in his castle and fumed. He, Lord of Annandale, heir to the old king, King Alexander the second, had been passed over by a bunch of scheming fools. The Comyns had something to do with it, of that he was sure. Well, he would show them that they ignored him and the Bruces at their peril. He seized the royal castles in the south west of Dumfries, Wigtown and Buittle which all belonged to the Balliol family. Then he sat and waited events. As he said to his son, "We must safeguard what is ours. Without a strong man to sit on the Stone of Scone who can tell what will happen?"

The Guardians, alarmed by the events, sent a delegation to France to seek out Edward of England and ask his approval of the arrangements they had made for Scotland's administration until the little princess could be inaugurated. The English king listened to the news with sympathetic understanding and approval, and the delegates began their return journey to Scotland in confident mood.

Edward was a very busy man. He had many commitments in his French territories and a tight timetable to subjugate the Welsh, who were putting up an irritating resistance to his power. At least for the time being the kingdom to his north could play at government. It suited him that no noble should become too powerful and when he, Edward of England, could spare the time, he would show them how a real king would govern. Meanwhile he would send orders to his spies to keep him informed.

The Bruce family owned many estates in England. When they heard that the English king had agreed to the peaceful arrangements for Scotland's government, they prudently withdrew their claims to the throne of the kingdom of Scots.

That summer the two boys went home to Elderslie with their Uncle Crawford and the adults agreed that dedication to the church would be a most beneficial career for the boys and the family. They should be sent to Dundee to finish their education. Perhaps an understanding of law combined with the right patronage would enhance their prospects.

Lady Margaret sat by the great fireplace with a distaff spinning. William had worried her, as sometimes he could be a little headstrong, but he kept his own council and was not led by other boys. He was a leader, even when he stood aloof from the crowd. Margaret could hear all three outside wrestling. She continued her spinning, dreaming her mother's dreams.

E dward of England on his return from France completed his conquest of Wales, and by 1289 was ready to assert his mastery over Scotland. The Scottish Council agreed to his proposal of a marriage between Margaret, their princess, and Edward's son, another Edward, and he sent a representative, post haste, to the Pope asking for dispensation to the marriage because they were cousins.

A treaty was signed between English Edward and King Eric of Norway: the young princess was to return to Scotland. Her prospective father-in-law gave orders for a fine sturdy ship to be refitted in Yarmouth paid for at his own expense. Edward's plans were meticulous and, to relieve King Eric's fears, the Bishop of Durham was ordered to sail with the ship to escort the young maid. In Oslo the bishop distributed lavish gifts to Eric's councillors, to sway their council and advise their king to dispatch his daughter – without delay – to Scotland. Edward had stretched his nets far and wide.

But King Eric was worried. He loved his little girl. She was so fragile and vulnerable. If he sent her to Scotland as the Scots were requesting, she would be at the mercy of any self-seeking, cunning and manipulative nobleman. Who would guard the interests of his little maid in a foreign land? Poison in her food, a pillow over her face, it was so easily done. He had good cause to know how greedy nobles could be. She was little more than a baby.

The Scots would have to wait a little longer.


E lspeth, Jack Short's widow, had spent the day gleaning. Now in the late evening she was eating her meagre meal before sleeping. She sat in the doorway of her cot. Her aching back was resting against the doorpost. The dog was sitting in front of her begging his share. Suddenly it jumped up barking and dashed excitely up the track. She heard the dog yelp. The visitor, whoever he was, had kicked it. Then the figure of a man came into view. It was her son Jack.

Their relationship had not been a loving one, but he was her son and she always hoped that this time he would greet her with tenderness. She got wearily to her feet and walked towards him smiling and happy. "Has your lord given you leave, Jack?" She asked. "Are you going to question me before I've even got my feet over the threshold, mother?"

She had heard that irritable tone before and knew that this would not be the visit she yearned for. Nevertheless she put her arms around him and he lowered his head slightly to receive her kiss.

He was twenty-three summers now, not very tall, but powerful, well built and with dark hair. He was not handsome, but there was a roguish look about him which she was sure attracted the lasses. He was wearing a rust coloured jerkin and brown homespun cloak. He carried his belongings over his shoulder and his shield was attached to the bag. His claymore was strapped to his back and battleaxe swung at his belt.

She built up the fire and busied herself finding him a cup of ale. As he lowered his bag it clanged. He looked at her and grinned. "The tools of my trade mother, but this time I haven't forgotten you." The gift was wrapped in his spare cloak. It was a good-sized leg of mutton. His mother's eyes lit up. She had not had such a fine piece of meat since her man had died. She forgot her aching back and prepared to cook the meat, while Jack sat drinking his ale.

Jack stopped with his mother for two days. He stayed close-by and told her not to mention his visit. Early in the morning of the third day Jack rose and told her that he would be leaving shortly. "You'll be going back to the castle, Jack?" "No, I'm bound for the south to seek service. The English always need a good soldier."

His mother looked horrified. How would she manage? She was getting old now. What would become of her without a son and daughter-in-law to give her a seat by their fire? Jack Short looked irritated, but instead of attacking her as was usually his way, he shrugged sullenly. "Mother, I will find a place and when I am sure all is well, I shall send for you. Have no fears on that."

Since this was the first time he had ever expressed any intention of caring for her, she accepted his promise and smiling happily prepared a small bundle of food for his journey. As he was about to leave she gave him the small silver ring which his father had given her. He put it on a thong of leather and tied it round his neck. She watched his retreating figure down the track wondering what he had done that he must go away to the south.

She went into her byre and looked at the two goats, both with twin kids at their heel. She took down an earthenware crock from a small shelf and milked them, before letting their kids out of their pens, then drove the animals out. Her youngest boy had died two years earlier. He had never been strong. He had become thin and pale, and his skin was always cold and damp. Occasionally he would get fevers, which would go as quickly as they had come, and he had an irritating cough. She had taken him to the infirmary at Paisley Abbey. The monks had given him syrups and hot poultices, but after a week when the boy began to cough blood they shook their heads and said that it was God's will. She had prayed to the Virgin that a miracle might happen, but he had died just before Christmas during a spell of very misty weather.

Lady Wallace had been kind to her, but during the long winter nights when she sat alone, she often considered her plight. If Sir Malcolm had turned a blind eye or demanded his share of her man's short measure, as many other lords did, perhaps her Jack would be with her still. Her life would have been so different as wife of the miller of Elderslie. She would be a fat and jolly grandmother instead of the poor thin thing she now was. As for his beatings, many men beat their wives. What were a few bruises compared to a full belly and grandchildren around the fire. The years had dimmed her memory.

Jack Short followed the route taken by William when he had visited Uncle Wallace in Borthwick Water. Along the road he joined a party of Highlanders driving their cattle to Berwick. An extra pair of ears and eyes was useful, especially those of a trained soldier. The Highlanders were journeying from Skye and had been taking the same route for many years. They were flamboyant fellows, who enjoyed a drink and a good yarn at the end of the day, but he could not fault them in the care that they took of their beasts. There was always a guard posted at night for the shaggy animals were valuable.

"Why go all the way to Berwick, man? What's wrong with the markets in Glasgow or Stirling? Why make work for yourself?" asked Short one day. "Money, Jack. We get a better price from the butchers in Berwick. There are fat merchants there who'll pay virtually any price for meat from fine healthy beasts like ours. Lots of foreigners are there, you'll see. All with money to spend." The easy going islanders liked Short. He was a useful man to have around.

After Peebles Jack decided to continue with the group to Berwick and then to go south. He would be faster alone but there was safety in numbers. Usually he was suspicious and uncommunicative when questioned about himself, but the drovers were proving useful to him and he would probably never see them again. So when the leader said, "Trouble with a lassie, was it?" Short had answered truthfully, "Yes, she was another man's wife." The Highlander laughed and said no more but Short had not told the whole truth. As he turned back to collect a heifer, which was slipping behind the main herd, Short smiled to himself as he thought how he had fooled everyone.

He had seen her at the White Ship Inn where he went often. A big red-haired woman, older than himself, with a knowing smile and bold eyes. The first thing he noticed were her big firm breasts, with the nipples always erect under her thin linen dress. She had well-rounded hips and thighs on which a man could get a good grip. She smiled saucily at him and he wanted her, but her husband was the landlord of the inn.

When Short was off duty, he sat eyeing the woman over his drink. There were plenty of other women available at the inn and he made free with them, but he wanted her. One day he was sent on an errand to the tanner in Renfrew and on his way back he saw her. She had been to the market and was walking back towards the inn. She smiled and he greeted her. "Will you be visiting us tonight then, Jack Short?" "Perhaps." There was no need to let the woman think that he was too eager, although he was surprised that she knew his name. "I'll see you then," she smiled coyly at him and pushed out her breasts.

That evening he sat as always with his ale. Late in the evening when he got up to leave she followed him out into the yard. There were many convenient shadows and he pulled her to him but she whispered, "Not here, Jack Short, but if you're free in the afternoon the day after tomorrow I'll slip away and meet you at the bothy up at the back." She pointed in the direction of the hill. Yes, he knew the place and thought he could find reason to leave the castle. He fumbled at the front of her dress. "Just you wait, Jack Short, and I'll make the waiting worth your while". She pulled away from him and went back towards the inn.

Thus began a convenient arrangement governed by the physical desires of Short and the innkeeper's wife. Love did not develop in either, just a greedy hunger for lusty satisfaction. Both were very careful in arranging their meetings, changing the times and places for their trysts. Yet although love had no part in their unions, jealousy did. She was fearful lest he should see a younger woman. Jack was jealous of sharing her with any other man, including her husband, and they often argued. Then one pleasant spring day when they had been lovers for about six months, Short was sent on an errand to the miller and there he saw the miller's sixteen-year-old niece. She was small, dark, quiet and shy. He found every possible opportunity to return to the mill. He even made himself pleasant to the miller and found himself thinking about her soft smile when he was on watch. After two months he was as near to being in love with the girl as it was possible for him to be with anyone.

His interest in the miller's niece could not be hidden for long. Tongues wagged and on a pleasant afternoon in late summer, when he was keeping an appointment with the inn keeper's wife, he found her angry and in belligerent mood. "Tired of me are you, Jack? Think you can replace me with a child, or are you after the mill when the old man dies? Is that your plan then? I hear you came from a mill, Jack, until your father danced a jig on a rope's end."

"Watch your bloody mouth woman," Short's comrades would have known to shut up at this point, but like Jack, she was used to getting her own way and persisted with her taunts. "I'm not frightened of you. Perhaps the miller would like to know about you. We do good business with him and he's a greedy man."

Short lashed out at her and sent her staggering. For a few moments there was silence in the small hut while they stood glaring at each other. Then she flew at him scratching his face, kicking, screaming, threatening to tell the sergeant-at-arms that he had attacked and raped her: her a respectable married woman. "Who do you think they'll believe me or the son of a murderer?" she screamed. Short grabbed hold of the woman, placed his hands firmly around her throat and began to squeeze. When she lay silent at his feet he smiled. "You can't say anything now, can you?"

He looked around the hut: he had to hide her body to give himself time. There was nowhere in the hut, but outside there was a stone enclosure for sheep. He dragged her outside and hid her under a pile of broken stones. He was on duty that night, but one of the men owed him a favour so as usual he went to the inn and sat drinking. A customer asked the inn keeper where his wife was. For a moment the man hesitated and then said, "She's in bed with a headache." Why should he tell them that she never told him anything and did as she pleased.

Short left and went to the bothy, retrieved her body and carried it to the shelter of the wood where he buried her. He returned to the castle but knew he would have to move on. Sooner or later she would be found and perhaps she had confided in someone about their meetings. Women often did. So he asked for permission to see his mother.

From the prosperous town of Berwick, Short crossed into England with a party of northerners who had sold wool in the town and were returning to their homes. The leader of the drovers had introduced Short to them as a reliable man and, like the Highlanders, they were pleased to be joined by a man who was so useful with the bow and sword. Short made himself pleasant and amenable, and the good merchants arrived back in Newcastle impressed by his honesty. Their leader, Henry de Tynne, suggested he should continue his journey to Durham and seek out the Bishop of Durham, Anthony Beck.

"Tell his steward that I have sent you and recommend you to him," he said. "I have served him on many occasions and his lordship is always in need of a good soldier."

Anthony Beck, Bishop of Durham, was confirmed as Lieutenant of Scotland during the reign of the child Queen Margaret, Maid of Norway. The Scottish barons were nervous. A child on the throne was a dangerous situation. They had agreed terms with King Edward that Scotland was a separate kingdom from England and that no Scottish Parliament could be held outside its borders. All Scotland waited to welcome the Maid of Norway to her realm.

On the Sunday after Michaelmas the great earls of Scotland, Angus, Atholl, Lennox, Menteith and Ross assembled in Perth to greet the Bishop of Durham and the Earl of Surrey. The citizens of Perth lined the streets to watch the nobles dressed in fine velvets, jewelled and plumed. If any frowned or shook their heads to see the English nobles and their large following of men-at-arms they remained silent. The happy throng was in holiday mood. The great men of the kingdom were preparing to meet their new Queen, who was at last sailing from Norway.

"Well, I say it's a shame, poor wee mite, being sent away by her father to a foreign land and she no more than a babe," said a large buxom woman in the crowd to any who cared to listen. "I hear she's a weak wee lassie," said someone standing near her.

Yet most of the crowd were too busy cheering, feasting their eyes on the magnificence of their leaders' clothes, to worry if their errand was right. Scotland's earls accompanied the representative of England at the front of the procession. The English men-at-arms rode at the rear. All were well-armed and riding fine strong horses. They did not look unfriendly and some grinned good-naturedly at the welcoming crowds. In the final rank rode Jack Short, the Bishop of Durham's emblem on his tunic and shield.

The following day the Bishop of St Andrews, accompanied by the Bishop of Durham and numerous nobles, set out on their journey to the isles of Orkney to welcome the little girl, but rumours were already spreading that the maid had died. The two Englishmen discussed the possibilities if the rumour should prove to be true. The bishop had seen Margaret in Oslo and he had told King Edward that he did not think the child would live to womanhood. "She is so pale and thin, my lord. Her lips are blue and when she runs to play she is breathless and weak." He shook his head, "I cannot see that such a sickly child can survive for long."

If the news were true the crown of Scotland would be worn by the strongest man, and who stronger than the King of England? He had subdued Wales and to force Scotland to recognise himself as overlord seemed natural and sensible. England's northern border could never be safe if the Scottish barons fought among themselves for the throne.

Anthony Beck and the Earl of Surrey waiting impatiently at Leuchars for news of the little queen were somewhat alarmed by the restlessness of the waiting Scottish earls. The bishop wrote to his royal master informing him that Robert Bruce, Lord of Annandale, had arrived in Perth with a large following and that the earls of Mar and Atholl had already left presumably to raise an army. "I advise Your Majesty to come to an understanding with John Balliol provided he accepts you as overlord."

The bishop sat back in his chair and listened as his clerk reread the letter to him. Yes, it set out a clear picture of the problem and the letter was sealed. How quickly the situation has changed, he thought. Just a few days previously the Scottish nobles had ridden together, united, acknowledging the cheering crowds. Now they were split into warring groups. He sighed. Politics never ceased to amaze him. He must act quickly and contact John Balliol. Jack Short, dressed as a Scot, carried the bishop's letter to England.

The Earl of Surrey came in. "A messenger has just arrived. There are disturbances in Moray. They don't waste time, do they?" He jabbed a thumb in the direction of the north. "The throne must be secured for my son-in-law, Balliol, before the earls have time to attack strategic strongholds. Balliol is pleasant enough, but he hasn't the stomach for military campaigns, so Durham, we must gain his throne for him."

William and John Wallace arrived in the monastic school at Dundee in the late autumn. Margaret Wallace had been ailing during the past few months and had expressed a wish to pray at the shrine of the blessed St Margaret at Dunfermline. So the family took pilgrim's staffs and walked humbly with others to the holy place. Lady Margaret unburdened her soul to the saintly queen, seeking comfort from her sacred relics. Then they continued their journey to Kilspindie to stay with her brother-in-law who was a monk of the Benedictine Order.

Elderslie had been left in Malcolm's charge. Tom and Alice had moved away to their own manor five years earlier, but they were close enough to give advice should the young man need it. Tom had inherited his estate from his eldest brother, who had died childless. Tom's first wife had died leaving him with a son also called Tom, who was a year older than William. When his parents had left Elderslie, young Tom had preferred to stay with the Wallace household, and the two young men ran the estate amicably between them.

The Wallace brothers lodged in Dundee with their father's friends, with whom he also had business dealings. The Blair household was lively. Master Andrew Blair, cloth merchant, lived in one of the new-style houses built from sound stone, with its own cellars and a walled garden at the rear, where Mistress Blair grew sweet smelling herbs and lavender. The older sons worked with their father, but the third son, John, the same age as William, attended the monastic school and was destined for the church. There were two young sisters. Isabelle the eldest at thirteen had bright red hair and a freckled face. She was a lively young thing, more interested in following the young men than helping her mother sewing, spinning and preparing the food and preserves. William was unused to living in a household with young girls, but found it pleasant in the winter evenings when they gathered around the fire. Isabelle was clever telling riddles and stories, and had a clear and pleasant singing voice.

On the day when the nobles paraded through the streets of Perth, William, John and John Blair were staying at Kilspindie and went to Perth to watch the procession. It was a brave sight with proud banners flying in a light breeze. "The English have splendid horses, even the men-at-arms have good mounts," commented John Wallace. It was a good-natured parade. The nobles were laughing and talking to each other waving gauntleted hands at the crowds.

In the evening the three young men stopped at an inn. It was full of lively English and Scots men-at-arms, talking and laughing, boasting, telling yarns. The three were not looking for brawls or trouble and after finishing their drinks they left collecting their shaggy beasts from the stables and rode home to Kilspindie.

It was here that they heard of the death of the little queen. Scotland was without a sovereign. William's great uncle shook his head sadly, "We knew good times under the old king, lad, but without God's guiding hand the nobles will squabble, take sides and the strongest will take the throne, but the people will suffer. This is a sad day."

The Blair household discussed what the future might hold. Master Blair, as a merchant, said to his sons and guests that an uncertain future would prove bad for business. He had recently returned from Berwick. "The English are much in evidence there. I think it's from the south that we can expect trouble. I saw the English king once. A warlike man he is. He has taken Wales and I think he will do the same with us."

William looked at the older man and said, "But we are a free people, sir." "Since when has a people's freedom stopped a strong man taking what he wants. If we don't have a strong man to lead us, we will be prey to any who wants to feather his own nest," replied Master Blair. "Then we will fight, sir." The older man smiled sadly, "Lad, in wars all men are losers". Then as an afterthought he added, "Particularly the merchants. How can we trade when armies fight?"

Yet as the year passed and season followed season the Blair household noticed little change in their lives. The fields were ploughed, the crops sown and harvested and Master Blair prospered but in the south Edward of England played arbitrator to the Scottish succession.

# The Bridal Wreath

In July of the year following the death of the little queen, Master Blair returned from Berwick where he had journeyed with his eldest son. He returned full of news of the great assembly which had been held at Norham. "We saw old Bruce ride away looking like thunder. I say he should be our king. He's old, but spry, and the Bruce kindred are all hardy men. Their claim is as good as that of the Comyn men." "Who do folk say will be our future king, sir," asked William. "Balliol as he is in direct line. The sooner it's all decided the better for trade."

Shortly afterwards William and John received a message from their uncle and they sought permission from their tutors to set out for Kilspindie. The weather was beautiful. The heather was purple on the hills and the air, heavy with its perfume, mingled with the pungent smell of thyme. They rested for a while, allowing their ponies to drink from a stream. William lay back against a tussock gazing at the blue sky with his head cradled on his arms. Bees were busy, and he could see an eagle soaring upwards in the caressing breeze. John had stripped off his clothes and was swimming in a nearby pool. "Come on, Will. It'll make you feel good." "Nay man, let's get going and find out what ails our uncle." William was always single-minded.

When they arrived at Kilspindie it was plain from their uncle's face, when he came to greet them, that it was not a great disaster which had overtaken him. "Hallo, Uncle Crawford, are you well?" He looked up at his nephews. His sister had certainly produced a fine-looking brood. William looked larger than when he had last seen him. He had broadened and seemed more like a man than a beardless youth.

"Aye, Will, but I have received news from your father." William looked sharply at his uncle. "Nay, lad, your parents are well, but they have heard that William Wallace, your great uncle has died, God rest his soul," he crossed himself, "and he has made you his heir, William." William remembered his great uncle with affection. He knew that Uncle William had lived a good long life, but was sorry that he had not been able to say goodbye. "Your father wants you to go home so that you may visit your inheritance and put all in good order."

The following day William and John rode back to Elderslie. They had not been home for some time and it was good to see their kinsfolk and the manor once more. Murdo was waiting for them. It was he who had brought the news of his old friend's death. William was shocked to see that Murdo looked old, grizzled and gnarled like an ancient oak. William towered over Murdo yet he remembered looking up into his fearful face. It did not seem that long ago. Now it was he who offered the assisting hand to the old man.

Sir Malcolm, with his eldest son and Tom, were all busy harvesting, but there were many hands to do the work so William and John could be spared. The two set out with Murdo for Borthwick water. It was nine years since William Wallace had ridden to Borthwick. Now he was a striking young man riding to his own manor with his younger brother at his side. Once again they slept by the ruins of the Roman fort. He wondered idly why the Roman commander should have built it in such a remote spot. It did not appear to guard any dwellings but was at a road junction.

Janet and old John came out to greet them. John had been working in the mill and was covered in dust and flour. Janet hobbled out. She was more lame than when William had last seen her. There were tears in her eyes as she greeted William. He reminded her of his uncle. Old William Wallace had not kept many followers, as the manor was not large, but when they all sat down at the boards to eat that night there were eight men including Murdo and John. Janet had two women to assist her in running the household. Neither was very young.

Janet had been expecting them daily and in readiness she had cleaned and decorated the hall. The earthen floor had been swept and fresh herbs and sweet smelling meadow grass had been spread about. After their meal they sat drinking. Murdo went to a carved oak chest and lifted out the two handed sword Vengeance and a fine shield. "These are part of your inheritance, Master." William took the sword outside and, laughing, swung the great weapon cutting the air with ringing slashes. "Well John, do you remember when we were boys how we admired this." He caressed the blade with his fingers. "We couldn't even lift it from the ground then, Will," replied his brother.

In the hall Murdo said, "He also asked that we should give you his battleaxe and cloak." He handed William a heavy two-headed axe and the red woollen cloak William had seen his uncle wear on that snowy day many years earlier. "He asked that he should be laid to rest wearing his chain mail, and this we did." Murdo got up abruptly, "I'll be away to my bed now," he said gruffly and disappeared. Janet had dewy eyes, but said she hoped that Master William would never have to use his sword in anger.

The following day the young men went out to oversee the livestock and harvest the crops. The oats and barley looked as if they would produce a good yield, although the manor could not be described as wealthy. The flock was well cared for and the fleeces in the shearing shed were of good quality.

William spent the next six weeks working with his men bringing in the harvest. There were repairs to be carried out to outbuildings and plough, as well as other implements to be looked over and sharpened ready for the new season.

He managed to hunt with his brother and they met John the Outlaw. He was arranging his snares and greeted them cautiously, unsure if the new master of Borthwick remembered him. He need not have feared. William Wallace was not a man to forget old friends, nor was he a man who chose his friends only from among the useful and powerful. He remembered John and hailed him courteously, introducing him to his brother as John the hunter, a neighbour and old friend of their uncle. They talked about hunting and John told them where they might find an old twelve-point stag. William thanked him and said that he would arrange for his skins to be taken to Berwick as his uncle had done. John the Outlaw watched the two young men. He was pleased that under the new master his life would remain undisturbed.

Once the harvest had been brought in, the men fished in Borthwick Water, which ran through the estate, while the women smoked the catch ready for winter. They had felled a stout oak. The branches would be used in the smoke house. The trunk was cut into short lengths for storing: William had plans that would require some well-seasoned wood.

They were sitting outside oiling some leather harnesses when John the Outlaw arrived carrying a bundle of furs on his shoulder. "Good day to you Master William, Master John," he touched his forehead in a salute.

Janet had seen him arrive and brought out ale, bread and cheese. She was at her happiest caring for the men. John the Outlaw thanked her. From his bag, he brought out a pair of boots, made from otter skins with the fur inside and tied at the ankle with leather thongs. "These are for you, Janet. They will keep the chilblains away in the winter."

Janet was delighted. She always suffered sorely in winter from chilblains. John also took out the pelts of stoats, in their snow-white soft winter coats, each with a black tipped tail. "These are for the lady, your mother," he handed them to William. "They will go well around the hood of a cloak or the cuffs of a dress," he added.

William was taken aback with such a costly gift. Sold in Berwick, the man would receive a good price for such rare and beautiful skins. "You should keep these for yourself, John, the wealthy like to dress themselves in such," said William, but the man shrugged. "The rich have enough fine furs and velvets. They'll not miss these."

In the third week of September the brothers set out to return to their father's manor. The weather had turned. It had rained heavily the previous day, and dark clouds, intermittent rain and a blustery wind chased them back to Clydesdale.

William was pleased with the arrangements he had made for the management of his estate which he left in the care of Murdo, John and Janet. He was still uncertain what he wanted to do with his own future. He had been happy enough to enter the service of the Church because it had been his parents' wish that he should dedicate his life to Christ. He enjoyed his studies at Dundee and knew he was a good student. His tutors said he had a sound understanding of the law. His inheritance would make entry to the Church easier. Now he felt uncertain and in doubt.

That autumn he returned to Dundee with John his brother, staying with the Blairs. John Blair was to enter the Benedictine Order that winter and eager that his friend should join him, but still William hesitated. He spent time at the monastic school teaching the younger boys, assisted copying documents in his bold handwriting and continued his own studies.

In November Scotland at last had a new king. John Balliol had been declared the rightful heir by Edward of England and was inaugurated at Scone on the thirtieth day of November. John and William Wallace accompanied by friends, Duncan of Lorn, Neil Campbell and John Blair on his last outing before entering the Church, joined the crowds lining the route from Perth to Scone to watch the procession. There were many Englishmen among the company. "The English seem to be with us a great deal these days," William remarked to his friends. "Their own homes can't be so braw that they spend so much time with us." "It's our lassies they're interested in, man," said Duncan.

That evening everyone celebrated their king's inauguration. William and his friends sat at the boards of the Crossed Keys drinking. A party of English men-at-arms were gathered around the fire. It was the best place in the inn. They sprawled on the benches and around the table. One large fellow stood with his back to the fire warming his haunches, his drink clasped firmly in his hand. They were very noisy and their presence subdued all Scots in the inn. William had been scowling in their direction for some time and John Blair noticed his friend's increasing temper. William was not usually quick-tempered, but once angered he could explode, especially when he had had a drink or two. John, anxious not to be involved in a brawl, persuaded them to leave.

Isabelle Blair was sixteen and preparing for marriage. She had been betrothed at Christmas to the eldest son of a burgess of Berwick. The betrothal feast was to take place at the bride's home. The parents and groom arrived before William and John set out for their uncle's house at Kilspindie, where they were to spend Christmas. William did not take to the groom. He thought him arrogant, but Master Blair was pleased with the betrothal and dowry arrangements – and Isabelle seemed happy.

The English king subdued any criticism in his choice of John Balliol as king by remaining in Scotland with a great following. He was pleased with himself and patiently awaited the outcome of his careful plans. He doubted that the Scottish nobles would suffer that fool Balliol for long, and he was sure they would begin plotting and scheming long before the celebrations were over. Balliol was amiable and too ready to see everyone's point of view. When Edward finally returned to his own land, he left behind a sufficient number of his own subjects to keep him well informed and to instigate just the right amount of restlessness among the Scots.

Just before the Christmas feast, Edward ordered the Bishop of Durham to attend him. They discussed Scotland at some length. "Durham, we must remind that Scottish idiot that he owes his throne to us. Have you news of any problems in which we may interest ourselves?" The bishop smiled, "Leave it to me, Sire, I know a way we can disturb him."

In his own apartment the bishop summoned his clerk and began dictating a letter to Master Roger Bartholomew, merchant of Berwick, who had been in his pay for sometime. He sat for a while staring into the flames of the fire with a goblet of wine cradled in his hand. His master should have taken the Scottish throne. Gifts of land, money or an heiress in marriage and Edward of England could be wearing the Scottish crown already. The death of Queen Eleanor had certainly unsettled his master. Well, time and God would heal his mourning and hopefully his judgement.

The Lord Bishop's intelligence network was extensive and well rewarded. Master Bartholomew responded to the bishop's instructions almost immediately. He was greedy as well as malicious. The Scottish courts had recently passed a judgement against him so he appealed to Edward of England, as overlord, to review the Scottish judgement. Edward with remarkable speed and great benevolence reversed the judgement. The slight to King John and Scotland's independence was plain.

King John, meanwhile, tried to maintain an aloof dignity ignoring the malicious whisperings of his lords and the obvious goading from the English king.

T he following April, after John was made king, William Wallace gained his majority. He had spent the winter in Dundee working at the monastic school, but his doubts about a calling for the Church had continued and he planned to travel to his estate for the spring sowing. During his journey there something happened which was to make up his mind and change the course of his life.

John Wallace remained in Dundee while William went home to Elderslie. His parents were to accompany him on the now familiar journey to Borthwick Water. Malcolm had married the previous winter and his parents decided to leave the young couple for a while in the privacy of the manor.

They stopped at Lanark. The busy town was brimming with English soldiers. Sir Malcolm was anxious to see his old friend Sir Hugh Braidfute, whose manor was in the north of the town with the rocky Cartland Crags towering behind. It was a pleasant estate, well husbanded by Sir Hugh. Since William had inherited his own estate he was taking a greater interest in farm management.

The estate had another interest for the young man. Sir Hugh's daughter Marion had grown to womanhood. William attracted the attention of the lasses. He was very appealing with a pleasant smile, well-mannered and kindly. Indeed, a man in whose company a woman felt safe. In Dundee he had visited taverns with his cronies and the easy girls who made their living in them had noticed the tall, striking young man, but his reserved nature had kept him from straying into too many liaisons.

There had been Agnes in the Blue Boar by the harbour. In spite of her profession, William found her to be a cheerful and kindly soul. They had met during the previous year. Sometimes when the weather was good they met outside the town on the banks of the Tay. She brought wine, bread and cheese which they would eat after making love on the soft turf for a bed. Agnes knew her kindly lover would go out of her life and she made the most of his attentions while she could. William enjoyed Agnes. She was a quick-witted girl, full of fun, someone who could made him laugh and he was sorry when he had to say goodbye.

Marion Braidfute was altogether different. Tall for a girl and willow slim, she had hair the colour of ripened corn and blue eyes like the periwinkle flowers that peep out of the woods in spring. She was shy but welcoming.

He watched her as she helped her stepmother and the women of the household to serve the guests. She filled William's goblet and smiled at him.

William lost his heart that very moment.

It was three days later that Sir Malcolm mentioned to his wife that William did not appear so impatient to get to his own manor. Margaret Wallace laughed and put her arm around her husband's ample waist. "That's because Marion has caught his eye, husband. Do you think Sir Hugh would consider such a union between our families?"

Malcolm Wallace looked enquiringly at his wife, surprised that she took William's change of heart so lightly. He had thought the young girl comely but for many years now they had both set their minds on William entering the Church – and a wife for his second son had not entered their plans. William's estate could not be considered large and moreover was in a relatively inaccessible part of the kingdom. Sir Hugh could certainly make a better match for his only daughter, who owned the manor of Lamington in her own right.

They stayed at Lanark for a week. On the evening before their departure, Hugh Braidfute walked with his old friend to the far end of the manor, to see one of his fields which was being prepared for sowing. It was a fine evening after an April shower, and the damp earth smelt fresh. Sir Hugh said, "William has a liking for Marion." "So my wife has pointed out to me," replied Sir Malcolm. "Marion inherited her mother's estate of Lamington. She and her stepmother do not always see eye to eye. I would like to see the maid settled with a good husband: she will have seen eighteen summers this year and is ready for marriage. What do you think, my friend, of a match between your lad and Marion?"

"He is a good son, but I have never spoken to William about marriage and I do not know what his wishes might be." He laughed. "Perhaps we should find out what her feelings are first. I have found women to be quite unpredictable in such matters." Hugh Braidfute said he would speak to his daughter, although he had noticed how she looked at the young man. It was decided that the Wallaces would visit again on their way home to Elderslie in the autumn to discuss the matter.

William showed his parents his manor of Borthwick with great pride. The sowing was well under way, as was the lambing. The flock had survived the winter well and they had not lost too many ewes or lambs to foxes. John and Murdo were advanced in years, but they still husbanded the manor as they had in old William Wallace's time. Nothing was too small to escape their attention: woe betide any man who shirked his full share of the work or left a job half done.

Janet likewise watched the serving women and when the young master returned, the manor house and barns were in good array. She was not ashamed to show a sensible woman like Margaret Wallace around. Janet had worried, however, that her master's mother would be critical of her management and the bunch of household keys that had jangled at her belt for nearly forty years would be taken away. Lady Wallace just smiled, sat herself at the fire with a piece of fine embroidery and told Janet to continue with her duties.

William was busy from dawn to dusk, taking a personal hand in everything. One afternoon while he was out with the shepherd helping him trim the ewes' hooves, John the Outlaw arrived and greeted them cheerfully. During their conversation William asked if John knew of paths through the forest which would take him quickly to Lanark. "Aye, it is possible. If you want to make such a journey, I can show you part of the way." William smiled and straightened himself, releasing the unwilling ewe. "I have a little business there and don't want to wait till the autumn. We will have broken the back of much of the work here by Tuesday next. Can you show me the way then?"

The following week William Wallace went courting. Sir Malcolm had not spoken to his son about the proposed match and William told his parents he was going hunting for a few days. His mother smiled inwardly and, after William had gone, she told her husband that William had taken his best linen surcoat, which she had embroidered around the neck and sleeves, and the red woollen cloak with the silver clasp which he had inherited from his great uncle. Her husband stared at her. "Where could the lad be going? There's nobody to impress here but sheep and deer."

"Why, he'll be heading for Lanark, Malcolm. Young men will journey far and long if their heart tells them." Then they sat in silence remembering their own youth. Malcolm patted his wife's hand and smiled.

William's journey was light-hearted. The weather kept fair and before entering the town he stopped to wash in a stream and remove the mud from his boots. He put on his fresh surcoat and entered Lanark with anticipation. Lanark was busy, the market bustling and lively. He had brought some pelts that Murdo had cured and asked him to sell, but went first to the Braidfute manor. A troop of English soldiers passed him going north and William was forced to ride off the roadway to make room for them. So many Englishmen roaming around annoyed him, but today he was going to see his love and the English could be damned.

Marion's stepmother, who did not appear surprised to see the young man, greeted him. "Good day to you, Master William". William smiled bowing stiffly. "Mistress Cecilia, I came to Lanark to visit the market," he tapped the bundle strapped to his saddle, "and since my business brought me so close to you, here I am." He made the last statement hesitatingly, unsure what explanation to give. It was unusual for William Wallace to be lost for words. He was not a lady's man and did not woo women for his own entertainment – as some men did.

Mistress Cecilia smiled, "Come you in then and take some refreshment. I will tell Marion to serve you." Once in the hall he stood awkwardly by the fire, feeling rather foolish. Marion came in bearing ale, bread and meat. In her company he relaxed. She laughed at his jokes as he told her about his manor and people and the fearful one-eyed Murdo. As the afternoon wore into early evening, he sat with the family to eat their meal before taking his leave.

"You are not stopping long in Lanark, Master Wallace," asked Marion's stepmother. "Nay lady, I must return to my estate. There is much to do to put the place in order." "And will we see you again?" she smiled looking at Marion, who blushed casting down her eyes. "Surely lady, if my business brings me to Lanark. I will call on you if I may."

Cecilia Braidfute thought that William Wallace would certainly find himself some business that would require urgent attention in Lanark. When it was time to depart, Marion came into the stable to help him saddle his horse. When he was ready to depart he said to her, "Marion, if I ask my father to speak to your father for me, would it please you?" Her face lit up: "Aye, William, it would please me greatly."

William led his horse outside, hesitated near Marion for a moment, then mounted. "Goodbye William," said the girl, and he nodded to her. She touched his booted foot and smiled. He took the road to the inn thinking about his love as he went. He would have liked to have taken her in his arms, feel her slender body close to his and smell the sweetness of her soft yellow hair, but Marion Braidfute was not Agnes. Marion would be his wife and he must hold himself in check until her father, witnessed by God, their families and friends placed her hand in his.

A joyful young man journeyed back to Borthwick the following day.

As he led his horse down a steep and stony forest path he met two tough-looking fellows. The younger man held a brace of capercailzie, the other a snare, both had bows and full quivers. William loosened the fastening that held his battleaxe to the side of his saddle and greeted the men. "Good day to you William Wallace" said the elder. William was surprised to hear his name, "You have the advantage of me." "John the Outlaw has told us about the new master of Borthwick Water." They introduced themselves and talked about hunting. William had a flagon of ale which they shared, before moving off up the bank and into the forest.

He was very busy for the rest of the spring and early summer. The lambing and the haymaking had gone well. The sheep were sheared and then taken to fresh pasture. His father looked through the fleeces. "It's a fine flock, William. The market for wool is improving every year." "I have a mind to travel to Berwick one day, father, to see the wool merchants and the foreign weavers for myself. The estate is not large, but I think it could be made more prosperous than it is."

The following morning father and son, accompanied by John the Outlaw as their guide, went hunting. Murdo and John seldom went far into the forest these days. Murdo complained of aches and pains in his joints, which made him stiff, and old John suffered from poor eyesight and was unable to aim an arrow at a target. Quite close to the estate William brought down a young stag: it was rare for him to miss his quarry.

When they were sitting by the bank of a small stream, relaxing before returning home, William broke his long silence about Marion Braidfute. "Father, I have seen the maid I wish to have as a wife. Will you speak for me?" "Tell me first who she is, William."

When he told his father the young woman's name, Malcolm smiled. "Your mother said you were smitten by that young maid, Will. You are a lucky man. Her father and I have considered such a match and we intend to discuss a marriage contract on our return journey in September. You know the girl will have a sizeable dowry, William. She has inherited her mother's estate at Lamington."

William looked annoyed, "I don't consider an estate good reason to be wedded to a shrewish wife. It's Marion's sweetness which I will marry." "Well, son, don't fret: I'll see what bargain can be struck."

The week following the conversation with his father, William Wallace set out for Lanark. This time he made no secret of his destination nor the purpose for his visit. He trimmed his beard and hair and carried clean clothes. On his arrival the family behaved towards him as if he were already a member of their kindred.

Marion was so sweet. She made him feel like a king, but her parents were careful that they were not left alone and were given no opportunity to make a clandestine meeting. When the time came for him to take his leave, he managed to whisper to her that in September their fathers intended to discuss a betrothal between them.

In early September Sir Malcolm and Lady Wallace returned to Elderslie, calling on Sir Richard Wallace of Riccarton who promised to support his brother in the matter of William's betrothal.

When the leaves turned to gold at the end of the month, the two gentlemen set out for Lanark. It was undoubtedly a good match for William, second son as he was. His estate of Borthwick Water was not overly wealthy and its relative remoteness made it unattractive as a place to live all the year round. It was apparent, however, that Marion wanted the match and Sir Hugh was an indulgent father. He knew the Wallace kindred and thought William would make a suitable husband for his girl.

The bargain was struck: Marion would bring her property of Lamington as a dowry. If she died without an heir the estate would return to the Braidfute family. If William and Marion had a living child on Marion's death the manor would go to her eldest child. A contract would be drawn up and the betrothal would take place at Christmas.

It was a most satisfactory outcome. The three men shook hands and drank a glass of good French wine to the union of their two families. Young Tom Johnston was sent to Borthwick with the news that William should go to Lanark for his betrothal at Christmas. "Tom can keep him company until then. The lad is sorely in need of young people on that manor of his," Sir Malcolm told his wife.

The week before the feast of Yule William Wallace, accompanied by Tom, set out for his betrothal. It was cold and crisp with a heavy hoar frost as they travelled through the Selkirk Forest to Lanark. William knew the forest well now and he was a welcome guest in the cottages of banished men along his route.

He had been busy during the autumn having journeyed to Berwick with six pack ponies carrying fleece and furs, mostly otter and fox pelts. He called at the house of Isabelle who was heavy with her first child. Her husband helped William to sell his fleeces and skins as William had never visited Berwick before. It was a lively place, bustling with merchants and traders and the harbour was packed with vessels from all over Christendom – even at a time of the year when the sea was at its most wild and cruel. There were many foreigners, not just among the sailors, but Flemish weavers as well. He was very impressed by Berwick.

With the money from the sale of his fleeces and skins he purchased betrothal gifts: a gold ring with the inscription *A gift from William*, and a length of linen lawn to match the colour of Marion's eyes, enough to make a wedding dress. He had not spoken a great deal to Isabelle. As a married woman it was not quite proper when her husband was not present, but he had asked her about her new home. She had been very excited. "You can buy anything you want, William. Bread, beer, bangles or brocade. It really is a remarkable place, Will, and so many people to talk to. My parents are coming to visit us for the birth of my child. I do hope mother likes it here too."

On the eve of Christmas, William Wallace and Marion Braidfute were betrothed in the hall of the manor. Sir Hugh placed Marion's hand in William's, who gave her the betrothal ring. The priest was present and witnessed their fathers signing the marriage contract and it was agreed that Marion should become his wife on the first Sunday after Easter.

She looked so fair. Her unbraided hair was flowing around her like a mantle of gold. She wore on her head a gold circlet, a sign of her maidenly virtue. The warmth from the fire and the cup of wine which William and Marion shared brought a flush to her cheeks. Her eyes sparkled with the excitement of the occasion. The benches and tables were moved and they danced and sang deep into the night. William and most of the men were full of wine and cheer.

When many of the guests had succumbed to the wine and snored on the benches around the hall, William, his brother John, Tom Johnston and other young men attending the festivities were banished to the stables to sleep and William had to endure many jokes and jibes. "Go to her, Will, perhaps the women who sleep by her have taken too much wine. Go and slip in beside her, go on man. She'll be softer company than we are." "Be quiet you lechers, I can wait till spring."

Everyone laughed and there was some horseplay before the young men fell asleep. In the darkness William lay in the soft hay, listening to the snores and grunts from the men around him and the animals moving around in the barn below. His loins ached with yearning for her. Finally the wine sent him drifting into a deep sleep.

Sir Hugh suggested that the Wallaces and their followers should ride with him to Lamington to see the manor. Lady Wallace declined the invitation. She was rather tired and it was a cold day, but Marion accompanied William riding proudly at his side. "When I was a child we often lived at Lamington, William. It's wonderful and beautiful in the summer."

The manor of Lamington was of a good size with fine barns and storehouses. Some required rethatching, but the hall itself was comfortable with a magnificent fire burning when they arrived. The Yule log was a stout holly and the smell from it and the roasting venison drifted to the rafters.

As they rode back to Lanark Marion asked, "William, when we are married could we not live at Lamington? It's a fine manor and we could make a good living there."

William had been thinking much the same, but was pleased Marion had herself made the suggestion. Borthwick was so remote. It was dark when they returned to the Braidfute manor and William assisted Marion to dismount. In the darkness, sheltered by their ponies, he pressed her to him and gave her a lingering kiss. She was soft and very slender in his arms.

On the twelfth day of the Yule feast the betrothed pair took a fond farewell of each other. William returned with Tom to Borthwick; his parents and John to Elderslie. He helped his mother to mount her bay mare and she bent down and kissed his forehead. "God bless you, my son, take care on your return to your own manor."

Before departing for Borthwick, he sought Sir Hugh, "Sir, I have thought carefully and believe that we should make our home at Lamington. My estate is distant and there would be little comfort or company there for Marion. My own men are trustworthy fellows." Sir Hugh thought it a sound plan, certainly until they had settled together. "It takes time to adjust to married life my boy, ask any married man and he will tell you so."

Marion walked a short way with him along the track that led from her father's hall. Tom had discreetly gone on ahead and the young pair walked slowly holding hands in the cold crisp morning. Marion looked sad with tears brimming in her eyes. "Don't be so sad, lassie. The time will quickly pass and we shall soon be as one." She smiled looking up at him. They kissed; then William let her go laughing. He mounted his horse and said, "I must be away, Marion. Another kiss like that and I won't be able to leave you. Then your kinsfolk will think I'm a man without a backbone. Farewell, my sweet." "Goodbye, Will. Take care."

It was a wonderful spring day on the twenty fifth day of April with the trees dressed in soft green and the bell of Lanark church inviting people to witness the marriage between William Wallace and Marion Braidfute. The groom and his men stood at the entrance waiting for the bride and her kinsfolk to arrive. The bridal procession came into view with Sir Hugh leading his daughter's pony. Marion's stepmother had washed her hair in lye to clean and lighten it and it gleamed under her veil of fine white gauze, which was held in place by the maiden's circlet. The blue material that William had bought in Berwick had been made into a gown, with a close fitting bodice embroidered with flowers around the neck and sleeves.

"You look lovely my dear," her father had said as they rode from her home for the last time. She felt rather frightened. William Wallace had not been the only man to ask for her, but he was the only man she had wanted to marry. He was amiable and she felt secure in his company. Her stepmother in a rare moment of tenderness towards her had patted her hand just before their departure and said, "Don't be fearful, Marion, William will make you a kind and sensible husband."

So here she was riding to her wedding. There could be no man better than her William. She touched her necklace. It had been her mother's; garnets and fresh water pearls linked on a silver chain with a silver cross. Her father said that it had been his wedding gift to her mother. On her finger was William's ring. Both trinkets were her most treasured possessions. As the church came into view she could see

William waiting among the groomsmen. He was so tall and strong, so noble and gallant. Her toes tingled with joy when she thought of him.

William's parents, uncles and cousins were already in the church to await the bridal pair, but William waited with some of his young men. The Wallace kinsfolk had come to Lanark in force to support the Wallaces of Elderslie.

William set Marion down while her family and followers went happily into the church. With her father holding her left hand, William her right, and followed by his merry groomsmen, they walked up the nave of the church towards the altar already laid with the communion chalice gleaming in a beam of sunlight. Her father squeezed her hand and, in response to the priest's question, said he gave his daughter as wife to William Wallace. He left her side and went to his place on the men's benches, followed by William's supporters.

The young couple stood before the cross, making their vows to each other. Even William Wallace's large bulk looked small and insignificant when kneeling before God's altar – as other men had done before him – and taking onto himself the responsibilities of a married man. When they had taken the sacrament and received the priest's blessing, William led his bride out of the church into the sunshine, with the congregation following and the wedding festivities began.

The wedded pair led the united families to the manor of Lamington. Some of the young men galloped ahead, bringing the news to the estate folk that their new master and their mistress were on their way home.

The manor house was set on a hillside with pasture sweeping down to the river. Marion knew and loved every nook and cranny, especially the old oak in front of the house that she had climbed before she realised that girls were not supposed to do such manly things. She loved the stables where she had kept her pony and where the old bitch had whelped and nursed her puppies. Marion had a way with animals and two of the pups had grown up with her. Now she was back to make her home in the dear old place. William and Marion took the high seats at the head of the table with their parents, parents-in-law and other relatives around them.

"Long life and good fortune to you both," said Sir Richard. There was a chorus of agreement inside and outside in the yard, for there was not enough room in the hall for everyone. The toasting and feasting continued and outside minstrels played all the old favourites. As the afternoon drew into evening, William and Marion led the dancing.

He had never been that fond of dancing and laughed in an embarrassed way. "Really, William, you have two left feet," his mother had once declared, but a man had to dance at his own wedding.

As night approached some of the young men began sniggering and found an excuse to go to the chamber which had been prepared for the husband and wife. A full moon began to climb high into the night sky and Sir Hugh quietened the gathering raising his goblet to his daughter and son-in-law. "It's time you were about your business, William." Marion blushed, William looked embarrassed and his guests collapsed around him in laughter. "Marion, you must go with the women and prepare for your husband and God bless you both this night," said her father.

Lady Cecilia and Lady Margaret took Marion by the hand to lead her to the bridal chamber. She hung her head and held back a little as was proper, but then she laughed looked over her shoulder at William and went willingly with the ladies. In the bedroom they helped her to put on a fine linen shift and Lady Margaret brushed Marion's hair which spread around her shoulders before she climbed into the bed and sat waiting for the men to bring in William. There was a fire in the hearth and the flames were throwing lively shadows around the room.

On the chest standing in the corner the ladies had laid the wife's linen coif and a new leather belt embossed with silver with the keys of the manor hanging on it. These were ready for Marion to wear when she awoke in the morning. There was a lot of noise and ribald jokes in the hall and outside in the yard. Marion sat patiently while the men were removing some of William's outer clothing and boots, and wrapping him in Uncle William's red cloak. As the door opened Sir Malcolm and Sir Hugh led in a rather red-faced William. The young men stood around outside the door. "Go to it, Will," declared Adam Wallace. "If you need any help, just let me know," said another. "Don't forget what I told you, Will, and you'll manage," said John Wallace. All were eager to show what experience they had had with women.

The two old knights led him to the bed, took his cloak and said goodnight to the young people. The parents left firmly closing the door behind them. William could hear his father's stern voice outside ordering the young men to leave the bridal pair in peace and to go and enjoy the dancing. Marion's old hounds settled down outside the door prepared to guard the room until their mistress should reappear.

After the excitement of the day the two looked at each other. The expectation that William had felt in church appeared to have left him and he hesitated. It was Marion, despite her shyness, who made the first move to break the tension between them. She smiled gently turning back the sheet on the bed beside her. William took hold of the covers and turned them down so that he could get into bed. Between the sheets where William's ample back would lay sat a large frog. They both laughed and the frightened frog jumped off the bed, hopping away into the safety of the shadows. "Perhaps we should search the bed. Maybe they've put toads at the bottom, Will," laughed Marion.

Suddenly they were relaxed, smiling into each other's eyes, oblivious to the music, singing and shouting that was going on outside. William took her in his arms, shyly at first, then with mounting passion and desire they consummated their love. When Marion gave a cry of pain as William made her his wife, an ecstasy of joy and love engulfed him.

William was not a man to sit around feasting for long. As soon as it was decent to do so, he began organising the sowing and work on the estate. As his father was fond of saying, "If the master is not seen to lead, how can he expect to be followed."

Marion was anxious to show her husband how well she could manage a household. There were always dishes of curds in the cheese house, sides of meat roasting or being smoked, and twice a week she baked bread and pies. After haymaking they intended to visit Borthwick, check on the manor and introduce Marion to the folk there.

There had been only one black cloud on William's horizon. In May, after his marriage, the news went around the country that the English king had called on the Scots to support him in his argument with the king of France. They were squabbling over the lordship of Gascony. 'Why should we be involved in another man's fight?' was the general opinion, particularly when that man was King Edward of England.

"The Lord Stewart has been ordered to attend with mounted knights and men-at-arms," said John Wallace when he was at Lamington for the haymaking. "He has refused to go which is a relief to father and Malcolm for they say they'll not fight for an English cause." "What is our king's reply to the English king, John?" "He's ordered the English out, man. They must all go, which is a blessing. Every tavern from Glasgow to Dundee is crawling with Englishmen. They have even set up a committee to help our king rule. He's a weak man, Will. We should get ourselves another king." William turned sharply on his brother, "Be quiet man. You're speaking treason. Besides to champion another king will bring confusion and unrest. We must be united or we'll be prey to the greed of the English."

They had been working since early morning and the sun was high. William could see Marion and her women coming across the field carrying food and drink for the men. Her dogs were racing off across the field after a hare. Time to call a break. Marion had brought bacon, bread and beer and they all sat in the shade of the oak. "This is a fine piece of bacon, mistress," said old Neil. "There's nothing quite like a good bite of bacon washed down with beer I always say."

They dozed for a while. Marion was sitting with her back against the tree and William was lying with his head resting in her lap and gazing at the branches and leaves overhead. "We'll be ready to leave for Borthwick Water in three days, Marion." He yawned, closed his eyes and fell into a light sleep. Most of their people were also asleep. Her dogs came bounding back. They had been unsuccessful in their hunt. Her dogs usually were as she fed them too well. She threw them some pieces of rind and scraps of bread. Then they also sat down, scratched, yawned, sprawled on the warm earth and slept.

William left Tom Johnston in charge of his affairs. The shearing had to be done yet, but Tom was as dependable as his father. William, Marion and John set out for Borthwick.

In the late autumn on his way to his uncle at Kilspindie John Wallace visited his parents' home. Life was changing. He would have to come to a decision about his own future. Elderslie was crowded once more. His sister-in-law had produced a healthy son and was again pregnant. His parents were talking about building a dower house and there would not be room for an unmarried son. Perhaps he would enter the church. God willing, William would become a father by March and he had asked John to persuade their mother to come to Lamington in the New Year to assist Marion at her lying-in.

Lady Margaret found winter travelling difficult, but she could not refuse her son's wife, particularly since the girl did not have a mother of her own. At Christmas she sent one of the men to Lamington with small gifts, a flagon of the best French wine, an embroidered shift for Marion and a beautifully illuminated Psalter, which once had belonged to her own mother, for William. "The master and mistress will come to you in the first week of February" said the messenger.

The winter was hard that year with driving rain and drifting snow followed by gale force winds. The freezing conditions brought much hardship to the people. For four weeks towards the end of January

William and his people remained close to the manor. No one could struggle far afield and many deer and other wild beasts came down from the hills searching for food. They could be seen eating bark from the trees at the forest edge. Their hunger and desperation was making them fearless of man. Occasionally the howls of wolves were heard close to the manor.

As Marion's time drew near William became concerned for his parents. Marion was very heavy. He feared it might be a matter of who was the stronger, his parents battling through the snow or Marion keeping on her feet with so large a burden. He was worried about her. During the past two or three years he had become quite skilled in animal husbandry, spending time with his shepherds and knew well the difficulties which a mother faced as she gave birth. As they lay in bed one night he placed his hand on her abdomen to feel the movements of his child. Certainly it moved vigorously and was large, but he was sure the shape felt wrong. Could it be that she carried her child upside down? He found himself things to do about the barns to keep his mind occupied.

Old Neil came to him one morning carrying a cradle. It was carved with magic signs to bring good luck to its occupant. "I've made this for the mistress. It's good and strong so you'll be able to put all your babes in it." "Thank you, Neil. It's a fine piece of work. Let us hope my mother arrives before her grandchild does."

The mistress was pleased with the cradle and had it taken into their bedchamber ready for the birth. They lay in bed that night listening to the wind as it found every opening, buffeting at the thatch and shutters. Marion clung to William kissing and winding herself around him. Eventually unable to bear the longing that she aroused in him he took her arms gently from around his neck. "Nay, Marion, my sweet. You are so big now and so near your time that I dare not love you as I would. You must lie quietly and rest." She lay limply at his side and then in the darkness he realised that she was weeping. He leaned up on his elbow kissing her wet, tearful face. "What ails you lass? Are you in pain?" She flung her arms around his neck. "Oh, Will, I'm so frightened. You do love me, don't you. You won't leave me when the time comes, will you, Will?" He tried to soothe her as much as he could. When she was a little quieter he fetched her a cup of the wine that his mother had sent. Taking a hot poker from the fire he warmed it and gave it to his wife. It had a calming and relaxing effect and she went to sleep quite quickly lying in his arms. He lay holding her, but had a bad feeling in the pit of his stomach that would not go away.

Two days later his parents and two retainers arrived struggling through the snow. They were cold and tired, but in good heart. His mother took over the household. She oozed confidence and bustling efficiency that seemed to reassure Marion. William watched his mother slightly amused. His father saw the look on William's face. "Your mother is enjoying herself, son. She feels rather useless at Elderslie now that your sister-in-law has taken over. I think we will have difficulty in getting her to leave when Marion is once again on her feet."

During the night on the first Sunday in March Marion's pains began. Years later, when William had seen and experienced much suffering, if he closed his eyes, he could still hear her cries of anguish and his mother's voice trying to coax and calm her. All that day and night Marion laboured.

"She has opened fully and I can see and feel the child, William, but she makes no further progress. I have tried everything, even shaken pepper under her nose to make her sneeze." It was well known that sometimes the mother's sneezing dislodged the child but all to no avail. "William, she is calling for you. Come and sit with her." William looked embarrassed but obediently followed his mother. As they went to the chamber, he confessed to his mother what had worried him for sometime. "Mother, is the child coming feet first." "Aye, Will, it is and I can't move it."

"Then I must try and pull it out from her, mother, while she still has strength left in her." "Will, I have heard that men do this sometimes, but always the child has died and sometimes the mother." She looked fearfully at her son. "Mother, we have no alternative. If we leave her she will surely die."

Marion lay pale and sweating, her hair wet at the temples. She held out her arms to her husband who lifted her slightly and gently embraced her. "Oh, Will, please help me," she sobbed. "Be still, precious, and we'll see what can be done."

Margaret Wallace gave her daughter-in-law a cup of warmed spiced wine to hearten her. When the next pain came, William forced his fingers around the child and began to pull down one leg, then the other. Marion screamed and screamed, but he did not let go. He allowed her to rest and when another attack of pain gripped her he pulled. "Once more, sweetheart, and I think your suffering will be at an end."

With William's mother on one side and Neil's wife on the other to give her support she pushed, William pulled and the child slithered feet first into the world. The women came to the father's assistance and took the lifeless body of his son from him, while he turned to comfort his prostrate wife. For a while she lay in a state of shock, bleeding heavily and unable even to cry at the loss of her child. William knew he had damaged and torn her flesh, but at least she was relieved of her burden. After twenty minutes or so the afterbirth came away, the bleeding seemed to lessen and the women were able to tidy and clear away the mess.

Margaret Wallace busied herself caring for her daughter-in-law and for the time being it looked as if they had saved Marion. They gave her a few spoonfuls of broth, sponged her face, rebraided her hair and put warmed stones by her feet. All through this William sat holding Marion's hand. She tried to move a little but he stopped her. "Rest quietly, sweetheart, you have bled and must lie still." Then she cried, "William, our child, I want to see him." He looked at his mother, she nodded and went to the cradle where they had laid the child before he was taken for burial. Both parents looked and mourned.

Marion lay-in for some weeks. She was weak and her flesh had to heal. William's parents remained so that Lady Margaret could nurse her. On the first pleasant spring day in April, William carried Marion outside and she sat in the sun with her husband. Her dogs were overjoyed at their mistress's presence and bounded around in the sunshine. After her first outing Marion began to improve rapidly. She was less lethargic and not so inclined to bouts of weeping. By the beginning of May Sir Malcolm, growing restless, suggested that it was time they returned to their own manor.

The night before their departure Lady Wallace went to William who was in one of the barns. She felt embarrassed at having to speak to her son on such matters, but was sure that it was necessary. "Will, Marion is a loving and kind wife, but she was injured by her confinement. It would be unwise for her to be brought to bed again too quickly. She must be given time, my son, to become whole again." William grinned ruefully, "I realise that mother, but children come when you least want them." "William you must keep yourself apart from her for a month or two. I know it is not an easy thing for a man to do. Your father and I were young once, but I am sure you will not regret your self-restraint." "Marion will not like it, mother." "Then you must be strong for the two of you, my dear. Sleep in the barn during the summer, where temptation will not come your way. When she is fully recovered you may once more share a bed."

Marion was not pleased. She cried and accused him of not loving her, but eventually agreed that it would be wise for a month or two if they slept apart. The household noticed, but any comments which they tried to make were quickly stopped by old Neil and his wife.

In early August William and Marion set out together for Borthwick. It was nearly a year since he had last visited the estate and now that his wife was stronger was anxious to see the manor. The weather was fine and they stopped at midday by a lochan to rest and eat some food. Their ponies were left to graze and they lay near the water's edge in the shade of a huge pine. The only sounds came from a curlew calling some way off and the drone of bees in the heather. The water reflected the blue of the sky. It was a perfect day.

Marion was hot after the exertions of the journey. "Come on, Will, let's bathe before we eat." She laughed at him in that familiar coy way she sometimes had, drew off her shoes and began to undress herself. William watched her for a while, then he also undressed and the pair ran into the cold water. Afterwards, they made love for the first time since her confinement. At first carefully with tenderness, for he so feared to hurt her, but gradually William forgot his inhibitions and they lost themselves in the energy and love of youth.

When at last they were quiet, allowing the breeze to caress their naked bodies, William looked into his wife's sparkling eyes and said, "Marion, I believe you planned this." She laughed and threw her arms around his neck, "Oh, William Wallace, I do love you."

The old people at Borthwick were sad to hear of William and Marion's loss, but Janet said, "Time will dim the pain, my dears. There will be more babies and not that far off, I'm sure."

Murdo and John had finished the shearing. The wheat and barley were ready for harvest if the weather held, and even Marion helped, working beside her husband. He reaped and she tied and stacked the stooks. She regained her health and he thought he had never seen her looking lovelier.

Some repairs needed to be done to the roofs of the hall and barn. As the old people found it difficult to climb ladders, William spent a week overseeing repairs and where necessary carrying them out himself.

Then they all celebrated the bringing in of the harvest. The table groaned under the weight of the feast. Murdo and John entertained them with yarns about their youthful exploits. Marion sang with John the Outlaw, who had helped with the harvest. They were all very merry and feasted late into the short summer night.

In September William led a string of ten pack ponies to Berwick laden with fleeces from Borthwick. He told Marion about Berwick and she was anxious to go with him and see it for herself. They stayed at the Sign of the Blue Boar near the market place. It was a well kept inn suitable, William thought, for a married woman. While William bargained over his fleeces and pelts, Marion wandered around the market wondering at the wealth of the place, staring at the foreigners in their strange clothes and listening to their even stranger speech.

When all his business was completed they went to see Isabelle and, to William's intense joy, John Blair was also visiting his sister and her family. John looked so serious in his coarse brown robe and shaven tonsure. It was well over two years since they had last met. Both had changed: William was now a resourceful, steady husband and farmer; John rather severe but well settled into the austere monastic life.

Isabelle was a busy and comely housewife. Her eldest boy was nearly two, her second son ten months old and, she whispered to Marion that she was again with child due she thought in March or April of the following year. She was a proud young wife and mother. At her belt swung the largest bunch of household keys Marion had ever seen.

It was a stone-built house, lavishly furnished with brightly coloured wall-hangings and cushions on the settles. At table the young men talked about trade and the threat from the English. Isabelle's husband was of the opinion that they should be careful how they behaved towards the English. "The English king is warlike. He has subdued and ravaged Wales. Do we want that? What will happen to our trade if we are at war? Show me a country constantly at war and you will find a poor and desolate place."

"By all accounts England is neither poor nor desolate," said his brother-in-law. "Ah, England takes the war to others. The war is never fought on her soil. We should keep the English as our friends. They are reasonable fellows," he said. "Have we not treated with the English and bowed to their king? If we are not careful they will think us weak fools," said William.

The young merchant looked angry, "Isn't it better that we are prosperous fools than dead heroes?" William's face reddened, but he answered, "Freedom is something we should value. For a man to trade he must first be free to do so."

John, who knew his brother-in-law's views, changed the subject. They parted on good terms and William and Marion suggested that the family should visit them when business permitted, but all winter rumours and counter rumours persisted throughout the realm, but Lamington and its folk slumbered.

Edward, King of England, paced up and down. "Those cursed turds, double dealing treacherous cowards." He stormed around his council chamber. Anthony Beck stood and waited. The king would calm down. Then they could plan. He had picked up the parchment that Edward had thrown angrily on the floor. It brought news from one of Beck's informants. The Scots were about to ratify a Treaty with Philip of France. Edward had learnt about the Treaty when it was first mooted in October of the previous year and had made strenuous efforts to stop it, but now it was to be ratified and it was this that made him so angry.

"Well Anthony," he thundered, "they'll regret it. By God before this year is out they'll have reason to wish they hadn't played the fool with Edward of England. Send out orders for the army to be ready for my inspection in March at Newcastle on the Tyne." He had stopped stamping up and down the room and now calmly rapped out his instructions.

"We'll need provisions. Get my eastern shires to provide these. Yarmouth, Lynn, Boston, Wainfleet and Grimsby have the vessels. They'll ferry stores up the east coast. Get my orders out immediately. All must be ready before the spring comes. Yes, by God, no one plots behind my back and gets away with it. That fool Balliol. His nobles lead him by the nose. Well, they've given us the opportunity we've been waiting for, Anthony. We will take Berwick first, a ripe peach waiting to be plucked." "I'll see that Berwick gives you cause for displeasure, Sire." "I leave all the details to you my friend," said Edward.

Beck withdrew. He had served Edward long enough to know that he had already decided on his strategy. He expected the necessary arrangements to be carried out meticulously. Beck settled to work: Berwick first. Among his many retainers were a number of well-paid Scotsmen. In return they supplied him with information or services where a Scottish tongue was vital to the success of a mission. He ordered five of his spies to report to him, among them was Jack Short. Short had prospered during the past few years in England. He had carried a number of messages between his master and his Scottish contacts and had ingratiated himself with Beck as a man capable of anything – if the price was right.

"You are all familiar with Berwick." They grunted or nodded their assent as befitted their characters. "A party of six English merchants will be leaving the burgh early on Friday morning. You are to intercept them as near to the city as is safe. You will make sure that only one completes his journey. Their goods and money are yours." "How will we know the right party?" asked Short. "The leader of the group is Gilbert of Boston. There is also one called Richard of Wrangle. They all come from Lincolnshire. You must leave tonight. Take what provisions you need from the stores and good strong horses. When you return you will receive ten marks." His orders were explicit and could not be misunderstood.

Two days later, in late February 1296, a group of cheerful, prosperous and quite harmless merchants, on their way home to the bosoms of their families in Lincolnshire, were brutally set upon, murdered and robbed by a band of villainous Scots. That was the story which Richard of Wrangle, the only survivor of the attack, told in every town and village he came to on his way home. His brother-in-law, John de Nasingges, owned three ships at Boston and when ordered by the sheriff's clerk, Richard Hetherington, to prepare his ships to transport the king's provisions along the coast to Newcastle, he loaded his ships with zeal. His sister's husband would find him a loyal kinsman and a loyal subject to his King. John voiced the opinion of all true Englishmen, "the Scots must be taught a lesson."

Throughout eastern England the king's sheriffs and their clerks travelled around the shires raising a wartime levy. Carcasses of beef, sides of bacon, corn, beans, barley, oats, bran, for an army cannot march on an empty stomach.

The Scots were not sitting meekly waiting for the English to attack. Their passions were also aroused. They were tired of English interference in their affairs: the English must be put in their place. In the name of their king, the feudal lords of Scotland and their followers met on eleventh March at Caddonlee, four miles north of Selkirk. That is some did. For there were those among the Scottish nobility who were undecided whether they should fight on the side of Scotland or England – too many held lands in both Scotland and England, and their loyalty was divided or unsure.

While the English mobilised their considerable resources, the Wallace kinsmen prepared to obey their Lord Stewart's command for service. John left Dundee and went home to Elderslie. The three men prepared their kit and weapons, while Lady Margaret and her daughter-in-law, like wives and mothers throughout Scotland and England, prepared clothes and food for the journey; yet at night they lay awake worrying and praying that it would be their men who returned. When the time came for the men to leave, the two women fought back their tears. These could flow later. Now they had to be brave. Sir Malcolm and ten of his own followers, good men who he had known all their lives, left the Elderslie estate on a blustery March day to join their lord and other Scots loyal to John Balliol.

That same day Lady Margaret, her daughter-in-law and grandsons, went to Paisley Abbey to pray for their men. Margaret Wallace knelt before the statue of the Virgin and begged her, as a mother, to watch over those whom she loved.

"Holy mother, you knew a mother's pain. Watch over my sons. Safeguard their father and bring them safely home.
"Hail Mary, full of Grace,
 The Lord is with thee,
 Blessed are thou among women
 And blessed is the fruit of thy womb, Jesus.
 Holy Mary, Mother of God,
 Pray for us sinners now and at the hour of our death. Amen."

Over and over, she repeated her prayer, turning her rosary around and around in her fingers until her knees were sore from kneeling on the cold slabs. Eventually her son's wife put her arms around Margaret Wallace's cold shoulders, "Come mother, you'll catch a chill." Margaret Wallace kissed her rosary, crossed herself and wiped away her tears with the corner of her coif. "Thank you my dear. I wish I had gone with them, but Malcolm would not have it. Who will care for them if they are wounded and we're not there? John was so excited. You'd think he was going to a tavern to meet a lassie."

Once again the tears began to roll down her cheeks. Outside she sat on a low wall and watched her grandsons playing at her feet, while her daughter-in-law talked to other women who had come to the abbey to pray for their menfolk.

William Wallace left Lamington to present himself at Caddonlee. His blacksmith had made a helmet and some light armour and he carried his shield, bow, battle axe and had strapped to his back the magnificent Vengeance. He said farewell to a tearful Marion who was again with child which she expected in early June. He had tried to persuade her to go to her father's house in Lanark, but she refused to leave her beloved Lamington. "I have my people here. Neil and his wife will help me with all things, Will." In the end she promised that if he had not returned to her by the first week of May she would go to her father.

William Wallace, Robert Boyd, Adam Wallace, Tom Johnston and men from Lamington rode across country following the paths through the Selkirk forest to Borthwick. The old people greeted them with kindness. They had heard from John the Outlaw of the events which had overtaken Scotland, and Murdo and John were busy sorting and sharpening weapons and other paraphernalia of war. William grinned ruefully at the old men creaking and groaning with rheumatism, and at their age preparing themselves for battle. "Murdo, John, it isn't necessary for you to carry arms." "Ah, but the manor of Borthwick must send men against the English. It's not enough that the master should fight," said John. "Have no fear, we met John the Outlaw. He will come with us from Borthwick. As it is, you may need to look to your own safety should things go badly for us and Scotland."

They spent that night at Borthwick. It was raining and cold. In the morning the journey would be difficult for both men and beasts. John the Outlaw arrived early. He had a full quiver of arrows and carried a battle axe. Janet brought him a helmet which had belonged to her old master and provisions: smoked bacon, sausages, cheese, oats and flour. William left instructions for the defence of the manor, and the old men with a tearful Janet wished them all God's speed and a safe return. The little party set out on the last stage of their journey.

The Scottish army camped on the hillsides north of Selkirk. The banners of the earls were fluttering bravely in the wind. The Wallace kinsmen collected together, uncles, cousins, many William had not seen since his marriage. They took their turn in keeping a lookout for the English, sharpened their weapons, told yarns and discussed fighting strategies – as all soldiers do. Around the camp fires there was the usual grumbling about the food or lack of it, the mud churned up by so many feet and hooves, the fleas and the work which they had been forced to leave undone and would not now get done. In spite of this they enjoyed the gathering and the exciting prospect of getting back at the English.

The Lords Dunbar, Angus and Bruce had refused to obey the command to arms and they and their followers were not present at Caddonlee. Rumour had it that the Bruce was marching with the English but, in the battle fever which existed, this did not seem to matter.

A council of war was held to discuss tactics attended by Sir Richard and Sir Malcolm Wallace with Lord James Stewart. Afterwards Sir Malcolm spoke quietly to his sons, "They disagree on every point. How can we fight a war if we cannot agree on one single thing and we are leaderless. No one will make decisions for us all. They cackle like old crones." He shook his head sadly and prodded the embers of the fire with the toe of his boot. "Anyway, the outcome is that seven earls are to take a part of the army in a foray across the border through the western marches and attack the English in their own land. The rest will remain here to protect our eastern coastline. They believe that the English will be distracted by our attack in the west." "What does the Lord Stewart think, sir," asked William. "He believes we are wasting our time, lad. He says the English king is a cool-headed fellow and will not easily be diverted from his plans. Time will tell. Meanwhile our lord has chosen to remain here since this is where he believes the main attack will come." After the army split there was little to do except train and wait for the English to make the first move.

Edward received news that the Scots were attacking English towns and villages in the north-west in grim silence. Two days later his great army crossed the border, set up camp at Hutton, close to Berwick, and the following day the English king himself rode to the gates of the poorly fortified town, except for the castle, and ordered the citizens to surrender or face the consequences. A few of the defenders gathered on the walls eager to catch sight of the English king but when his herald asked for their reply they laughed and jeered. The king said that other little towns in other campaigns had tried to call his bluff and they had regretted it. So would Berwick.

The next day, Easter Sunday, a man-at arms watching at the west gate saw an army approaching. There was a slight early morning mist. He rubbed his eyes. Surely the pennants flying at the head of the column were those of Scotland, "Aye definitely the Scottish emblem." He ran to a comrade. "Look, over there." The man followed the direction of the pointing finger. "Our lads, our lads are coming to join us." They agreed. It was definitely the Scottish pennant of the Bruce family. "I think they're asleep at the castle. You run with the news that they have sent us reinforcements from Caddonlee. God be praised."

As the man ran with his news he yelled to everyone he saw, "Our lads are coming. We have seen their banners." The citizens along the lane leading to the castle felt instant relief. It was difficult to get a goodnight's sleep with the English just a few miles away. Now here were their own men ready to defend them. The news spread to the street of the bakers, and to a man they began preparing extra dough for bread for hungry soldiers.

The lookout watched the approaching army. It certainly was large with many mounted knights. The mist lifted and the sun glinted on shields, lances and the proudly fluttering leopards of England. The soldiers stood bemused. How could this be? They had seen Scottish banners. Holy mother: the gates. They had opened the gates wide to greet their saviours, not the English.

He ran down the steps. "Close the gates, it's the English. The English are coming." Everyone was in utter confusion. Was it their own people or the English outside the town? Whatever chance there had been to organise and compose themselves was gone. The gates swung to as the men gathered on the walls to watch their enemy approach. The English army positioned itself around Berwick. Its citizens watched with horror at its size and strength. There were perhaps twenty-five or thirty thousand foot-soldiers and at least five thousand mounted knights.

Sir William Douglas, governor of Berwick Castle, had been eating his breakfast when the news was brought to him that reinforcements had been sighted, but within ten minutes he heard a commotion and shouts in the streets below the castle walls, "The English, the English." "Why can't somebody make up his mind who it is paying us a visit," he grumbled. He finished buckling his sword as he clattered up the steps to the castle battlements.

The English were still positioning their forces, but well out of range of Scottish arrows. He thought that if reinforcements failed to come, he could not hope to hold Berwick, the pearl of Scotland. Looking out towards the sea he searched for English vessels, but could see none. There were a number of foreign ships in the harbour. Some were preparing to leave when the new tide came. Douglas gave the order for the men to go to their posts. They must await the first move by the English.

King Edward began his attack in unpretentious fashion. A hundred or so foot-solders attacked the north gate. They were easily repelled. A party of twenty-five mounted men charged the south gate and retreated noisily around the walls of the city. Small groups here and there detached from the main army and flung themselves at the walls. While the English commanders positioned their forces, the skirmishes continued. Edward sat passively on his great black warhorse and watched. His army consisted of veterans who had seen action in Wales and France. He knew he could rely on them. It was the reaction of the Scots that interested him. The walls would be easy enough to breach. Hardly walls at all, just earthen mounds with wooden ramparts. The cavalry could break through when he was ready. He had used the banners of the Bruce family on his approach to Berwick to cause confusion. A similar tactic on campaign in France had worked well. It never failed to upset the enemy.

All that night the English continued to harass the besieged town, softening it for the main attack. It came the following morning when the cavalry smashed through the defences and into the town. Behind them poured the foot-soldiers.

The Red Hall was a large and impressive stone building, easy to defend and difficult to set on fire. The Flemish weavers retreated into it with their families. A party of English cavalry called on the defenders to surrender. They jeered and one of the young craftsmen defiantly took his bow and let fly. He was an excellent shot but an unlucky man. The arrow lodged itself in the eye-slit of the helmet of a knight who fell from his horse. A cheer went up from the Flemings.

They could not know that the knight they killed was Richard, Duke of Cornwall, cousin to the English king. To kill a member of the royal family was an affront to Edward himself. "No quarter," he roared. "No quarter, young, old, male, female." Those of his advisers with softer hearts shuddered when they heard his order. "They must be taught a lesson, Durham," he told the bishop.

The carnage began. Knights and foot soldiers, without check on their actions, ran from house to house raping, killing and looting. The Red Hall finally burnt along with those who had taken shelter within, men, women with babes at their breasts, children: all were consumed by the fire or by English swords. The Red Hall did not suit Jack Short and half a dozen of his cronies. They headed for the merchants' houses where there would be rich pickings.

Isabelle's husband had shepherded his heavily pregnant wife, children, mother-in-law, who was visiting the family for Isabelle's lying-in and female servants into the cellar. There had been many ships in the harbour. He knew one or two of their captains and he was sure that he could get passage for his family, but they would need to go after dark. He told his mother-in-law to barricade the cellar door while he went to the harbour to search for a boat. He would return as quickly as possible. As he set out for the harbour he told the men-servants to defend the house. With his sword in his hand he made his way along the narrow alleyways to the harbour. As soon as the master was out of sight his men ran away.

Jack Short had been quite successful in his search for loot. He took mostly jewellery or money, nothing too heavy or cumbersome. Then he saw a merchant's house which seemed to be without occupants. There was some good silver plate that one of the men took but they could not find either money or jewellery. Plainly the owner had hidden it.

There was a smell from the kitchen of freshly baked bread. Fighting had made them hungry. As they entered the kitchen they heard a child crying from behind a door which lead down to a cellar. It did not take long to smash it down. A light burning in a sconce on the wall allowed them to see the women cowering against the far wall clutching the children.

"Well, what have we here, mates? There's not one for each, but we don't mind sharing, do we?" As the men came towards them the serving women ran trying to find places to hide. They were raped, fighting, kicking and screaming. Mistress Blair stood in front of her daughter and grandchildren. "Have mercy. God will reward you with eternal salvation. Have mercy on defenceless women and babes," she cried in anguish.

Jack Short and a comrade stood and laughed. "We'll take our rewards now, mother, and not wait for God." Mistress Blair had a small dagger and struck at Short as he moved forward. Behind her Isabelle and the children were screaming.

Short, angered by the cut on his hand, grabbed Mistress Blair, swung her round and slit her throat. Poor Isabelle was stricken with terror, but tried to push the two small boys behind her. Short grabbed her by the hair and pushed her onto the floor beside the body of her dying mother. He pulled up her skirts and raped her. Over his shoulder she saw his companion pick up her younger son and bash his head against the wall. The elder boy had slipped between the man's legs and ran to his mother thumping Jack Short on the back. His comrade came over and casually slit the small one's throat, tossing his body into a corner.

"Come on Jack, I want a turn." Isabelle had ceased to scream and lay silent under the man's thrusting body. Once Short had satisfied his lust, her children's murderer took his turn. The cellar had grown quiet, but still he poked at her and she lay staring at the lime-washed vaulted ceiling. The soldier finished his brutal act and adjusted his clothing and belt. The woman lay at his feet a pool of blood forming around her hips and thighs. He looked around him. The other women lay across the cellar floor and he could hear his companions upstairs drinking. A drink, a good drink of wine would suit him nicely. He did not bother to kill Isabelle. She could not survive long. He could see her blood pumping out onto the floor. He ran up the stairs and joined in drinking and eating. The events below had brought on an appetite.

It was nearly dark when Isabelle's husband managed to make his way back, hiding whenever he saw or heard the English. There was fighting in the streets and houses were on fire. He could hear the screams of women and children. At one point he had to seek shelter in a pigsty. The English had so much food and drink around them that for the time being they had left the animals in peace. There was a church nearby where many people had sought sanctuary, but it had been torched and as the trapped souls tried to escape they were cut down. The air was heavy with smoke and the smell of burning flesh.

His house was not on fire and at first he was hopeful that all would be well, but when he went through to the kitchen his heart sank and he knew he would be too late. The door of the cellar stood open. He began to feel sick. At the top of the steps he stood staring in horror at the scene below. Isabelle lay as the Englishman had left her in a pool of blood around her sprawling legs and staring with sightless eyes at the ceiling.

The young father saw his little boys, discarded and crumpled. Their yellow hair and fair skin was speckled with blood. He knelt beside his wife rearranging her skirts for modesty's sake. He put his hand on her abdomen, but could feel no movement within and he cradled her in his arms, tears rolling down his cheeks; then he picked up the bodies of his murdered babies and lay them in their mother's arms. "God speed you to his heavenly kingdom my sweet ones." He crossed himself. The small coffer that he had given to his mother-in-law for safe keeping lay opened on the floor. The silver coins were gone.

Meanwhile the assault on Berwick Castle continued and Douglas and his men fought off each new attack. During the lull between each assault the defenders of the castle could hear the massacre continuing in the town below. As night fell the flames were seen far out to sea. The slaughter went on throughout the long night and in the morning Sir William Douglas surrendered. At least the sacrifice of Berwick Castle would bring an end to the agony of the civilian population of the town he thought.

Douglas was wrong in assuming this. Edward did not order a halt to the sack of the town. That went on until the Bishop of Durham was persuaded by others to talk to the king, "Sire, we are coming into the third day now. The castle has surrendered. We must not allow this to continue." "Must not, Anthony? We must not allow these savages to poke fun at the king of England. But perhaps they have learnt their lesson. I will issue the order."

The news of the fall of Berwick, the surrender of its castle and massacre of the population became known to the Scots at Caddonlee as survivors struggled in with their terrible tales. Roger Livingston,

Isabelle's husband, stumbled upon the bodies of his father and brothers before making his way to the harbour. One of the ship's masters knew him well and his vessel was anchored a little way out from shore. It was bound for Flanders, but Roger refused the captain's offer of sanctuary until the troubles had passed. How could he seek safety when he had witnessed Isabelle's suffering and the mutilated bodies of his poor babes left unburied and unrevenged. The captain had a family himself and sadly shook his head, "Very well, my friend, I understand. We will drop you further down the coast and you can avenge your family's murder."

Roger made his way across country to Caddonlee. The first soldier he met on guard duty was one of James the Stewart's men who took him to his lord. Roger told his story slowly, stumbling from one horror to the next. Some gathered around to listen. They were outraged although they had heard similar tales from other survivors. Roger finished his tale and sat exhausted before a brazier, then fell into a fitful doze. He awoke with a start to find William Wallace standing in front of him. "Is Isabelle with you?" Roger shook his head.

William said nothing but took the man's arm and led him to his own fire. When he heard Roger's story he thought about his own pregnant wife and Isabelle as she was when he had first seen her, an unwed girl, happy, carefree and full of life.

The news of the massacre spread throughout Scotland while in the west the Earl of Buchan marched his men into Cumbria killing and burning as they went; but at Caddonlee the Earls still argued. What was needed was a decisive victory against the English. "We must strike back," was the general opinion, but how and when differed from one camp fire to the next.

Edward's army moved slowly northwards towards Dunbar. The Earl of Surrey with a detachment of cavalry and archers went ahead to secure Dunbar Castle at all costs. The Scottish garrison of the castle, hearing of the massacre at Berwick, sent an urgent appeal for help.

William Wallace was on guard duty when the order finally came to march north-east towards Dunbar. At last they were moving in the right direction to cut off the enemy's advance into the heart of Scotland.

They took up a defensive position at Spottismuir on a hillside commanding the valley and the approach to Dunbar. Wallace was with his own men from Lamington. His cousins together with John Wallace and Roger Livingston joined them. The Scottish army was drawn up in a disorderly and undisciplined mass. One hundred and fifty mounted knights were positioned on the left and right flanks. William's father, brother Malcolm and Sir Richard Wallace were among the knights.

It was the twenty-fourth of April, William Wallace's twenty-fourth birthday. A priest moved along the ranks of men giving absolution. Wallace went down on one knee to receive the blessing. He wore chain mail and a padded gambeson. His helmet had a light chain mail protection for his neck and he carried a shield, which gave extra width and height to his already powerful frame. He held firmly the claymore Vengeance. His battleaxe hung at his belt. He stood with his men. They were a good bunch. All were freemen from his own area, but they had had little training with either sword or spear and most had no protection from enemy attack.

William had spent time training his own men while they were still camped at Caddonlee and he had instructed them how to slash, cut and thrust. When one or two grumbled he replied, "Do you want to meet an Englishman and be unable to give him as good as he gives you? Come man, put more effort into it. Don't take your eye off your opponent until you have killed him. Nay, use your shield. It's for your protection."

It was a good clear day and they had chosen their position well. Now they must wait for the command. Wallace saw the English cavalry come into view crossing the valley in front of them. They were in orderly ranks and seemed to know what was expected of them. He hoped he had done enough to train his own men. The watching Scots saw the English cavalry divide into groups and many began jeering, banging their swords on their shields and generally making a great din. Suddenly an excited shout went up, "They're retreating. The cowards are fleeing." William watching said to John the Outlaw standing on his right, "If they're fleeing, its an orderly retreat."

The excited Scots, first in ones and twos, then in groups, began to move forward. Roger Livingston, standing among the crowded men, with sword drawn watched the English and remembered his family's shameful end. He saw many men breaking ranks and running down the hill towards the English. What was Wallace waiting for? He pushed past his comrades and began running towards the enemy. "Come back man," yelled Wallace, but Livingston ignored him.

The English had brought up a company of archers, who drove stakes into the ground in front of them before sending their arrows into the advancing Scots. Wallace noticed how keenly accurate they were. He watched and waited with his men restless around him. The trumpet had not sounded the advance. A few of the Scots had already reached the bottom of the hill. Roger Livingston was among the leaders. Some of Scotland's mounted knights began to move forward. Foot soldiers followed without command to advance. Well, right or wrong, they were engaging the enemy. He must lead his men forward if they were to fight together.

Holding his claymore aloft with a mighty bellow 'forward,' Wallace led his men into battle. They tried to keep together as Wallace had instructed them, but as they plunged downwards the enemy arrows showered around them and some men fell. Wallace heard the English trumpet give a shrill call and their cavalry turned towards the Scots and began their charge, hooves thundering and lances sloped. As Wallace and his men reached the valley the English cavalry crashed into them scattering some, trampling others. Wallace gave himself up to the passion of battle, making space around himself, cutting down all foolish enough to confront him.

A knight pulled his horse around rushing at Wallace, who impaled the Englishman's mount. As the animal went down its rider was caught by the leg and Wallace dispatched him with a powerful blow. A mounted man-at-arms came at him with lance lowered, but Wallace had time to step sideways. As man and horse turned he brought the claymore across the soldier's right arm. The force was so great that the Englishman lost his balance and fell to one side. Wallace ran alongside and, before the man could recover, he delivered another blow across the throat which severed the head.

Wallace glanced around him and saw John the Outlaw backing away from a mounted knight. William ran to his aid jumping over dead and dying men. The Englishman turned to Wallace who swung Vengeance and caught his victim across the chest, cutting deeply into the knight's chain mail, blood spurting out. He went limp still sitting astride his war horse. William pulled the man off, jumping into the saddle. Astride the horse he had a clearer view of the progress of the battle. They were being forced back by the English who had an overwhelming advantage with cavalry and archers. Once more he hurled himself into the thickest of the fray. From time to time he caught sight of his countrymen fleeing towards the hills and the cover of the trees. A large party of Scottish knights fled the field. The battle was lost.

He bellowed to his men, "Retreat! Retreat to the hills!" As they tried to leave the battlefield, Wallace went to their assistance dispatching many of their opponents. Vengeance sang its deadly song as it cut through the air. Only when as many as he could see were safely retreating did Wallace dig his heels deeply into his mount's flanks and left the battlefield.

He kept the men together as they fought their way towards the safety of the Lammermuir hills. Of his original twenty five, only thirteen remained, three of whom were wounded, two not seriously. His cousin and brother were not with them. They reached the safety of the trees where the English cavalry would not bother them. The noise and clash of weapons and screams of pain from men and horses receded.

He would not allow his men to stop until they had put some distance between themselves and the pursuing English. Eventually they reached a small stream and he allowed them to rest. He sat on a rock by the side of the water. The men were lying or sitting. Several had removed their boots and were busy bathing their feet. They said very little. It was peaceful except for droning insects and the horse cropping at the grass with its bridle jingling as it moved. Yet just two hours before they had been running for their lives. It had happened so quickly. The Scottish bravado was victim of the ruthless discipline of the English. There was little point in dwelling on it now. He must think what should be done. Presumably survivors would regroup somewhere, but for where should he and his men head? They needed food and news.

"Men, as I see the situation our army has been defeated, our position overrun and probably our leaders killed or taken prisoner. We must survive to fight again for I swear to you that the next time William Wallace meets the English on the field of battle it will be the English who will turn and run, not Wallace and his men." There was a chorus of comments from the listeners. "Well said, master." "Such talk is fine, but what do we do now?" "What about my land, who'll work that?"

Wallace raised his hand to silence them. "One step at a time, men. Our first task is to find food. I have a manor at Borthwick Water in the Selkirk forest and it is well stocked. Has anyone any better plan?" They all looked at one another, but said nothing. Wallace led his men south-west. They made good time and just before dark arrived at a hill overlooking the village of Lauder.

It looked quiet enough. The English did not appear to be there. Wallace left the men sheltering by some rocks for it had begun to drizzle. He rode down to the village church. He thought that the priest would surely give them food and shelter for the night. There were already nine men who had sought sanctuary in the little church and a few more turned up in the night. By the morning there were twenty- seven dazed and subdued men accepting what hospitality the small village could offer them. Some decided they would return to their own homesteads, but a few who were without land followed Wallace to Borthwick at least until they could find out what was happening.

They left early for the priest was anxious that they depart because he feared the English. He had his flock to think of. They travelled across country using forest paths but keeping away from all farms and manors. In the evening they arrived at Borthwick.

The old people knew nothing of the events that had overtaken Scotland. They described the battle at Dunbar to Murdo and John who sat with tears in their eyes, but Janet and the other women were kept busy cooking and baking for so many. The news spread – as bad news does – and the following day men began appearing at Borthwick. They were tough looking men used to forest life. One or two of them Wallace knew by sight: they were outlawed men of the forest. They had come to listen to the stories about the battle at Dunbar.

Wallace spent his time organising the quartering of so many men on the manor. The smithy at Borthwick was not large but sufficient for the needs of the estate. Wallace, looking over the weapons which they had with them, said they would need to be repaired and some new ones made. Two of the men were journeymen-smiths and they quickly set to work under Murdo's eye. He was pleased to think that he was useful.

A few days later Wallace told them he was going to Lanark and then to Renfrew to the castle of James Stewart. Perhaps there he would get some news. He left John the Outlaw in charge because he knew the forest so well.

The horse taken on the field at Dunbar was a powerful warhorse. It would draw attention if he was seen riding such an animal. He travelled on foot first to Lamington. Marion was now very large with her child. She was in the cheese room making the first cheeses of the season and stood by the vat stirring the curds. A shadow in the doorway blocked the light. Without turning her head she called out. "How can I make cheese if you stand there blocking the light." Wallace came into the room putting his finger to his lips as the startled maids looked at him, then he put his hands over Marion's eyes saying. "I'm back, sweetheart." Marion turned flinging her arms around her husband's neck. "Oh, Will, you're safe: God be praised. We have heard such terrible tales." "The English can't finish me, sweetheart," he answered.

She left her women to continue the cheese making and arm in arm they went into the manor. Marion had intended to go to Lanark the following day, but now that she knew that William was safe, she declared she would stay on her own manor, saying, "The English will certainly go to Lanark, Will. How will we survive the winter if the crops are not sown and harvested?" "This is not work for you now, sweetheart," he replied.

"At a time like this we must all do what we can. Surely the English will ignore me and mine." He patted her hand and replied, "Let's hope so."

After what had happened in Berwick, Wallace was no longer certain that Marion would be safer in a town. He did not tell her about Isabelle and her children. It would serve no useful purpose in her present condition.

Some of his men who had left with him for Dundee had not returned and he spent time talking to their kinsfolk, giving them what comfort he could. Then he left for Lanark. The little town was tense with rumour. Every traveller had a tale to tell. Wallace went directly to his father-in-law's manor. "Ah William, you at least are a level-headed fellow. Is it all true?" Wallace told him his own story and Sir Hugh sat listening, clearly outraged by the news. "Then everything else we have been told must also be true. The castle at Edinburgh surrendered, Will, and the English are moving northwards."

"What about the king and our own lords, sir?" asked Wallace. "What has happened to them?"

"They say well over one hundred knights including the earls of Menteith, Atholl and Ross are prisoners of the English. The king?" Hugh shrugged his shoulders, "I do not know." Wallace looked gloomy.

Sir Hugh continued, "How can we fight if all our leaders are dead or prisoners?" "We will have to find other leaders, sir." "That is no easy task, Will. A man's born to lead." "Well, sir, we cannot sit idly on our hands and watch the English take all that has been given to us by God."

"You have the fearless talk of a young man, William, and I cannot argue with that." He changed the subject. "What are you going to do now?" "I'm going to my father's house and then to my Lord Stewart." His father-in-law lent him a shaggy pony and, with his best wishes for a safe journey, William left for his father's manor.

Sir James Stewart, the High Steward of Scotland, received his old friend Robert Wishart, Bishop of Glasgow, with much sorrow. The eventual outcome of the battle of Dunbar had been obvious to Sir James as he watched the deadly accuracy of the English archers from the hillside. The cold discipline of their cavalry made the end inevitable. What point was there in remaining to watch the slaughter? He had withdrawn from his position and returned to his castle at Renfrew.

"This is a sad business, James. The English have had much influence in recent years. They have set themselves above us, interfered in the running of our kingdom and involved themselves in our spiritual lives and our churches. Our religious houses are not free from their meddling. Now with this latest disaster they will take the kingdom."

"There's little we can do Robert. We've suffered heavy casualties and without leaders the power is with the English. Be sure King Edward will extract promises and hostages from our nobles before he allows them to see the hills of Scotland again. Now they will march across Scotland and nothing stands in their way." "You have liege-men, James. Those men will follow you." "My friend, if I thought I could stop the English once and for all, do you think I would be sitting here talking? No, we are a divided kingdom. Why, the Bruces are riding with the English. Their banners were seen at Berwick. The only people whom I could gather around me now would be the fellows who cut the hay. How do you think they would fare against English knights?"

As they gloomily discussed their realm's future there was a knock on the door and the house steward announced that William Wallace had arrived. "Send him in man," he turned to Robert Wishart. "This man was at Dunbar, Robert. It may interest you to hear what he has to say."

Wallace bowed to his liege lord, but to the bishop he dropped to his knee and kissed the out-stretched hand. "Be seated, William Wallace. You survived Dunbar I see." Wallace sat in the offered chair. "Well, what can I do for you?"

"Sir, when and where are we to stop the English?" They were surprised by his direct and forthright speech. "As yet I cannot tell you, Wallace. We were decisively beaten at Dunbar. You must have seen that for yourself."

"Aye, but I have men staying at my own manor waiting only for a signal from you, lord. We shall attack and be gone before they have a chance to rally." Sir James looked surprised, "How many are you?" "As yet, it is true, not many, but we await only a command from you and I believe that others will follow to rise against the English."

"You cannot fight Edward of England's army with a handful of men, Wallace." "True, but we can attack when they least expect it, and many more will join us when they hear of our successes. Besides, the king of England cannot keep his army in Scotland forever. Sooner or later he must return to his own land. We are a free people. We must fight on."

Normally James the Stewart would have laughed and sent the man away, but he knew and respected the Wallace kinsmen. Hardy men they all were and these were not normal times. The passion and honesty of Wallace's statements moved the Steward of Scotland, but Robert Wishart answered Wallace, "My advice, my son, is to go to your manor and prepare yourself and your men, but be patient. Let the English do their worst. We cannot overcome them at present. Wait and they will dance to our jig. Come and talk with us again in the autumn. I will send word to you."

William left somewhat perplexed. It had not been quite the interview that he had expected. His lord and the bishop were as confused as he was, but the eventual outcome of his visit was to change the course of his life and his country's history.

Lady Margaret Wallace wept with joy when her son rode into the courtyard. "Blessed Virgin, he is alive and well." She ran out to him. "William my son, is all well with you?" He laughed, "All is as well as it can be, mother. Have my father and brothers returned safely?" "I am a very lucky woman, William. You are all safe."

After Elderslie Wallace moved on to see his uncle at Riccarton, then returned to Lamington a disillusioned man. The country was in chaos. Men could not agree on the right course of action and the kingdom's leaders were either dead or imprisoned. As he urged his pony along the road to Lanark, his thoughts went round and round in his head. Try as he might he could not forget the humiliation which England had inflicted on them at Dunbar.

Lanark was a hubbub of noise with refugees coming from the east, carrying belongings, herding livestock and fleeing before the advancing English army. Wallace asked his father-in-law to come to Lamington for safety, but he refused and Lady Cecilia would not leave him. Wallace returned to Marion that evening and the following day went to Borthwick.

He sat over his food talking to Tom Johnston and making plans for the future. The men at Borthwick discussed Wallace's plans. They were as divided and confused as the rest of their countrymen. But the outcome was that they would disband and return to Borthwick after Michaelmas when the situation in the kingdom would – hopefully – be clearer.

Wallace asked John the Outlaw to remain at Borthwick to steward the manor and give support to the old people. The lambing was nearly over as was the sowing, and Murdo showed Wallace the pikes which they were forging. They were as long as two men with deadly iron spikes.

Wallace rode along the track that led down to the manor of Lamington. He could see Neil and some of the men by the edge of the forest. They had been felling trees and cutting them into logs. As he drew nearer to the hall, Neil's wife came out and walked along the track to greet him. "Good afternoon to you, master. The mistress reached her time an hour past and she has delivered a fine lassie."

William rode into the yard, for a moment unsure what to say to her. It was unexpected and a little before her time, but when he saw her lying in bed, with the child at her breast, looking pale but radiantly happy, for the first time since he was a small boy he wanted to weep for joy.

The women gave him his child: she was small but perfect. The child's head fitted into the palm of his hand. He put his face near to hers. She was warm and pink, with such tiny features and so vulnerable. He put the child back into the mother's arms and dropped on his knees beside them. "Sweetheart, she's perfect, just perfect. You are well and not in pain." She smiled a contented and triumphant smile.

"I am well, Will. It was easier this time. What shall we call her? I was thinking of Margaret after our mothers." At this moment William could refuse his wife nothing.

For a short while Wallace gave himself up to the joy of parenthood, work on the estate, haymaking, shearing and in the evening when his toil was done watching Marion nursing their daughter. Once or twice a week he went to Lanark, sometimes to sell an animal, but usually just to hear the latest news. The castles of Jedburgh and Dumbarton had surrendered in May; and in June the garrison at Stirling abandoned their posts. Then in early July, under pressure from King Edward, John Balliol, King of Scots, known as 'Toom Tabard', renounced his claim to the Scottish throne.

# The
# Avenger

The English army continued a leisurely progress to Elgin then turned south to Scone. To show his supremacy, King Edward ordered the sacred Stone of Destiny, the Stone of Scone, to be taken south and placed under the coronation chair at Westminster Abbey for all to see. When he arrived at Edinburgh, the same fate awaited the Scottish royal regalia and state documents, but the greatest sacrilege of all was yet to come. The revered and holy rood of St Margaret was also sent to England.

At the end of August Edward held a parliament at Berwick where he ordered all landowners to sign an Act of Allegiance to himself. He appointed the Earl of Surrey to be Governor of Scotland, Hugh de Cressingham became Treasurer and William Ormesby the Chief Justice, and he awarded many Englishmen with official posts. William Hazelrig became Sheriff of Lanark and every town and castle in the country was to be garrisoned with English soldiers.

King Edward was pleased with his arrangements. He had covered every possible eventuality. Even King John Balliol and his heir were now safely in the Tower at London. In the early autumn Edward returned to England, leaving behind him a well-ordered kingdom. As he said to Sir John Warenne, Earl of Surrey, before he left, "Resist? How can they resist? I have all that would resist safely under lock and key and those who remain have neither the stomach nor the wit. No, Surrey, you won't have any trouble – but if you do: stamp on it hard."

The Earl of Surrey groaned. At his age he could do without the responsibility of this God-forsaken place. It never stopped raining and the dampness brought on the ague. As soon as his royal master was safely in England, the earl left Scotland for the comforts of his own estates in Yorkshire. He could sit by his own fireside, hunt in his own forests and leave the administration of Scotland in the capable but greedy hands of Cressingham and Ormesby, who had every intention of making their fortunes in that kingdom.

Thus was the humiliation of the kingdom of Scots completed.

The English arrived in Lanark at the end of July. The town's people stood and watched malevolently as the mounted men trotted along the street and up to the castle. Wallace stood quietly by the drawbridge and in the evening he returned home angry. He was out in the far field directing his men in bringing in the hay when he saw a horseman riding towards the manor. He left Neil in charge and returned home. His brother Malcolm was unsaddling his horse. He looked tired and upset. It must be something serious to bring him from his own estate. "Hello, what ails you at such a busy time of the year?"

"I wish it were a happier visit, Will. Nay, nothing ails our parents, but I need to speak with you." Marion had already greeted her brother-in-law and was busy arranging refreshments for him. She brought out beer, meat and freshly baked rye bread. The two men sat on the old bench outside the door in the pleasant sunshine.

"The journey was difficult, Will. English troops everywhere. I was stopped and questioned many times. You've heard that we must all pledge allegiance to the English king." Wallace nodded. "Our father refuses to give such a pledge, Will, and I in all honesty must follow his example, although I fear the consequences to our families. I have spoken to Uncle Crawford at Ayr. He intends to swear allegiance but father cannot be moved. Mother stands by him and says that he must do what he thinks is right." He paused and Wallace said, "If this is so, Malcolm, I have already decided to follow father's example. I will not be a liege-man to the king of England, but as Marion owns Lamington in her own right, I will advise her to sign for the safety of herself and our daughter." He continued, "it is right that we should stand firm against the English, Malcolm. Can you not send your family and our mother to a relative for safety, at least until the English are occupied by more important things than taking revenge on women and children?" "That I intend to do. I'll escort my family and mother to Uncle Crawford at Kilspindie. I'm sure they'll be safe there."

"Malcolm, I'm not going to stay idle. When all the harvest is gathered, I'm returning to Borthwick to meet men who want to continue the fight against the English." "Will, take care. There are English spies everywhere. Anyway how can a handful of men resist an army?" William looked angry. "We are a free people. I shall fight their rule even if I have to do it single handed."

The two said little more on the subject. Malcolm Wallace's faint-heartedness made him feel guilty and he was overshadowed by his younger brother's bold statement, but then William always had been fearless even when they were boys. They walked around looking at the crops. Everything appeared peaceful and normal.

Andrew Moray was as devastated by the rout of the Scottish army at Dunbar as Wallace. He brooded, turning over and over in his mind what they had done wrong and how they could have turned the defeat into victory. The strutting arrogance of the victors irritated him no less than it did Wallace, but for Andrew Moray the shame of defeat was more difficult to bear. He had been captured and throughout the summer languished in Chester Castle. He was frustrated by inactivity and heard only news which his captors wanted him to hear.

One morning towards the end of September, he sat morosely awaiting the arrival of his food. He could hear the jailer coming along the passage with his keys jangling. The man was disagreeable and rarely spoke to his prisoners. As he placed the bowl and tankard on the bench, he glanced over his shoulder towards the sentry who lounged against the wall looking down the passageway. The gaoler seized the opportunity and took from his jerkin a small leather purse, gave it to Moray and left hurriedly.

Andrew Moray opened the bag with nervous fingers. It could not have come from his father or uncles since they, like himself, were prisoners of the English. Inside he found five marks and an unsigned letter. He read:

'During the night after you receive this letter a vessel will be waiting at the river estuary to take you north. A friend will come. Follow him and he will guide you.'

Moray paced his cell restlessly, forgetting about his food. Who had sent the message? Was it just another English trick? Impossible: his ransom was worth more to the English than his death. He sat and ate. Well, trick or not, he would rather take his chances trying to escape than rot slowly in prison.

It had been dark for some hours when Moray heard a noise in the passage and his door opened. The gaoler stood there. He said nothing but beckoned. Moray followed, taking a homespun cloak which the man offered, and allowed himself to be led to a side door. "My boy awaits to guide you to the river." He indicated the other side of the moat which Moray was to swim and did not wait for thanks. Why should he? He was working for good gold and not a cause. A lad of about ten waited in the shadows and greeted Moray as he came out of the water.

As they left the castle behind the moon came out from the clouds lifting the young man's spirits. It was good to be free once more. The path leading to the river Dee was muddy and there was marshy ground on either side. "Take care, master, the earth be very soft here," said the boy.

They reached the estuary and he followed the boy to a small fishing boat moored at some distance from the others. A dark figure stepped out from the shadows. "Here lad, give your father this," he gave the boy a purse jangling with the final payment. "Welcome, Andrew Moray," it was a Scottish voice. "Quick, we must hide you and leave with the tide. We'll talk later, sir."

Moray was bundled into the bottom of the fishing boat and covered with nets, lobster pots and a spare sail. The dawn chased the tide from the estuary of the River Dee and the small boat began to rock gently in the ebb. The fishermen rowed out. As they pulled away from the land the sail was hoisted and they began tacking northwards. "You may come out now, sir." They pulled away some of the fishing gear. "We have some dry clothes for you here." He handed the young man some coarse peasant clothes. "Who must I thank for my freedom and why?" asked Moray. "The first part of your question I can answer, Robert Wishart, Bishop of Glasgow. For the answer to the second part of your question you must bide awhile until you meet with him."

"How am I to get home?" "We are to sail further along the coast where horses and a guide will be waiting. Then we shall travel mostly at night using little known paths."

Andrew Moray returned to Scotland and two weeks after his escape was ushered into the presence of Robert Wishart at the abbey in Paisley. Moray fell on his knees, kissing the outstretched hand. "My lord, I must thank you for my freedom."

"I am told that apart from very wet and windy weather your journey was without incident, my son" "My lord, I hardly noticed the weather in my eagerness to get home." A servant gave him a glass of wine and he was offered a chair by the fire. Robert Wishart sat opposite regarding his guest in whom he was placing such hope. Moray was fair-skinned and had a crop of dark, unruly hair adorning his stocky figure. He was not a handsome man, but he had a pleasant, dependable look.

82

"My son, you know that our king is imprisoned in the Tower and nearly all men of consequence have paid homage to the English king. The English occupy all positions of importance throughout Scotland, and English spies are everywhere, even in the Church." Moray nodded but said nothing.

"At Dunbar we lost all who could lead us, but that does not mean Scotland has lost her heart. The will to resist still lives in the people. They will fight if they are asked to do so. That is why I have arranged for your escape." Moray shifted in his chair and smiled but still remained silent. "I have news from many parts of the country. In Inverness a burgess, Master Pilche, is organising resistance and I am in touch with him, but you are skilled in the arts of war and your family is loyal to our king. The people will follow you." Moray sat for a few moments. "My lord, I am honoured that you have such faith in me. I have a few scores to settle with the English," but the bishop continued, "After Dunbar a young man came to the Lord Stewart and myself asking how he could continue the war. I have sent for him and should like you two to meet, but first refresh yourself."

Wallace had been surprised by the bishop's summons. He had taken care on his journey to Paisley for he had not signed allegiance to King Edward and there were always patrols stopping travellers. "Wallace, this is Andrew Moray, lately prisoner of the English and like yourself anxious to throw them out of Scotland." The young men were of similar age and, from the beginning of their acquaintance, understood each other. Wallace told Moray of the meeting he was to have shortly at Borthwick with like-minded men. "Our first concern will be weapons and food," said Wallace. "I must have sufficient stores to keep the men from robbing our own people." "Then you'll have to take it from the English," said Moray.

They talked well into the night discussing warfare and the following day they parted for their own homes. They would begin harrying the enemy during the coming winter and spring and as soon as possible join their forces.

The Bishop of Glasgow was pleased with his efforts and reported to James Stewart, "Now we will have to wait and see if our choice of leaders has been wise."

Wallace took a tender farewell of a tearful wife and daughter. He journeyed to Borthwick through the Selkirk forest with his brother John, Tom Johnston, Adam Wallace and Andrew Neil's son. As the autumn changed into winter, the manor rang with the noise of men spoiling for a fight, banging and hammering in the forge.

Just before the beginning of Advent a troop of English cavalry left Roxburgh Castle, escorting two English officials and a string of pack horses to Edinburgh. The road was bad. There was thick mud in the deep ruts after the autumn rains and the soldiers were forced to ride slowly. In some places they dismounted, walking through the mire and often had to leave the track altogether. They spent a night at the village of Lauder before continuing their journey early next day.

The road followed the river which was in flood. The sides of the valley were steep and heavily wooded, and there was a light mist, cold, grey and clinging. The captain sent three of his men on ahead to check the path, but the company had been forced to dismount and lead their reluctant animals. One of the scouts returned saying the road was blocked by a fallen tree, but that beyond the way looked better and they would be able to ride.

It was necessary to move the tree since the pack horses found it difficult to cross, and the steep sides of the valley and fast flowing river made their progress hazardous.

The experienced soldiers recognised the sound of whistling arrows that struck their targets before any could take cover. Four men went down dead or wounded in the first flight, three more in the second. Out from the misty trees charged the Scots. Each man had chosen his victim and fell on him before the English had time to rally.

Wallace rushed at the sergeant, who had mounted and was wheeling his horse around to face his attacker. Wallace held Vengeance firmly in two hands and as the Englishman slashed at him he received the blow across the blade of his claymore. As the man turned his mount, Wallace struck him across the shoulder, blood poured from the wound and he slumped forward. The horse trotted away further up the track then stopped. Its rider was lying across its neck with the blood running down the animal and staining the earth red.

The English bringing up the rear had been floundering through the mud when they were attacked. Three tried to run forward to help their comrades but were brought down by more arrows from the trees. Two men tried to seek shelter among the trees but were quickly cut down. The two officials had already crossed the fallen tree when the attack occurred. In the confusion, they tried to escape up the road, away from danger, but Wallace saw them and jumping onto a riderless horse gave chase. Both were soft-skinned clerics, not fighting men. After a short pursuit he reigned in his mount and returned to his men. Perhaps it would be useful to have two survivors who would spread the news among their kind that the Scots were attacking again.

Two soldiers had tried to escape across the river but their dead bodies floated past Wallace as he returned. The pack horses, weapons and clothes of the English were collected and Wallace and his men disappeared into Selkirk forest.

Wallace was with his family at home in Lamington for the Christmas feast. His mother was with them. The servants of Sir Richard Wallace of Riccarton had escorted her to Lamington. Since the murder of her husband, she had aged. Her rich chestnut hair was streaked with silver, her face drawn and pale. She spent much of her day by the fire spinning, singing quietly to her granddaughter, rocking the child's cradle with her foot.

Sir Malcolm Wallace had steadfastly refused to swear allegiance to the English king, although his brother-in-law Crawford, still Sheriff of Ayr, had begged him to change his mind, if only for the sake of Lady Wallace, but he had remained loyal to King John and to Scotland's cause.

The English tried in every way they could to force all Scots to sign, but their patience began to wane and tales of murder and missing landowners began to spread across the kingdom as autumn gave way to winter. The Wallace family took refuge with relatives and old Tom Johnston had stewarded the estate at Elderslie. A troop of English soldiers had appeared at the manor, just after Michaelmas, searching for Sir Malcolm, but had left without harming the buildings or livestock. The sergeant in charge of the troop said, "Tell Wallace if he won't bend his knee to the king as his liege lord he better look to his safety."

At the beginning of November, Sir Malcolm had travelled to Elderslie to check on his affairs. He set out early taking two serving men with him. The weather was bad, a leaden sky and brisk north-westerly wind made their progress slow. They reached Loudon Hill by mid morning and at a sharp turn in the track saw a troop of English soldiers coming towards them. Retreat would bring attention to themselves, as they were greatly outnumbered, so they continued. Perhaps the English would pass them by. They heard the singing flight of an arrow passing and landing harmlessly behind, but the warning was clear. On their left the River Irvine wound its way towards the Firth of Clyde. The bank of the river offered some shelter. It was heavily wooded, but to reach cover would be difficult across open marshy land. There was nothing for it but to brazen it out.

All might have been well for they looked like harmless travellers: an elderly knight and his servants – but for an unfortunate coincidence. Among the English men-at-arms was Jack Short. He recognised Sir Malcolm from some distance. There was a reward for the betrayal of the king's enemies and he felt a personal hatred for the Wallace family and Sir Malcolm in particular. So he spurred on his horse to the side of Sir Andrew Fenwick, who led the company, and betrayed his countryman.

Sir Andrew was the type of soldier who liked to be sure of his facts before taking any action, but when the man said he had been reared on the Wallace estate he accepted the truth of the statement.

The two groups met. The English superior in numbers surrounded the Scots and Sir Andrew challenged Sir Malcolm calling him by name. Malcolm Wallace drew his sword. The encounter was short and bloody. When the English resumed their journey, Malcolm Wallace, knight of Elderslie lay dead – stripped of his clothes – at the roadside. Passing traders found his corpse that afternoon and took it to Riccarton.

William Wallace said little to his wife and mother about his father's murder, but to his brothers and cousins he vowed revenge and was consumed with hatred for Fenwick and all the English race. His father had been an honourable man, careful in his duties to his superiors and a fair lord to his own people.

After Sir Malcolm's funeral feast, William Wallace took his bow and went alone into the forest. He remained away for two days and Marion became alarmed for he had never stayed away for so long before. Old Neil had seen her worried face as she gazed long and hard across the fields towards the forest. "Don't you fret, Mistress, the master will return once he's decided how to avenge his father's murder."

Late in the afternoon, when it was raining heavily and beginning to get dark, William returned. "Oh, Will, I've been so worried for you," said Marion. "How wet you are. Sit you down by the fire." She knelt and began to draw off the sodden boots. His feet were cold and the heels sore with blisters. While Wallace drank a long draught of mulled ale, Marion bathed his feet rubbing goose fat into the sore parts. He bent forward and took her hands in his, "Sweetheart, you're a good lass and I don't deserve you."

He pulled her towards him kissing her roughly with hard passionate lips. She could feel the anger in him and it frightened her. So she hung back startled and wide eyed: she had never known him to behave harshly. Margaret began to cry and she pulled herself from him to comfort her child who was a bonny maid, big and strong for her age.

When she spied her father sitting in the carved oak chair, she held out her arms to him. Marion carried her over to the big, sad man. "Come then, Meg, come and cheer up your father." Marion left them together to prepare food for her man.

At the beginning of February 1297 a messenger from the Bishop of Glasgow arrived at Lamington requesting Wallace to attend him in the following week. He took his wife and daughter to Lanark where they were to await his return. Marion was reluctant to leave her own manor, but this time Wallace was firm and would hear no excuse.

"I cannot tell when I shall return, my love. I am sure you will be safer under your father's roof than alone in this isolated manor. The folk here cannot protect you against the English should it become necessary." Marion was expecting another child in late June and had been ailing, unable to keep food inside her. Her women said that this time for sure it would be a son. Wallace knew what the English did even to women and children, and there was little protection at Lamington. After leaving Lanark he travelled with his mother to Paisley, and then he would escort her to the care of her brother at Kilspindie. He took these precautions for it was his intention that the English would get to know the name of Wallace.

The Bishop of Glasgow greeted Wallace cordially. To Lady Wallace he was kind and sympathetic. Later when they were alone he said to Wallace, "I heard news of your exploits by Lauder, my son." Wallace grinned. "It was a pleasure, my lord, but it is only the beginning."

"I have heard from Moray. He will be ready to begin his own activities in the north in March. Will you also be ready in the spring, William, and on how many can you rely for support?" "Some thirty will follow me. A few are at my manor of Borthwick and there are others who await but a nod. For myself I will fight alone if necessary. I await news of my father's murderer. He will not die quietly in his bed." The Bishop stirred adjusting the cushions at his back, "Perhaps I can help you there. Many people bring me news. When you have settled your mother in a place of safety, visit me again."

When mother and son were about to part she kissed him. "God be with you, William." She watched sadly as he rode away. His tall square body was bent slightly forward over his horse as he urged it to a canter. The wind caught hold of his red cloak billowing it around him. How like his father, she sighed. At the bend in the track he turned and waved to his watching mother and uncle, then was lost from their sight.

Lady Wallace looked up at her brother. Taking his offered arm they walked back together. "Come now, Meg. William is a good son and a sensible man. Why look so worried?" "He's been so angry since Dunbar and now with his father's murder I fear what he might do. Am I to lose all those I love so much?" Her brother made no reply and she continued sadly, "Why must he stand against the English, when those above us accept them as their lords? We have our land and kin to care for. What can we do against so many? Is it not better to bend the knee in homage along with everyone else? No good can come of this," again she sighed. Her brother had his own views, which did not agree with his sister's, but he said nothing for he knew that it was a widow's grief which caused her to speak so.

Wallace went to Dundee to the Blair's house. He was delighted to find his friend John visiting his family. His father had taken the deaths of his wife, daughter and grandsons badly and John Blair confided in Wallace that they had to watch the old man constantly, particularly if the English approached. "He is no soldier, Will. They would cut him down before he could strike a blow."

Wallace spoke openly of his intentions to continue the fight. "There's a lot of unrest in the town, Will. If the nobles don't give the lead soon, I think the people will rise themselves. All they need is a leader."

Wallace stayed in the town for a week meeting old friends and discussing plans late into the night, until John Blair warned him to show more caution. "Will, there are English spies everywhere, men who would betray their own kindred for a few marks."

Many years later when John Blair sat in Dunfermline Abbey and wrote down the life of his friend he remembered Wallace's reply. How typical it was of Wallace, who was so direct and without guile. It was both his strength and his weakness. "John, if we're too cautious and spend time looking over our shoulders, we'll not have time to get on with the job of sending them back to where they belong."

During the last week of February Wallace returned to Paisley. The bishop was warm in his greeting inviting Wallace to sit himself by the fire. "I have received news of Fenwick, your father's murderer," Wallace looked hard at the bishop. "In a week Fenwick will be in charge of provisions and reinforcements leaving the garrison in Carlisle bound for Ayr. It will be a wonderful opportunity for you at a time of your choosing," said the bishop.

The Bishop of Glasgow had reached middle age and had a deep understanding of his fellow man. Young Wallace, he had noticed, was a man who inspired loyalty in others. He said to his steward, "If yon laddie survives long enough, there will be many who will love him."

After his meeting with the bishop, Wallace went straight to his cousins at Riccarton and Craigie, then made haste to his own manor at Borthwick. There was no time for rest. He must prepare the ambush for the English and for Fenwick in particular. With his brother John and fifty or so friends and kinsmen they assembled at Loudon, grim and determined. They had already met the English at Dunbar and Lauder, and were becoming skilful in the arts of warfare.

It was wild country and near the top of a ridge Wallace blocked the track with boulders leaving only sufficient room for single-file passage. Sheltered by the wild landscape and in the cold and rain, they awaited their quarry. When two days had passed the column of pack horses and men was sighted moving slowly along the muddy road. From their vantage point they counted at least 150 mounted men and almost as many pack animals. Wallace scanned the leaders looking for Fenwick. That was probably him, he told his brother, pointing out a tall well-armoured knight riding at the head of the column.

Yet another fall of rock, Fenwick observed. There had been much rain during the winter and Sir Andrew Fenwick had found all the roads crossing the borders blocked here and there by landslides of mud and rocks. However, the hills sheltered many rogues and robbers and, as an experienced soldier, he unsheathed his sword staring hard at the misty view unfolding in front of him. The only sounds came from his own men. He pulled up his horse sending the pack horses and first troop of men-at-arms through in single file led by his sergeant. Satisfied that all was well, Fenwick followed. An arrow found the gap between the sergeant's iron helmet and leather jerkin piercing his neck. The man next to him fell from his mount as the animal reared with an arrow embedded in its chest. At the same time the silent and desolate moor revealed its deadly secret. From behind the rocks leaped the avenging Scots, armed with battle axes, pikes and claymores, shouting their battle cries.

Wallace had positioned half a dozen good archers high on the hill and they continued to bring down escaping men and beasts. The narrow track quickly became blocked with the dead and dying, and those at the front could not turn about to give assistance to the men coming behind. In the confined space Sir Andrew Fenwick hacked at the attackers and was about to turn his mount once more when a tall, well-armed Scot sprang in front of him, calling him by name.

Plainly this Scot had cause to seek him out and he accepted the challenge. He tried to keep his advantage skilfully wheeling his horse, but the Scot nimbly sidestepped and slashed at Fenwick's mount bringing the animal down. Fenwick struggled clear.

"Get up, Fenwick. None will say your death was not in fair fight." He stood waiting for Fenwick, 'Vengeance' clasped in his powerful hand. The two men circled, lunging and slashing at each other with the ringing sound of metal striking metal. Around them men fought and died, and arrows continued their deadly flight. Englishmen at the rear of the column attempted to push forward to aid their comrades and the once lonely moor rang with the noise of frightened, wounded animals and desperate, fighting men.

Wallace had the advantage of age and height. Fenwick backed away until his back was against the rocky escarpment. He brought up his sword in a swinging arch to fend off Wallace's attack, missed his footing in the stony ground and fell. Wallace's claymore reached its mark and blood poured from a wound in Fenwick's side. He tried to regain his feet, but fell back with blood pouring from his mouth and nostrils. Wallace looked down at his enemy and was about to deliver the final blow when a shout from the fighting men drew his attention to Tom Johnston desperately fighting off two Englishmen. Wallace went to his aid and it was Robert Boyd who delivered the coup-de-gras to Fenwick.

After Fenwick's death the English tried to flee, but the narrow path made this difficult. A few at the rear turned, galloping back the way they had come, leaving pack horses and half of their number dead or dying. Wallace climbed to the highest point to watch their confused retreat. He was calm, unlike the anger he felt after Dunbar or the elation at Lauder. The men below were shouting and laughing, searching and stripping the bodies of their enemies. Tom came to him, "They have found wine, Will. You must come down and take command before they're the worse for drink. The English will return with reinforcements." He nodded in the direction of the retreating English survivors.

Wallace stirred, never a man to waste time dreaming, and followed Tom. They had stripped Fenwick's body. It lay grotesquely white on the blood soaked earth. Boyd held the English knight's leather boots which he offered to Wallace. "Here, Will, his goods are rightfully yours." Wallace waved them aside irritably and looked distastefully at the man's body. "It's enough that he's dead. Come men, make some haste. The English will no doubt search for us."

The pack animals and loose horses were rounded up and they left the terrible scene to the scavenging crows and soaring eagles. That night a storm blew in from the west, covering the tracks, and by the time the garrison at Ayr started its search, the goods had been divided among manors and farms throughout Clydesdale.

When an English patrol arrived at the manor of Lamington, the master was busy in the yard directing his men building a new barn for the early spring lambing. He could not be described as friendly towards the sergeant who came to search his manor, but the sergeant reported that all was in good order and it looked as if Wallace had been at home all winter.

Wallace had watched in silence as the English poked into every nook and cranny. His share from the ambush was already hidden in the forest, where the English would not find it. In the late afternoon he rode into Lanark to his wife and daughter. He wanted to spend the holy weeks of Lent with them.

On the Sunday following Wallace's revenge for the death of his father he went to the church in Lanark, where almost three years earlier he had joyfully made his marriage vows. Wallace stood among the men and looked across to the women's side of the church where Marion stood holding the child in her arms. Her pregnancy was heavy upon her now. She swelled with life and hope. The sickness which had plagued her in the early months had gone, and her husband thought he had never seen her looking lovelier. He smiled to himself when he remembered how soft and winsome she had been when she lay in his arms the night before. Then he remembered that he was in God's House, and looked towards the priest preparing the sacrament.

Two days later Wallace, accompanied by Tom Johnson, set out for Paisley. They led two packhorses loaded with furs and fleeces. The English were checking all travellers, male, female, young and old. It was no longer safe for hardy, young men to be travelling any distance from their estates without good cause, and they were stopped many times by patrolling soldiers who searched their baggage. By the time they arrived at the abbey Wallace was in an impatient and dangerous mood.

The bishop had heard, as had all of Scotland, about the ambush, but to hear the details from Wallace's own lips brought a gleam to Wishart's eyes. "And what are your intentions now, Wallace?" "I shall be meeting up with my men near Stirling," he grinned, "we shall let the English rest awhile, but will poke their fires occasionally. Have you had news from the north?" "It is a little early for them to be stirring from their firesides, Wallace. Spring comes late in Moray, but I have little doubt that with the first nesting birds they'll be up and about harassing the English."

Wallace and his men camped in the Gargunnock Hills overlooking the River Forth. It was still early in the year. The weather was clear and Stirling Castle could be seen away to the east, but that fortress was not to be his target, not yet anyway. They struck camp at dawn and he sent his cousin Adam with Tom Haliday on ahead to spy out the land. In the late morning they sat resting, sheltered from view by trees and looking down at Gargunnock Tower waiting for the return of his scouts. At about noon they returned to an impatient Wallace. "Well, Adam, what's the news?"

"The English are carrying out some repairs, Will. Carpenters are at work and they move in and out across the drawbridge as they wish." "Have they no guard then?" "Och, aye. There are two sitting at the entrance, talking and yawning and another in the middle of the bridge with a line out fishing." All those listening laughed except Wallace.

They were without horses and the final half mile or so to the tower was across open ground. To go in daylight would offer no chance of surprise and Wallace had no intention of conducting a siege. The two young men refreshed themselves, then went to Wallace. Their faces were eager for the expected fight. "Nay lads. The English will still be there in the morning. For now find a sheltered spot and rest quietly." They all moved off to the cover of trees to wait. It was a cold night with intermittent rain. For warmth they dug shallow pits in the earth and cut pine branches and bracken for shelter. They slept a little, but were pleased when Tom Johnston, who was on guard duty, awoke them as dawn showed in the east.

Quietly and quickly they moved across country towards the tower with Wallace in the lead. At the bridge crossing the River Forth they halted. The drawbridge had already been lowered and carpenters were busy replacing rotten timbers. The huge iron shod door was still closed, but the postern gate stood open. A sentry stood watching the carpenters, a large piece of bread in his hand. It had been a damp watch and he was waiting for his replacement. Then he would find a nice warm place beside the fire in the kitchens. He took another bite of his bread and wandered out onto the bridge. Wallace's arrow cut through his throat and he fell without a cry. The carpenters scattered as the Scottish force approached the drawbridge.

It was a lookout on the battlements above the gatehouse who first saw the attackers and raised the alarm. They tried to bar the door but it was too late. The English, still bemused from sleep, were at a disadvantage from the surprise attack. The captain of the tower, John Thirlwell, had only recently taken up his new post and had been secure in the knowledge that so close to Stirling he would be safe from Scottish attack. He had felt such confidence that recently his wife and three young children had joined him.

When he heard the commotion, he jumped from his bed, took his sword from the bench beside him and cautiously opened the door. The stairway appeared clear. He ran down trying to pull on his chain surcoat as he went. When he reached the bottom of the steps he came face to face with Wallace.

John Thirlwell, a veteran of France, was an able soldier but the fight with Wallace could have only one outcome for Wallace fought for a cause. Thirlwell lay slumped at his feet when he heard a woman's scream. Looking up he saw his victim's wife at the bend of the stair with her hair hanging loose around her white face. She wore a shift and her feet were bare. Behind her peeping from around her legs wide eyed and frightened stood three small children. "Go back to your chamber woman," commanded the man. There were just over a score of Englishmen defending the tower and within twenty minutes all were dead.

Wallace was in the courtyard. He had finished prowling through the rooms and outhouses, checking for fugitives, when he heard women's screams coming from the direction of the kitchens. He found the room in disarray, benches and baskets upturned, and freshly baked rye bread scattered across the earthen floor, but the meat still roasted on the spit. In the far corner a woman was struggling with one of Wallace's men, while another lying on the floor desperately tried to fend off his comrade.

"Leave them," bellowed Wallace as he grabbed the nearest man by his hair pulling him roughly away. "We are trying to drive the English from our land, not molest their women." The man, already impassioned by killing with lust throbbing in his loins, put his hand to his dagger but checked himself and looked sheepishly at Wallace.

Both women scrambled to their feet and clung to each other, weeping noisily. Wallace prodded them with his claymore and they obediently went outside to the courtyard. He called to his brother,

"Round up the women and children John and send them on their way. See that the men do them no harm." To Tom Johnston he said, "Search out for weapons, clothes and other stores. We shall take what we can and then torch the castle. Be quick. We have little time to get away to the hills."

An hour later a string of horses and ponies trotted into the cover of the Gargunnock Hills laden with booty while the smoke from the funeral pyre of the English garrison rose lazily into the spring sky. The women and children stood weeping and watching for some time before moving off towards Stirling. They were unlikely to forget Wallace's name.

Once safely shielded from spying eyes, Wallace turned west then north, fording the river in the late afternoon. Only when they were safely into the heart of the forest did he allow his men to rest, but he would not permit a fire. As night fell it became cold. Before sleeping John Wallace said to his brother, "Well, Will, what plans have you for the English now?" "The English king has a liking for Perth and Scone. I thought we could pay his men a visit. They'll not be expecting us up there." Tom Johnston asked, "What will you do with the ponies and baggage, Will? The ground is bad and they're slowing us down."

"There are plenty who will gladly take both beasts and goods. We shall have what we need and leave the rest at the Ferguson manor, near the River Earn. You remember David Ferguson who fell at Dunbar. His father has good cause to hate the English and will help by concealing what he can." The following day, after hiding what they could not use, they crossed the Earn.

The inn at Kinclaven was a busy place and popular with the English soldiers. Two young Scots arrived, each carrying smoked fish for sale. They managed to sell some, without getting a very good price, but appeared pleased with the transaction. Before leaving, they sat close to a group of English soldiers and had a drink. They left by the Methven road, but once out of sight, Wallace's spies took the hill path to rejoin their comrades.

Wallace chose the position of ambush with great care, concealing his men in thick woodland near the confluence of the Tay and Isla rivers. Sir James Butler was returning from Perth to his home in Kinclaven. It was a grey, wet day and they had to wait patiently for some hours. The men were becoming restless when the lookout reported mounted troops coming, perhaps a hundred or so. Wallace crossed himself, murmured a Hail Mary, took his bow and quiver and went to a position with a clear view of the road.

The battlements of Kinclaven Castle could already be seen. The English had begun to relax when Wallace opened the attack with a keenly aimed arrow. The affair was brisk and bloody. Wallace dispatched Butler, a man many years his senior and no match for the ringing claymore wielded by its master. When more than half their number lay dead or dying, the surviving English made a dash for the shelter of Kinclaven. As the drawbridge was lowered for the fleeing English, so the Scots followed. In the outer courtyard there was much noise and confusion. The men were shouting. Frightened horses and clash of weapons on shields added to the horror of the situation. As darkness fell smoke and flames rose to greet the stars and a small group of women and children, accompanied by two English priests, made their slow sad way towards Perth.

Wallace retreated into the Methven woods, but this time the avenging English were able to follow his trail. They prepared themselves to hunt down the murderers and flush them out, but in the heavily wooded country they were forced to fight on foot. The Scots skirmished and fled so that the English were never sure when to expect the next strike, but during one melee Wallace received an unlucky wound. An arrow grazed his neck just below his chin. It did not find any vital organ, but the wound became increasingly painful. Many of his men fell. They were good men who had fought with him at Dunbar. To save those who remained he gave the order to scatter. That way they stood a chance. Before continuing on their way Wallace spoke to his brother, "John, if I don't return, look after Marion and the babes. She'll need a brother's care." Under cover of darkness each went their own way.

As dawn broke Wallace reached the ford by the river Earn. He smelt wood smoke and in the early light could see the English camped near the water's edge, barring his way. Their horses were tethered close by in the shelter of a large oak. "Well, you buggers. It'll take more than you to stop me," he murmured.

Crouching low and seeking cover wherever he could behind gorse or rock, he made his way to the tethered animals. He had already mounted one and released others before the English became aware of him. He dug his heels into the beast's flanks and headed for the ford. They tried to lunge for his reins, but Wallace slashed to left and right. He heard the deadly song of an arrow but it passed him by harmlessly. As he reached the river bank a young knight rushed towards him, sword in his hand.

Wallace reined in his horse and struck the man a blow across his neck with such force that he severed head from body. The head spun into the river bumping and banging from rock to rock as Wallace fled across the ford pursued by his enemies. At Blackford his horse stumbled and fell. Wallace regained his feet but found the animal had broken its front leg.

"You'll not rise again laddie". He patted the great beast. It had carried him safely for many miles and he had no wish to leave it to the wolves. Drawing his dagger he cut the animal's throat then turned to continue on foot. He kept to a south-westerly route, dog tired, wet and cold. He had strips of dried meat in his pouch and he chewed these, but the wound in his neck was painful and he found swallowing difficult. He came to a small stream and tried to drink a little. The water was icy cold and he began to shiver uncontrollably. It was growing dark and he climbed into the shelter of some rocks, pulled his cloak around him and tried to sleep, his claymore ready by his side. It was dark when he awoke, stirred by the sound of braying hounds in the distance. In spite of the darkness he arose and continued his journey towards the Forth, but the baying from the hounds grew nearer and nearer.

In the early dawn he looked down at the Forth winding its way towards the sea. He was very wet and tired. His boots squelched with every step and his body ached from fever. He allowed himself to rest for a few moments on a fallen tree, looking across at the opposite bank that offered safety: he must make a final effort. The hounds were close and he could hear men's voices as they called to each other. The Forth was deep and wide at this point, icy cold from the winter's snows and he shuddered as he waded out from the bank. He had tied his sword, battleaxe and boots into his cloak which he strapped to his back. His chain mail he flung into the swirling waters where the English hounds could not find it. He gritted his teeth, each stroke an agony in the strong current as he reached out for freedom.

On reaching the opposite bank, Wallace crawled like an infant from the water and lay on the grass shaking with exhaustion and cold. Gradually he became aware of a boy watching him. He was about eleven and from his dress a peasant. He carried a string of freshly caught fish. Wallace realised that he had been seen and struggled unsteadily to his feet, but the boy came to him offering his arm.

"Sir, my home is near," he indicated the forest, but Wallace could see no cot or smoke. He wanted to tell the boy that he could manage, but the words would not come so sore was his throat. He took a step and fell. Across the Forth the noise from the dogs and searching men could be heard. He must take cover. The boy had run to a nearby thicket and cut a stout staff. As Wallace again struggled to his feet, he ran back offering it to him.

"Lean on it, sir. It'll help you along." Then, giving Wallace his arm for support, he helped him to the safety of the trees. He led him to a clearing where his brother was tending a charcoal pit and together they lay Wallace where he would get the benefit of the fire. Then the young man ran off to seek help.

Wallace was only dimly aware of his journey, carried on a litter, through the forest to their cot. The old woman, their mother, laid him on a straw mattress and removed his damp clothes wrapping him in wolf furs and placing hot stones at his feet. They knew who he was, calling him by name. His exploits at Gargunnock and Kinclaven had already spread and they treated him with great respect and kindness.

He found it difficult to keep his eyes open and his mind – like his body – felt numb. His head banged and no matter how hard he tried he could not speak. The woman put more wood on the fire. The sparks and smoke rose up to the roof vent and he drifted into a delirious sleep.

He did not know how long he lay there, but stirred a little when the woman tended his wound and when they carried him further into the forest. They had prepared a small shelter hidden in dense thicket. A charcoal brazier glowed in the darkness and the young lad sat quietly by him both day and night. The mother applied hot poultices to his festering neck, which caused him much pain, but most of the time he lay in a fitful sleep – until the third day when the fever broke. On the following afternoon, he heard rustling outside as someone approached. They had placed his sword at his side and placing a finger on his lips to warn the boy to silence he picked up the weapon. A figure bent low through the narrow entrance and Uncle Wallace of Dunipace appeared. "Well, Will, you've certainly been a fox among the chickens." Wallace managed a smile.

"All Scotland has heard of your success Will, but they say you drowned in the Forth. Your mother refused to believe it. She said she would know if you fell. Nay, do not be fearful, we have already sent a message to Marion". Wallace lay back on his couch, relief on his face. "It is hard for women," said his uncle. "Will, whatever the English say to the world, they continue to search for you and your men, there will be no future for you if you don't seek terms."

Wallace looked sharply at his uncle. "Nay lad, you must consider your family: you have avenged your father's death but you cannot pit yourself against the English king with just a handful of men." However it was plain that he was making no headway. Wallace was determined to carry on with his quest.

Two more visitors arrived shortly after their conversation. John Wallace and Tom Johnston were overjoyed to find William alive and, as they ate broth and bread which the old mother insisted that they should accept, the young men talked excitedly of the past raids and of raids yet to come. Uncle Wallace, watching and listening, marvelled at the ability of young men to be fearless in such dangerous times.

"Well, Will, what do you propose now?" asked Tom Johnston. "I must get away from here. These good people are in danger the longer I remain. I'll take to the forests for a day or two until the hue and cry has died down."

The widow was aware of the danger, but she was a mother and cared for William as if he were her own son. She had found an old wadmal coat that had belonged to her husband. It was shapeless and well darned, tight across his shoulders and short in sleeve and skirt, for Wallace was a giant compared with her poor man. It was the best she could do, however, and at least from a distance it would disguise him.

Uncle Wallace arranged for three shaggy ponies, nondescript beasts, to be tethered at the foot of the Dunduff Moor and the three young men rode into the hills until the English returned to their garrisons. Wallace set up camp in a small bothy on a hillside with good views. On the morning of the third day, they saw a young man riding along the sheep track which led to their eyrie. Tom urged Wallace to take cover until they should know if the newcomer was friend or foe, but Wallace went out openly to meet him with one hand extended in friendship, the other on his dagger hilt.

Sir John Graham's father owned the land around the encampment. He was a cautious man fond of saying, "Don't seek trouble laddie, wait till trouble seeks you". When he heard that William Wallace, leader of the hotheads, was hiding on his land he flared up angrily at his sons and steward and anyone else who was within earshot. "Damn his eyes. Does he think the English will let his stupidity pass without reprisals? We'll none of us be safe now. John, you find him and tell him from me that I'll not give him sanctuary and to be gone."

His eldest son did not agree with him. He was amiable and honest, long suffering of his father's irritable nature and the presence of the

English in every town and castle, swaggering around the land, arrogant in their demands, was more difficult for him to accept than his father's bad temper. The following morning he set out alone to see Wallace.

When Wallace came out openly to greet him, his decision to join his group was made. He had also felt the humiliation of Dunbar and they sat together for a long time talking about the future. "Surely you can gain fresh support from the men of Clydesdale and strike at the English while they still lick their wounds," said Graham. Wallace poked the embers of the fire while he pondered. He did not want to dampen Graham's enthusiasm. "The English will be on the alert in the area, Graham, and new men need careful training."

They parted on friendly terms and Graham promised to join Wallace after Easter. As he rode home his excited thoughts whirled around. Wallace himself had surprised him. He had expected an angry, violent man, interested in booty and glory, but Wallace was none of these. Unassuming and direct of speech, courteous and pleasant, all attributes which John Graham admired.

Wallace remained in the hills for a few more days. On the morning of the third day as the weather turned cold, wet and atrocious, they left heading south-west for Glasgow and Paisley. That year Easter was late, coming in mid April, and he had a great longing to celebrate Christ's resurrection with his family. He called at the Stewart's castle, but his exploits had preceded him. "Wallace, you have ruffled their feathers, keep it up," had been his lord's parting words.

Wallace travelled by remote paths to Lanark, arriving well after dark. The Braidfute manor was in darkness, but the dogs set up a ferocious barking and a house servant opened the door holding a lantern aloft. One of Marion's old hounds recognised his master and bounded out to greet him. Marion was already abed and Wallace, tired and cold, drank from the ale barrel, removed his dirty, smelling clothes and crept to his bed, pulling the coverlet and wool-filled quilt over him. He could feel the soft warmth of her body as she stirred, opened her eyes and in the glow from the fire saw her husband's comely face beside her.

"Oh, William, they told me you were hurt." She flung her slender arms around him covering his face with kisses full of joy. He winced when she caught the wound in his neck. "Nay, sweetheart. Calm yourself. You make it hard for a man to resist you". Marion was now well advanced with perhaps six weeks to go. He did not wish to cause her harm.

They talked for a while. Margaret was so big and bonny now and was trying to walk. Marion's pride rang in her voice. She had heard about the raids and the name of Wallace was mooted about the market place. Her father had told her not to venture outside where the English would see her. "William, I was frightened when they said you were dead, but I knew you were not. I would know if it were so, but you must take care, Will, for I am sure that they watch the manor."

He held her close. Her head was resting on his shoulder so that he could smell the sweet perfume of her hair. In the cradle by the bedside Margaret stirred but did not waken. It had been over a month since he had lain in a bed with a down mattress and soft dry covers. The warmth and comfort quickly overcame him and he drifted into a deep sleep.

In the early morning he lay thinking about what she had said. So they watch her. Margaret awoke and he padded round to her cradle. She was sitting up and looking at him. Then she remembered her father's face and smiled holding out her arms to be picked up. He stooped to her and she stood up, carefully holding the edge of the wooden cradle. It rocked and there was some danger that she would fall out. Her mother had woken and looked over the bed edge at her husband and child.

"Nay, Meg, your mother can take you. You are so wet," her father laughed rather sheepishly. Marion went to the door calling one of the serving women to take the child. The little girl was carried away protesting loudly, and husband and wife lay for a while enjoying the company and warmth of each other.

It was Lady Cecilia who brought up the subject which had been worrying Wallace ever since Marion had said she was being watched. Late in the morning when Marion was in the bakehouse and he was in one of the barns sharpening Vengeance, Lady Cecilia came to him, "William, I believe you must think carefully about her safety. The sheriff has sent his clerk around twice asking after you and I believe a man has been set to watch our comings and goings on the Crags yonder. Marion and Margaret will be safer at Lamington or at your own manor of Borthwick."

That night Wallace set out for Lamington. Marion followed the next day, openly and for all to see, accompanied by her stepmother and servants. An English patrol stopped them and were told that Marion was seeing to her affairs while she still could. The sergeant saw the lady's condition. He was a family man himself and had a gruff kindliness about him. "Well, take care down by the river," he said "the ground is bad. This nag nearly had me in the water and a drenching won't do you no good."

In the evening when they returned the party was one less for Margaret had been left with Neil's wife to foster. It was a hard decision for the young mother to make, but she consoled herself that it would be for a few days only. She would remain at Lanark until after Easter when William and his men would escort her to Borthwick

Wallace arrived in Lanark early on Easter Day. Tom Johnston and his brother John were with him. People were already astir and they could hear Matins being sung in the church. Wallace had an urge to receive the sacrament and to offer prayers for the souls of his men who had fallen in the woods of Methven. They were dressed in peasant clothes and remained near the back of the church, keeping in the shadows with the hoods of their wadmal cloaks pulled over their heads. When it was time for Wallace to receive the host, he moved up along the side isle waiting for the priest and dropped to his knees. The priest bent low holding the chalice and whispered, "The English are entering the church"

Wallace with head bent low, followed by Tom and his brother, turned to leave. As they reached the arched doorway an English clerk who had been watching the tall figure murmured to the sheriff and the men around him. Wallace sensed danger. Then hearing the excitement he quickened his pace. On leaving the church he crossed the market square into the narrow alleys. Any doubts, which the English may have had about his identity, were lost when they found how quickly he had vanished. A young woman, a stranger to Lanark, was asked by the English if she had seen three men running from the church. Since she did not know William Wallace, she told them that they had run into the alley of the sawyers. The men had been shabbily dressed. They had to be thieves. The English spread out but generally headed out of town towards the Braidfute manor. The sheriff was sure that was the way he would go.

As they ran Wallace's mind was racing. If they were caught in or near the Braidfute manor it would go badly for Marion and her people. "Make for the Cartland Crags," he called to his companions. As they left they took care to be seen heading for the hills and the English, who had reinforcements, searched the hills until nightfall. Sheriff Hazelrig was determined to catch Wallace, murderer of Butler, and returned to the Braidfute manor early the following day prepared to use force.

The Braidfute family had decided to show an innocent face to the world. Sir Hugh had already risen and was out on his estate with his steward. Lady Cecilia had gone with her women to the church and Marion was resting in her bed when the sheriff and his men began hammering for admittance. The frightened servants had no alternative but to admit them. Herding them into the great hall, the sheriff demanded to know where William Wallace could be found. Old Alexander, who had worked for the family for over forty years, said that William Wallace had not been seen for many weeks. The sheriff struck him a blow which sent the old man staggering backwards and he fell heavily against the table. The female servants clung to each other, while the old man was picked up and struck again. "Come on, old man, where is William Wallace? He was seen heading in this direction. It'll go badly for you and the women if you remain silent."

The old man's eyes rolled in his head. He had been shaken by the fall, but he continued to protest that Wallace had not been near the manor for many weeks. Marion's old wolf hound sleeping by her bed rushed out as she opened her door and hurled itself at the nearest man. It landed on his hastily drawn dagger, whimpered and fell dying to the floor. Marion threw a mantle over her shift and came to the top of the wooden steps which led down into the hall. Summoning up all her courage she spoke with as much dignity and confidence as her condition would permit. "My lord sheriff, leave my servant alone. He is an old man and knows nothing."

All eyes turned to the young mother with her pale face, lovely blue dark-ringed eyes and yellow, braided hair, hanging in two plaits over her breasts. That she was close to her time was plain. Firmly grasping the wooden stair rail, with considerable dignity, she came down the stairs. "We have come for your husband, madam, and will leave you in peace when he gives himself up," said the sheriff. "Sir, my servants have already told you that he is not here nor has been here for some time." Hazelrig, his voice rising, said through clenched teeth, "He was seen madam." "Then your informant was mistaken, sir, and I ask that you leave this house and us in peace. I have signed my allegiance to the king and you have no right to trespass in this house."

Hazelrig was used to having his own way in all things and this was too much to bear from a Scots hussy. He roughly took hold of her plaits and pulled her towards his sergeant. "Answer my questions woman or I shall hand you and yours over to my sergeant. He'll get an answer for me." Marion winced with pain and fear, but once again said, "I am telling you the truth, I have acknowledged King Edward as my liege lord. Surely you cannot believe that in my present state I have betrayed my oath. Leave us in peace."

Hazelrig, red in the face and exasperated by the woman's persistence, shrugged, looked towards his sergeant and left the hall. As he reached the door, he heard the women scream and the thud as the old man fell to the floor. Looking back he saw the old man lying in his own blood and the sergeant holding Marion so that she must gaze on his final seconds of life. "When she is ready to tell me what I want to know call me," called Hazelrig from the doorway.

The sergeant struck Marion across the face and she fell heavily to the floor. Her mantle dropped from her and her loose sleeveless linen shift revealed her heavy prenatal breasts. The sergeant standing over her pulled her to her feet, bending his face close to hers. She could smell his sour breath and tried to struggle from him. The room spun around her. She could hear the other soldiers laughing as her women began to scream again. There was pain in her left breast which the Englishman was squeezing. "Come lady, where is Wallace?" Marion felt dizzy. Her back was hurting and she had to bite her lip to stop herself crying out. A soldier came over, "Go on sergeant, screw her. That'll make her squeal."

The sergeant pulled her close to him. "Did you hear that they think I should fuck you? Look what's happening to your women. Tell me where your man is?" He spun her around so that she could see her four women. They were on the floor, skirts up over their shoulders, while the Englishmen puffed and laughed over them.

Marion began to sob shaking uncontrollably. The sergeant struck her again sending her spinning across the room. She could not rise even if he had allowed her to. She closed her eyes so that she need not look into his pitiless face. She had fallen by the fire and her right hand closed around the iron poker. With her remaining strength she brought it up and down catching the man a blow on the side of the head. It was unexpected and knocked him off balance but did not cause him serious harm.

She lay helpless as the man drew his dagger and casually drew the blade across her throat. The blood spurted out covering both the slayer and the slain. Marion shuddered and choked and bubbles of air formed at the corner of her mouth. Then she died. "You've done for her serg. She won't tell us nothing now," said one of his men. The sergeant cleaned his dagger on Marion's shift then went to the door. Outside the sheriff was sitting in the sun drinking from a small silver goblet.

"Well man, is she ready to speak?" "Sir, she is dead and said nothing." The sheriff looked annoyed. At least he could not be held responsible for the woman's death. He had given no order, nor had he been present. Anyway it was unlikely that any would question the death of the wife of Sir William Butler's murderer. Hazelrig got to his feet, "Kill them, kill everything and fire the place. Perhaps that will bring Wallace from his lair." As he spoke Sir Hugh and his steward came running towards the manor. The sergeant took a bow and arrows and brought down both men before they came into the yard.

Lady Cecilia and her followers were told of the catastrophe by the cowherd who had seen the English arrive and had remained hidden in the safety of the orchard. He had heard the screams and pleadings, the squeals of the pigs and squeaking from the geese. Then there was the ominous silence before the flames and smoke began to devour the evidence.

He ran as quickly as he could to the church to seek the lady. Her neighbours gathered about listening to the man's story. That it was true was clear from the smoke and flames which arose on the outskirts of Lanark. They said little to Lady Cecilia. With many English spies around a wise man kept his own council.

The priest, taking her by the arm, gave her the sanctuary of the church, but she spoke quietly to her servant. "Alan, seek out Wallace, before others give him the news."

Wallace had gone to a shepherd's bothy in the hills north of Lanark. He saw the smoke curling heavenwards and grew restless. Eventually he agreed to remain in hiding while Tom went into the valley to get the news. By the late afternoon his irritability had increased so that his brother found it a hard task to stop him from returning openly to Lanark. There was such relief when they saw Tom returning with another, but as they drew near their faces showed all was not well.

Wallace ran down the hillside to meet them, "Well, what news? Is she safe?" Tom, embarrassed by the pain which he was about to inflict on his friend, looked back towards Lanark where the smoke still spiralled upwards. "Come, Tom, don't spare me, what has happened?" Tom Johnston found the courage to look Wallace full in the face saying, "Will, the sheriff and his men went to the manor. They have fired the place and all who were there are dead."

The anguish and pain on his friend's face made him ashamed and he looked away. Wallace turned to Alan the cowherd saying, "Tell me all." The man told everything that he had seen and heard and when he had finished Wallace turned about and went up the glen, walking at great speed. The three men stood watching. Tom was about to follow, but John Wallace pulled him back saying, "Follow at a distance and see that he is safe, but let him be alone."

As it grew dark Wallace returned to the bothy. He said nothing but ate a little of the fish which they had grilled on the embers of the peat fire. When it was quite dark he said, "I am going to Lanark to see for myself and if need be to give Marion a Christian burial."

No man tried to stop him and he did not ask that they should accompany him, but some minutes after he had left John Wallace took his battleaxe and followed his brother keeping some distance behind him. It was a silver night. The full moon was riding across the sky casting shadows over rocks and trees. Wallace expected a guard, but after circling carefully around the manor he found none. Little remained of the once handsome Braidfute manor. Heavy oak beams that had supported the roof lay smouldering. The carcasses of slaughtered cows, pigs, dogs and geese lay around the yard. Young Jamie, who helped in the ale house, had been bound and thrown into the largest vat full of the fresh brew he had been making that morning. He floated on his back staring through the brown foaming liquid with sightless eyes. The gutted remains of the brew house were around him.

Wallace found the charred body of his wife recognising it by the ring that he had given her at their betrothal. He knelt rocking her gently in his arms. She had been such a tender loving wife. He wrapped her in his red cloak and bore her away from that terrible place to the church where he sought the priest. "Father, the body of my murdered wife who was close to her time. Will you give her Christian burial?" "We have already a place prepared for another. We will lay her there, my son."

Wallace followed him placing her tenderly in the grave. He then stood quietly, with bent head, his big frame shaking with silent weeping. The priest said the blessing to speed her soul's flight to paradise. The young widower crossed himself murmuring the *Pater Noster* and *Ave Maria* and began to shovel the dark cold earth into the grave.

The priest placed a hand on the man's shoulder. He should have found words to comfort the bereaved. Normally words came easily to him, but there was nothing he could say to ease Wallace's torment, so he stood quietly with him. "It's my fault father. If I had left the harrying of the English to my betters she would still be here to call me husband." "Did she ever try to stop you my son?" "Nay, but I should have cared more for my responsibilities to her than to fight for something which others held to be of so little account."

They heard light steps behind them. It was Lady Cecilia. She was carrying a wax taper, her face pale in its glow. He remembered then that she also mourned the murder of her husband and he took her hand. They talked about the little maid, Margaret, but he said he did not know what he would do with her. Better she knew nothing: then she could not betray them. He bowed low to her and wishing her well received the priest's blessing, then left for the hills.

When he had reached the top of the first slope he turned and looked down at the church tower silhouetted in the moonlight. He could hold his grief back no longer and flung himself onto the mossy track, fists clenched and body shaking with uncontrollable sobs. John Wallace, who throughout the night had remained with his brother, watched him and sat quietly by.

# Men of Courage

S ir William Fitzwarenne, Constable of Urquhart Castle, stood in his stirrups to get a better view of the rear of the column. Satisfied that his knights and men-at-arms were keeping together he settled down again to enjoy the pleasant spring weather and mull over the discussion he had had at Inverness Castle that day. They had left Dunain behind them and would soon see the dark peaty waters of the neck of Loch Ness tucked between the hills. He sniffed the breeze. He always enjoyed this time of the year. There had been good weather recently and the track was firm. He increased the pace to a steady canter. At this speed they could expect to reach Urquhart well before dusk. A small lochan came into view, sparkling with a million diamonds in the sunshine. The track began to slope downwards towards the great loch itself. Once through the pass, they would be safe along the edge of Loch Ness. With accoutrements jingling merrily, they began the steep descent.

There was a slight whistling sound hardly heard above the clatter, then unmistakably the whirr-r-r from a flight of arrows. The startled horses neighed, one or two reared, men shouted warnings to one another, others fell struck by the arrows. From behind rocks and heather came the men of Moray. In a brief moment the quiet May evening was filled with the noise of battle. Horses and men fell under the fierce but brief attack. Fitzwarenne and the men closest to him broke free and, on his instruction fled for the safety of Loch Ness and Urquhart Castle, leaving behind the dead and dying. The attackers, who were all on foot, quickly gave up the chase.

Andrew Moray watched the retreating English and then turned his attention to the dead and dying, his men and foe alike. Two English knights lay where they had fallen with serious wounds, but with God's grace they would live long enough to bring a handsome ransom to their captors. There were well over a score of loose horses which would also be useful. The men, laughing and exhilarated, stripped the dead. "You've done well, but let's gather what we can and get back to camp while we may," said Moray to his men.

Fitzwarenne and his men were angry and shaken by the audacious attack, but in the safety of Urquhart he regained his composure and gave orders for the guards to be doubled. The ambush was after all a small affair. The rogues would not dare to defy the king and openly besiege such a strong fortress. In the morning he would send out patrols to gauge the strength of the Scots.

Just before first light, movement from the landward side of the castle alarmed the guards high on the turrets. As the morning mists cleared they looked down at the brave faces of Moray's patriots. Grim and determined men, with neither fine armour nor deadly siege engines, driven only by a spirit which the English did not understand. Fitzwarenne arrived hurriedly on the battlements. Plainly they were under siege. "Damn their impudence, Ralph," he said to his sergeant. "Well we can sit here and wait." "I recognise some, sir, they're only merchants from Inverness. They'll be in a hurry to get back to count their money," he sneered.

Andrew Moray, joined by Alexander Pilche and other burgesses from Inverness, had drawn up his men on the three landward sides of the castle. Pilche's determined appearance had impressed Moray, but Pilche was a Fleming, not a Scot, and Moray wondered why he was prepared to risk his life and livelihood in other men's arguments. The previous evening they had discussed plans and Moray asked him what reward he wanted for his help. "Revenge for my kinsfolk and friends, my brother and all his family were in the Red Hall at Berwick." Moray gazed at the camped men around him, "It seems the English have made many enemies for themselves."

Moray had decided to lay siege to Urquhart because the Countess of Ross and her men from the west were close at hand ready to give aid to the English. If they were allowed to join forces with the English, it would be difficult for him to take the castle. The morning wore on. The English sat behind their raised drawbridge while the Scots, just out of arrow range, lit small fires and sat down to wait. Just before noon, a Scottish knight rode into the camp and was brought to Moray who knew him by sight. He was an esquire of David Ross, the Countess's eldest son. "Well, man, what brings you here?" demanded Moray. "My lord sends a message for the governor of the castle, sir." Moray laughed, "Really? And they think I will let you pass?" "My lord says that you will understand what a difficult position the Countess, his mother, is in. The earl is still a prisoner in the Tower at London and if she does nothing to assist the English all will be lost."

Pilche snorted angrily, but Moray smiled and waved him on, "Go on then, deliver your message, for all the good it will do you." The English listened glumly to the Scottish knight delivering his message before the raised drawbridge. So the Countess is camped nearby thought Fitzwarenne. "Why does your mistress suggest we surrender when our defences are so strong?" he shouted to the herald. "Sir, the whole country is in revolt and you are in a very difficult position." "Thank the Countess for her concern, but I believe the castle and my men can withstand any siege which Scots may attempt. Your mistress should be assisting us by attacking the king's enemies, not talking to them. Take that message to your mistress." They watched sullenly as the herald went back through his countrymen's camp.

"What foolery is this?" demanded Alexander Pilche. "Are we trying to force the English from this land or meet then in a joust." "The Countess is troubled by her husband's imprisonment. She must appear to give them aid for his sake," replied Moray mildly.

The following day Andrew Moray rode up the glen to the shores of the loch to talk with David Ross and his mother. He was greeted in friendly fashion for they had known one another since boyhood, and the Countess and Andrew's mother were second cousins. "David, I understand your position, but I must ask you not to interfere and not ask me to raise the siege. My family also has much to lose. I know my father would rather sweat in an English prison while I fight honourably for our kingdom."

The Countess looked sharply at him. "That's a very pretty speech, Andrew Moray, but my husband is old and ailing. He will not see his grandchildren if I don't seek favour of the English – and they'll take our land away to boot." Andrew Moray could think of many arguments against aiding the English but he held his tongue. He extracted a promise that the Countess's men would not attack Moray's force and in return he promised to allow her to seek out Fitzwarenne for old times' sake.

He rode back through the glen deep in thought. Damn the English to Hell! As long as the important families of Scotland owned land in England, with a foot in both camps, this situation would continue. He did not want to waste time laying a long siege to Urquhart. Besides a quick victory was important for morale. Back in camp he said to Pilche, "We will ask for a surrender, Alexander. If none comes in a week or so we'll consider an assault. We can't waste too much time here." He watched the expression on Pilche's face, "You should have been a soldier man, not a merchant."

Fitzwarenne refused outright any suggestion of surrender. Moray and Pilche sat down determinedly to the siege. The weather was fair and the men remained in good spirits, watching good naturedly the Countess's herald daily paying her respects to the English garrison. In her camp, however, the Countess fretted, pacing up and down, and plotting how she might please the English.

"Mother, calm yourself. Andrew will not attack us and he won't attack them either." But she could not stay quiet and by the end of the first week had persuaded her son to send provisions to the beleaguered English. She reasoned that if they could withstand the siege amply provided by the Countess of Ross, Andrew Moray and his men of Inverness would go home. She left her son the task of delivering the provisions.

Ten nights after Andrew Moray first laid siege to Urquhart Castle, the men of Ross successfully carried flour, beans, meat and bran to the beleaguered garrison. It was done silently, by water on a night of high wind and heavy rain, approaching the castle from the loch side and gaining entry through a small postern doorway on the landing stage. The besiegers heard the creaking of the oars too late as the rowers pulled away after completing their mission.

"This is tomfoolery," yelled Pilche. "Here we sit ready to fight, while the fellows up the glen give them supplies." Andrew Moray, angry and embarrassed by the deceit, had to do something to regain the respect of the burgesses of Inverness. As Pilche kept pointing out, the English could sit on their arses for a year and a day growing fat and laughing at them. "Well, if we can't starve them out we'll have to try and burn them out," Moray told Pilche.

Two nights later, as the English changed their guard, the Scots began their assault. In the half dark of the northern late spring they tried to scale the walls and many Scottish arrows found their targets beginning small fires within, but by early morning it was clear that if they continued, they would suffer many casualties and the outcome would be uncertain. Andrew Moray called off the attack.

Good men had died, but the English, too, had had many losses and Moray learnt a bitter truth that the attacking force would always lose too many men and they would always have to be the attackers. The English had the advantage. The following morning as day began to dawn the English looked from their battlements and found that the

Scots had gone. They laughed congratulating themselves on a job well done.

Moray led his force to Balconie Castle, a solid fortress belonging to the Earl of Ross. Its garrison, unaware of any danger, were relaxing after dinner when Moray attacked. It was over quickly. More a rout than a battle, and those who submitted and joined Moray outnumbered the men who did not, but the message was clear: you were either with the patriots or against them.

His men were elated and as the days passed excited groups came to join him. He divided his force, leaving some at Avoch while he and Pilche harassed the English wherever and whenever they could. Neither convoy nor garrison were safe from their attack.

Sir Reginald le Cheyne, Governor of Inverness Castle, waited for a reply to his urgent message to the king. Edward heard of the uprising in the north and angrily sent orders to suppress the rebels. He was a very busy man planning his campaign before waging war in Flanders. He was irritated for he thought had quelled the Scots at Berwick and Dunbar and that Scotland was his. Recently, however, he had received many alarming messages. Not least was the news of the murder of his Sheriff of Lanark by an outlaw named Wallace.

The king was at his residence at Ospringe in Kent and ordered that some of his Scottish hostages among them the Earl of Ross be brought to him. On their knees they solemnly promised obedience to the king of England and their assistance to suppress the rebels in Scotland. The following day, with the king's safe conduct in their pouches and escorted by English men-at-arms, they rode northwards.

The night following the murder of his wife, Wallace made haste to Lamington, arriving just before dawn. His little maid was still sleeping gently in her cradle. He held aloft a lighted taper, looking down at her innocent face. He turned to Neil's wife, "After you have collected her things, waken her for we must leave quickly." He went to organise the horses and his people. They must take everything they needed, including the animals, into the Ettrick Forest.

He had not visited Borthwick for some little time, but the old people had cared for it as if it were their own. When the master and his following arrived, they threw more logs onto the fire and Janet set about baking extra bread for so large a gathering. The news spread among the men of the forest that the master of Borthwick was back. They began to arrive at the manor to offer their support.

A few days later Wallace sent his daughter in the care of Neil's wife and a few chosen men to his mother at Kilspindie, while he went back to Lamington to await the moment when he would call upon Sheriff Hazelrig. The English had been to Lamington. Any stock left behind had been driven off and the buildings burnt, but there had been heavy rain afterwards and the fire had not taken serious hold. The hall had lost its thatch and the rafters and walls were blackened by smoke. He sought shelter in a bothy in the hills, overlooking the estate, to bide his time. One evening he stood looking down at the scar of Lamington. His face was harsh with anger. His mind had been dwelling on the sack of Berwick and the dishonour of Dunbar. "It won't be long, sweetheart, before your revenge," he murmured.

On a lovely morning in early May, Hazelrig, as Sheriff of Lanark, sat down in the high seat to hear pleas, issue writs and to pass judgements on Scots. It looked as if it would be a long day. There were many people gathered in the hall and the courtyard outside. He nodded to his clerk to indicate that he was ready for the first case. The session had been in progress for about an hour, but the people were more restive than usual and there was a lot of murmuring and fidgeting. He beckoned to his clerk, "Tell the sergeant-warden not to let any more in and to keep the peasants quiet." He waved his hand in the direction of the people.

The soldiers moved among the people in an attempt to stop their restlessness, but the murmuring grew louder. Suddenly a scuffle broke out near the back where some ill-clad peasants had been standing. The melee erupted into a fight. People standing nearby fled lest they should be accused of aiding the affray. Three men-at-arms were already dead as Wallace leapt towards the sheriff. The crowd scattered.

That it was Wallace could not be doubted for he shouted, "Vengeance for a Wallace: come out Hazelrig or can the English only fight women." A man-at-arms lunged at him, but fell heavily tripped by one of the crowd. He tried to raise himself but was again knocked to the floor. All around the hall other soldiers were brought down. Outside there was a hubbub of noise as Wallace's followers, quickly throwing off their disguises, attacked the English.

Using the noise and confusion the sheriff, with drawn sword, tried to escape through a side door, but his way was barred by the crowd, some of whom had taken weapons from the fallen English and stood defiantly barring his way. The Braidfute kindred had been well known and respected in the area. "Come Hazelrig. Turn and fight," snarled Wallace. The sheriff, his escape barred, turned to face Wallace. "At least you will be judged in your own court with a weapon in your hand. You gave my wife and her people no such honour." "You'll pay for this outrage, Wallace, you'll all pay!" the sheriff shouted at the crowd.

Hazelrig noticed that it was quiet outside. This meant that his men-at-arms had been overpowered. The crowd moved back leaving room for the combatants. The sheriff struck the first blow. He was a good swordsman and had taken pride in his skill with the sword. They circled each other and the clash of sword on sword rang around the stone walls. Wallace struck a blow that caught Hazelrig's left shoulder. The force sent him staggering and a roar went up from the watching crowd, but he regained his balance and Wallace renewed his attack. With his left arm hanging limply and losing much blood, the Englishman tried to fend off his avenger, but he was growing weak and as Wallace struck the fatal blow a great shout echoed around the walls.

Hazelrig's three English clerics and four remaining men-at-arms stood huddled near the side door. They were seized by the crowd and dragged brutally from the court. The noise and confusion were terrifying. The doomed Englishmen were struggling pitifully and begging for mercy. Ropes were found and thrown over beams in the stables. One of the clerics asked to see a priest that he may be shriven, but in the crowd's jubilation his request went unheeded. With trembling lips he began to say his Pater Noster as the rope was thrown around his neck. Two burly journeymen pulled on the rope's end and he was jerked roughly into oblivion amid much laughter and shouting.

Wallace stepped over the crumpled body of the sheriff and went out into the bright spring sunshine. The passion had passed. There was no exhilaration or satisfaction within him. His wife's murderers were dead, but he knew he could not rest until the English were driven back into their own lands. There would be no more Marions or men like his father or the townsfolk of Berwick, no more victims of the English begging in vain for mercy.

A few of the English had escaped the first onslaught but they were quickly rounded up and became the victims of much cruel sport. Finally they were dragged to the wooden bridge spanning the river and, with hands and feet securely bound, were thrown into the water. All the buildings that belonged to them were burnt. Wallace's brother came to him, followed by many men of Lanark, who gathered round Wallace, excitedly demanding that he lead them against the enemy. Wallace jumped onto a cart, his blood stained claymore still clasped in his hand. The men quietened, waiting expectantly, awed by his stature and leadership qualities.

"If you follow me, we will attack the English where and when we can. There will be no castle, manor or cot where they will be safe." A cheer went up, but Wallace quietened them. "Do not think that because of today it will be easy. The English king will use every means to hold onto our land. Ours is a just cause. Do not doubt that. But our only reward may be the memory of our deeds kept alive by our grandchildren and their children." If anyone listening thought he needed a more substantial reward, he did not say so and they shouted and cheered Wallace as their leader.

Wallace withdrew into the forest, safe from the attack which he had expected hourly, but none came. He made plans for his campaign and said to his brother, "We cannot keep the men here for long, John. They must see action while the passion is still within them."

News of his resistance spread rapidly and groups of men came to join him, some with weapons, but many without: ordinary men of little account but with a fierce desire to rid the kingdom of the enemy. Wallace, with the help of his closest followers, began to organise them and train them for war.

Wallace had impressed the young Sir John Graham when they had first met, and he was preparing to leave to join him when he heard of Wallace's attack on Lanark. Old Sir John, his father, had blustered and threatened, making much of giving his blessing only grudgingly, but had turned impatiently on his tearful wife saying, "Hush woman, our lad is made of sound stuff." She had bit her lower lip and said nothing, but her fears for her son continued to haunt her.

Graham arrived at the head of men from his own lands and greeted Wallace in friendship with outstretched hands, and his presence and respect for Wallace was noted by all. "We have come to give our support," he said warmly.

Yet it was the arrival on the following day of Sir William Douglas, with many mounted well-armed men riding in good order, which caused the greatest stir within the camp. Douglas was a great warrior. Ransomed from his English captors after Berwick, he was ready to give his support to Wallace. Surely if 'Hardy' Douglas was ready to fight with Wallace, other nobles would join the cause. Or so they said to each other.

Douglas, a dark bristling man, looked around. Most of the men who stood watching him were common folk, inexperienced in the arts of war and unlikely to make much of an impression on Edward's army. He sniffed. Well, if James Stewart and Bishop Wishart wanted him to give this rabble his support why not? It was a good season for war and he had never been a man to sit on his estates dangling his children on his knee. He was taken to Wallace, who was busy drilling men drawn up in a closely packed schiltron. Instead of pikes they had cut staves from the forest. Wallace occupied by the task in hand marched them forward. At his command the front ranks knelt with staves slanting. At his command they rose as a man, moved forward, stopped then once again knelt.

Wallace saw Douglas but made no attempt to break off the drilling until they had moved down the full length of the glade. Then he briskly dismissed them and walked to Sir William. He was respectful as was fitting, but made it plain that he would not hand over his power to another.

Three weeks after the slaying of the English sheriff, Wallace awoke early and sent word to Graham and Douglas to prepare their men to break camp within the hour. Both were startled by the abruptness of the decision, but Graham set about rousing his men and preparing to leave, while Douglas angrily went to Wallace, "What is this? Do you trust me so little that you command me like a common serving-man?" he demanded.

"No, my lord, but the less men know beforehand of our movements, the better our success. We ride today. I hope you and your people will ride with us, but if you would prefer to follow with the main force ..." he did not finish his sentence turning to continue saddling the horse at his side. "Am I to be told where we are bound?" asked Douglas gruffly.

Wallace glanced over his shoulder at the dark angry man. "We are heading for Scone, my lord." Then turned to continue his work. Douglas had to be satisfied with the blunt answer. Wallace left his brother and cousin in charge, with instructions to continue the drill with the remaining force. Wallace with a few chosen mounted men, Graham, Douglas and all their followers rode to Scone. His target was the English Justiciar Ormesby whom he had heard was residing in the Abbey of Scone.

It was late into the evening when they arrived. They did not halt but galloped up to the main gate which was still wide open. The walls were unmanned and the abbey was deserted. Torches burnt in wall sconces, and the bakehouse and smithy had fires burning. The high and lower tables had the remains of food scattered upon them: platters, bones, bread and goblets half filled with wine.

Wallace gazed around, "Damn them." Clearly they had news of his coming and left in some haste, Ormesby with them. His men ransacked the abbey and Ormesby's lodging, which had many luxuriously furnished rooms. Well, it was best to let them. There were rich pickings for all. In the carved high seat, usually occupied by the lord, there were embroidered cushions of vivid red and blue colours. Marion would admire such rare and lovely things he thought; then he remembered that Marion was in Paradise where such earthly frippery was of no account. He stirred. He must not allow himself to think of Marion. There was work to be done.

As he could hear shouting outside he strolled into the courtyard. Douglas's men had found some English priests who had sought sanctuary in the abbey church. Their sanctuary had been violated, but Wallace made no move to interfere watching as they were beaten and dragged to a makeshift gallows. Graham strode over to Wallace. "Surely we should put a stop to that," he nodded in the direction of the priests, but the warm humane man of their first meeting on the Dunduff moors was no more. "If we make an example of some of their clerics, the others will quickly scuttle back over the border and leave us in peace," he bluntly replied. "Come Graham, let us see what stores they have left. We will need all we can get if our numbers continue to grow at such a pace." He turned away as amid howls and yells the first of the English priests was hoisted into the air.

They remained at the abbey for a few days and many men from the lands around came to join them. On the third day the lookout called loudly that a small group of people, among them women, was approaching. Once within earshot they were challenged. "The uncle and mother of William Wallace beg admittance," was the reply. There was much excitement among the men at the gate for they held Wallace in high respect and here were their leader's kinsfolk.

Lady Wallace greeted her son with tears in her eyes. He bowed his head low that he might receive her kiss. Then he took his daughter into his arms, kissing and caressing the soft silky hair. He put the little maid down and she began to totter around the chamber on unsteady legs, holding onto the knees of the men who sat here and there to balance herself. Once or twice she was scooped up by a brawny arm and made much of by them until her grandmother claimed her, carrying her off on some woman's errand.

From his uncle he heard that James the Steward and Bishop Wishart had called for a rising against the English, who were said to have raised their northern levies and were marching up through the border country. Robert the Bruce was rallying his men, although no one knew – for sure – which side he would join, except maybe Bruce himself. There were murmurs of excitement from the listening men. "Are we to march south then, Master Wallace, to greet the buggers?" called a voice from the lower benches. "Nay, be patient for a little longer, Jack. We won't let the English rest for long."

Three days later at the head of his men, Wallace left Scone, moving openly across country. Douglas had already ridden south for Sir William had heard that his wife and children were being held prisoner in Annandale by Robert the Bruce, who had apparently come out for the English.

The sun had already dipped below the horizon in the short June night as Wallace sat by the fire embers talking with his brother, Graham, Tom Johnston and his cousin Adam Wallace. So many had joined them that the hillside was dotted with camp fires. "At first light we ride to Paisley," said Wallace. He grinned, "the English Bishop of Durham sits in Paisley Abbey and we'll help him to move house." "Then we'll need to get there before the English army can move north from Galloway," said Graham. "We'll arrive in good time. There are many who are blocking the path of the English." "Perhaps this summer we'll see their backs for good," said John Wallace. William shrugged but made no reply, took his wadmal cloak, lay down at a little distance from them and went to sleep.

The early morning sun shone on the helmets of the English men-at-arms guarding Anthony Beck in Paisley Abbey. His spies had kept him well informed of Wallace's movements and he had guessed that he was to be Wallace's next victim. In desperation, the bishop's clerk urged his master to leave for the south. "My lord, there is little time. He is only ten miles away. There is such confusion here. We do not know who our friends are. Soon there will be no place of refuge."

Slowly Beck picked up his gauntlets and adjusting his mantle replied, "I will not be hurried by a murderer and outlaw, Maurice. Have payments been made to my agents here?" "Yes, my lord, all as you directed." "Then calm yourself, I am ready to leave. Without showing sign of urgency the bishop rode from the abbey. As the last of his troops clattered out of the gates, flames began to leap through door and archway.

Wallace gazed at the once beautiful abbey which he had known since boyhood. Anger never far away welled up in him. "They will not be satisfied until all Scotland is blackened and charred." Nothing had escaped the arsonist, not even the doocot which had housed Bishop Wishart's bonnie white doves. A few of the birds had managed to escape and sat in a pathetic white line along the west wall. At that time of the year most had been sitting on eggs or were busy rearing their broods, but the flames had caught hold of the dry timbers of the doocot and quickly devoured everything within.

Some of Wallace's closest friends urged riding after the English bishop but Wallace argued that although capture of so important a man as Anthony Beck would be a bitter blow to the English, the Scottish army now rallying near Irvine needed their support.

The Shipp Inn, overlooking Glasgow harbour, was a bustling, prosperous place with good cellars, bakehouses and stables, frequented by sailors, merchants and all manner of travellers. Anthony Beck had resided at Paisley Abbey since the early spring. Jack Short was among his escort. Short had proved himself a useful man to his English masters and in a leather bound coffer he kept the rewards of his diligent service. Then the innkeeper suddenly died. Short, quick to take advantage of the situation went to the bishop, feigning the attitude of submission which he adopted so well. "Well man, what do you want?"

Usually the bishop would not have bothered himself with one so low as Short, but the man had proved unscrupulous and cunning in his service. It was a good thing these people were prepared to sell their souls to anyone with some gold, he thought.

"My lord, since Berwick, I have suffered sorely with my back and can't fight as once I did. With your permission and help I can still offer you service. If you'll assist me to buy the Shipp Inn here in Glasgow, I shall always have news for you."

There were many in Anthony Beck's pay and an innkeeper in this busy port might have certain advantages. Sooner or later all news good and bad passed through an inn. On the bright June day, when Beck rode away from Paisley, Jack Short was in the cellar of his inn tapping a barrel of ale. Short had sent news to his mother and she, poor soul, overwhelmed by the fact that her son was not only alive, but prospering had hurried to him. When first he greeted her, she saw only his well-fed belly protruding over his wide leather belt with the embossed silver buckle, the russet-coloured cloth of his coat and well-fitting leather boots. Her mother's pride failed to notice the mean, cruel glint in his eyes, the mouth turning down at the corners and the short clipped answers to questions, which denied further overtures of friendship. Nor did she question how he had come by such good fortune.

The Wallace family had taken her into their household and she had lived comfortably enough, but she had accepted their protection as of right and had grown morose thinking about her own lost home and family. In her son's household she could sit by the fire with a soft feather cushion at her back, and a beaker of red wine which helped to ease the pain in her joints. She was a very happy woman.

The Scottish army was encamped on the green slopes by Irvine. Banners and pennants of the nobles were fluttering bravely in the summer breeze. Wallace's forces had grown to many thousand, well beyond just his closest friends and kinsmen. They were common men of little account in the world. William Douglas accompanied by Robert the Bruce, who had now seemingly deserted the English, arrived and were camped side by side like good brothers in arms. James Stewart, the Steward of Scotland, Bishop Wishart and many others had also raised their standards at Irvine.

Wallace sat on a rock overlooking the scene. It was a brave sight. Men were busy sharpening and burnishing sword and shield, but Dunbar was still in his memory and he did not dare to hope that this time they would send the English back across the border. The English army was camped a few miles away and foraging parties from both sides had been sent out and made contact. Spies told Wallace that they were perhaps thirtyfive or forty thousand foot-soldiers and at least three hundred cavalry commanded by Sir Henry Percy, who had already sent a herald to speak to the Scottish leaders. Wallace allowed himself a fleeting thought of his little maid Margaret. If the English returned to their homes, he could take Margaret back to Borthwick or Lamington. It was a fine manor and would be hers one day. He checked himself as there was no sense in daydreaming. That would not oust the enemy.

His brother John wandered over to him and the two men sat side by side gazing out across the hills much as they had done when they were boys. "They have called all leaders to a meeting in the Steward's camp at noon, Will." Wallace continued to gaze at the lovely views, "Aye, I'll be there."

James Stewart had a fine tent in the shelter of some great oak trees. In the warm sun the sweet smell from the trees drifted lazily about.

Wallace accompanied by Graham had arrived at noon. He thought ruefully what a bonnie site the Steward had claimed for himself. Indeed the tent was so well equipped with stools, benches, tables and cushions that it was more like a hunting expedition than a council of war.

The other captains had arrived before him, Alexander Lindsay, Douglas, Wishart and Bruce, and had eaten a meal to which Wallace had not been invited. He bowed accepting the seat offered at the end of the table. Before his arrival they had been discussing the English king's demand that his Scottish nobles should accompany him on his French expedition that summer. Wallace sat quietly listening to their arguments. The meeting ended without any decisions being taken. Nor had they asked Wallace to contribute and hardly even acknowledged his presence. They agreed to meet the following day.

"Who are we fighting, John?" He asked Graham as they walked back to their own men. "Are we defending our land from foreign invasion or are we at odds with our liege lord who makes unacceptable demands? They are like a dog with two tails," he nodded his head in the direction of the noble lords. "Aye, but does the dog wag the tail or the tail wag the dog?" was Graham's reply. "Does that matter? Either way disorder reigns as it did before Dunbar."

They lapsed into silence. Wallace was feeling depressed after the meeting for which he had had such high hopes. The pattern was set for successive councils of war. Discussions centred around Edward's demands, and messages were given and received from the English army. The discussions led nowhere.

A week after Wallace's arrival they began to discuss battle tactics, but as he settled ready to contribute, friction between the nobles turned the gathering into a farce. The quick-tempered Douglas was the first to show his anger, banging the table with his fist and storming from the meeting, shouting as he went, "What nonsense is this? You're a bunch of bungling old hags, trying to feather your own nests and farting into the wind. I and my men are ready to fight. Cowards the lot of you." Bruce jumped to his feet, hand on dagger, but Wishart raised a hand to calm him. Wallace sat silent. None bothered to look his way. Sir Richard Lundie challenged Bruce, "Have a care, Robert. Do you want to give the English the satisfaction of knowing we fight among ourselves?" Bishop Wishart suggested that it would be better if the meeting broke up to consider their respective positions.

Time did not heal the discontent and disagreements. They met in small groups discussing and plotting. Wallace told his kinsmen that there were as many opinions as there were fleas on a dog. He kept himself aloof from the friction, spending more time with his men perfecting battle drills. Sooner or later the nobles would come to a decision without his assistance. In the long light evenings he sat with his brother and John Graham, for he admired the man's quiet common sense and good humour.

On the first day of July rumours spread that there had been another fierce argument between Bruce, Douglas and Lundie and that Lundie and his men were withdrawing from the camp. Worse was to come. Later that day it was discovered that Lundie had taken his followers to the English camp and was sitting with Percy and Clifford discussing the Scottish army.

This was the final straw for Wallace and he said to Graham, "John, should you prefer to remain, I'll not think less of you, but for me, I've had enough. I'll not submit my men to yet another defeat neither on the battlefield nor by glib tongues. We'll take cover in the forest." The following day Wallace, accompanied by Graham, Sir John Ramsay, Ruthven and all their followers, left Irvine to lesser men. As he led them from the confusion Bishop Wishart came to him with other clerics, among them Andrew Lamberton, whom Wallace had known for some years. "You are leaving the field, Wallace. Is that necessary?" asked the bishop.

Wallace did not reply immediately and chose his words very carefully, so that he would not give offence to a man of the church. His voice shook, however, and it was plain that he was upset. "Both you and my liege lord encouraged me and gave me aid to continue the fight against the enemy, and I have paid dearly for doing so. Yet when I sit at the council table and listen to my leaders I wonder who Scotland's enemy really is!" Bishop Wishart reddened and Wallace continued, "these men," he indicated his great following, "have risked everything to fight for this land. Yet you, who have so much to gain, smile and kiss the hand of our enemy." Wallace collected his reins, saying as he left. "Perhaps my friends and followers can put fear into the English for no others shall."

A few days later Wallace heard of the surrender of the Scottish army to the English without any hostilities between the two. The news shocked Wallace yet did not surprise him. His reply was swift.

Leaving the bulk of his army safely in the forest, commanded by his brother and Tom Johnston, Wallace accompanied by Graham, Ramsay, Ruthven and a chosen force of mounted men set off north to harry the English, burning and killing wherever they found their enemies. Perth fell and he left Ruthven as Sheriff and Governor of its castle. He pressed on to Cupar then north into Angus to Glamis with the banner of Scotland held high until they arrived at Dunnottar Castle on the coast of Kincardine. Many of the fleeing English had taken sanctuary there. The fortress was built on a near impregnable site and was strongly garrisoned: it apparently offered safe refuge from Wallace's fighting men.

Wallace reigned in his mount, gazing down at the formidable walls of the castle, the sea pounding the rocks below the cliff-girt walls. He did not give the English defenders or his own men time to dwell on the coming encounter. His archers from the forest were given the command and immediately began a sustained attack. Flight after flight of burning arrows caused fires to rage out of control in the castle for it had been a dry spring and summer. Battering rams opened the first gate. The English fought with desperate courage. With the sea all around, where could they run to? Their usual steadiness and discipline, which had proved so fatal to the Scottish cause, finally deserted them as the flames and smoke gained the upper hand.

Wallace was the first to storm through the entrance tunnel into the courtyard. Many English tried to leave through a postern gate, fighting each other to get through the narrow doorway down a precipitous path to the rocks below. Some sought sanctuary in the hall, but the thatch was burning fiercely and they rushed out again. The draught from the wide open door was fanning the flames.

Some women and children had been sent into the church for safety and they began screaming, wildly fearful of going outside, yet terrified to remain. A Scot came to the open door, dripping claymore in hand. He took a look at the sad scene within, smiled grimly, then slammed the door firmly shut, and wedged it. The pitiful screams could not be heard above the general commotion, and after a few moments the thatch and timbers fell inwards sending a shower of sparks and flames into the sky.

As Wallace entered he lay about him with Vengeance and all who came within his reach suffered the same fate. In one of the many storehouses he caught a young woman with a baby held tightly to her breast, hiding behind barrels of pickled fish. He raised the claymore high above his head. The woman, eyes wide with terror, cowered closer to the barrel as if it would give her comfort. Her face swam before him changing its form. He saw Marion's wide eyes pleading for mercy. Wallace lowered his sword and hurriedly left the place. Here and there pockets of Englishmen had been cornered and had laid down their arms, hoping they might be spared.

By the end of the afternoon all resistance had been crushed. Bodies lay about and the sweet, sickly smell of burnt human flesh hung over the smoking ruins. Wallace looked at the prisoners. There were a little over forty weary men and a handful of women with small children. Shouting and jeering from the jubilant Scots left them in little doubt of their fate. The women began to weep and beg for mercy but, since the death of his wife, Wallace's heart had hardened and he was less inclined to interfere on their behalf.

A few days previously their force had been joined by Bishop Sinclair, who now pushed his way through the crowd, "In Jesu's name, Master Wallace, spare these wretches." He waved towards the prisoners. A great cheer went up as another headless body sprawled on the ground. "Why should I save men who have inflicted outrages on our own people, my lord bishop?" "I would remind you of our Lord's teaching, Master Wallace, blessed are the merciful."

Wallace turned to John Graham, who was standing beside him, saying, "John, have the women and children locked in one of the storehouses. The men must suffer as we have." The bishop shook his head sadly, but had to be satisfied. That night as they sat eating Wallace said to the bishop, "My lord, the execution of prisoners is necessary. If we are to defeat the English they must be fearful of us. We must break their will so that they have no heart for a battle. At the moment – with just cause – they hold us in contempt."

Wallace allowed his men to rest for a day or two and he spent time on the battlements, staring out to sea and watching English ships passing back and forth to Aberdeen. On the evening of the third day he called John Graham to him, asking him to seek out Andrew Moray with a message. "Say I will attack Aberdeen harbour before laying siege to the castle. If he will join me, the castle will fall quickly and we can march south together." Graham grinned, "I'll miss the junketing in Aberdeen, Will." "Aye, but I trust none other with such an important task. Take men with you and keep to little-used paths." "We'll leave within the hour and travel by night," replied Graham.

The Sheriff of Aberdeen stood on the castle ramparts, watching the smoke and flames from the harbour. His sergeant said that William Wallace led the attacking force. The sheriff sucked his bottom lip. This attack was the final straw. Daily he received news of uprisings and rebellions throughout the north and east, and Andrew Moray was reported to be a day's march away heading towards Aberdeen. Sir Henry turned to his steward, "Keep all gates open, lower the drawbridge and offer no resistance when Wallace arrives and have the board laid for dinner that he may sup with us."

The next day as Andrew Moray rode into Aberdeen, he found a busy bustling place. Children running in the alleyways and the pennant of Scotland flying from the castle battlements, while at its entrance he recognised the large and impressive figure of William Wallace. He rode across the drawbridge to greet his fellow commander like a brother and equal.

Leaving Aberdeen and its castle in the care of Sir Henry Latham, Andrew Moray and William Wallace, at the head of their triumphant armies, surrounded by loyal leaders who had given them their support, pressed southwards. Their goal was Dundee, which was still in the hands of supporters of the English cause. They rode side by side and Moray, if he ever thought it, did nothing to show that Wallace was of inferior rank. They were joint commanders of the people's army. Both knew that soon they would be forced to face the English in open battle and they put their trust in God. This time, they hoped, Scotland would not be humiliated.

The gates of Dundee were firmly closed and the English sentries watched glumly as the Scots positioned themselves around the walls. "Take a look at all those buggers. If we don't get reinforcements we'll be well in the shit," said one. "Nothing to them, man. I've heard that they gave in without even a fight at Irvine." They continued their watch while the Scots settled into their positions.

Since the murders at Berwick, Master Blair had lived in a twilight world, drinking morosely and leaving all matters of business to his eldest son. As the news of Wallace's attack on Gargunnock had spread across the kingdom, he had stirred himself somewhat and had even spoken of joining the rebels. His daughter-in-law had patted his hand on one occasion saying, "Now, now, father Blair, no one expects a respected merchant like yourself to take to the hills."

Blair, usually a mild-mannered man, jumped to his feet, pushing the young woman roughly to one side, "Is the desire for revenge the privilege of the young only?" he snarled. When the army of Moray and Wallace laid siege to Dundee, the old man was beside himself with excitement. On the moonless night in early August, like-minded merchants and journeymen gathered in his cellar to plan the deliverance of Dundee into the hands of the Scottish army.

The following night at the darkest hour a hooded figure made his way to the eastern postern gate. The English guard was at the furthest end of his patrol. A pouch of gold pieces quickly passed to the gatekeeper and master Blair slipped out. On the following night dark figures made their way through the gate, which had been opened by the bribed gatekeeper, and Wallace's men filed silently into the sleeping town. English guards were despatched just as silently and it was not until they were at the walls of the castle that a dying Englishman screamed a warning. That morning Scotsmen patrolled the walls of Dundee, although the English in Dundee Castle continued to defy the Scots.

William Wallace awoke as the Blair's serving girl entered. She had a bowl of water for him to refresh himself, and carried his washed clothes and boots with the mud of his campaign removed from them. She was a comely young woman with full firm breasts and well rounded hips. She smiled coyly at him as she laid his clothes at the foot of the bed. "Is there anything else I can do for you, Master Wallace?"

It was almost three months since Marion's death and lust overcame him, but the Blair household had been friendly to him for many years. It would not be fitting to despoil their servant within their house. "Be gone, hussy. I have all I need." The young woman pouted and smiled, but left without saying anything.

He lay enjoying the comfort of the big bed. He had neither slept in one nor removed his clothes for three weeks. There was a light knock on the door. "Didn't you understand me, woman?" he roared, but the door opened and John Blair stepped into the room dressed in wadmal cowl, sandals and the shaven pate of his order. As Wallace washed, trimmed his beard and dressed, they talked mostly about his campaigns, but finally about Marion. Then Wallace said, "It is I who am doing all the talking, John, how goes it with you?" "My life is one of prayer and contemplation, Will. I have grown used to listening to others."

For three weeks the army laid siege to Dundee Castle and Wallace sent Graham south into the Ettrick Forest with instructions to march their foot-soldiers towards Stirling. His spies had told him that the English were massing a large army of some three hundred mounted knights and at least ten thousand foot-soldiers at Roxburgh. Their destination was thought to be Stirling. Just before Graham left he said to him, "If they come, John, we must stand and face them. Let it be near Stirling. There will be no more fading into the forests leaving the enemy in command. Our people need a victory."

On the fourth day of September Wallace and Moray led their army out of Dundee towards Stirling. Dundee and its castle were left in the care of its burgesses, and Wallace left them in no doubt of their responsibilities saying, "Sirs, we leave this town in your hands. It is important to us that those in the castle remain where they are and cannot aid their countrymen, who are at this moment marching on Stirling. We will not accept any excuses. Here the English are and here they must stay." He waved his hand towards the castle. "Failure will result in the harshest of punishments." Wallace, Moray and Pilche stood in front of them, grim and warlike. "Believe us, sirs, we do not jest."

They moved at speed passing through Perth, then on towards Stirling through countryside which only a few months earlier had been held by the English, and through which Wallace had passed secretly with a handful of close friends and kinsmen. Now with God's guidance he rode openly beside Moray and John Blair. North of Stirling they were met by John Wallace and Graham at the head of the archers and pikemen from the forest. Together they pressed on towards the town.

Moray looked at the motley, ill-clad and poorly armed army, who were expected to withstand the onslaught of the well-trained and well-equipped English. Wallace watching him grinned and said "They don't inspire confidence, do they? But I've spent many weeks training them and they'll stand their ground when the time comes. They're tough enough, with nothing to lose but their lives."

They crossed the Forth before the English had been sighted, and set up camp on Abbey Craig commanding the view of Cambuskenneth Abbey and the river with its causeway and wooden bridge. The land around was flat and boggy, and the Forth looped its lazy way towards the sea.

A tent had been erected for Wallace and Moray, and in the golden days of early autumn they sat together planning the forthcoming battle, as spies kept them informed of the progress of the English army. One evening Wallace sent for a man whom he knew well, a carpenter-journeyman by trade, who had proved to be a reliable and skilful man on previous occasions. "There are two possible places to cross the Forth, Hal, the ford further upstream which we are guarding and this bridge. Make the bridge unsafe, Hal, without it appearing to be so. I leave the details to you, but it is important that none know what you have done. Can you manage such a task?" The carpenter scratched his beard, paused, and said, "Leave it to me, sir, and it will collapse just when you want it to." He gave a slight bow in the direction of Andrew Moray before withdrawing.

On the ninth day of September the midday sun glinted on the shields and lances of the English army when it came into view. Andrew

Moray, with the practised eye of a knight, admired the disciplined movements and well-equipped knights and bowmen. They certainly will take some beating, but he had fought the English many times during the past four months and won, and with God's help would win again.

Wallace watched the approaching English with less detachment. At long last they were to confront the enemy in force. Together they watched the heavily armed knights. "If they are given the chance to charge, Wallace, we'll be in trouble." "Then we must see they don't," came the reply.

Through narrowed eyes the Earl of Surrey watched the slopes opposite and the ill-clad common Scots. "Are they trying to mock us," he said to Malcolm, Earl of Lennox. "Do they expect to take us on? They look as if they're more at home herding hogs than pulling a bow string."

Lennox, James Stewart and other Scottish nobles were riding with the English. Since their surrender at Irvine they had become good friends with their former enemies. Surrey turned to Lennox, "Surely you can command them to leave the field. Promise them that we will allow them to depart without hindrance."

Since Irvine the Scottish lords were doubtful that they could persuade Wallace to leave in peace, but they set off across the wooden bridge and rode through the Scottish camp. The men were silent and sullen. Many did not bother to stand, sitting with their backs turned as their nobles rode by.

Wallace and Moray did not come out to greet them and remained seated as the lords were ushered in. Only then did they rise and bow before offering benches to their guests. Neither Wallace nor Moray spoke, waiting to hear the envoy's message.

James Stewart, as the spokesman, began, "The English have a large and well-trained army. If you meet them on the field the result will be devastating for our own people. Consider your position. We have the Earl of Surrey's promise that you may leave without hindrance. Do not lead your men to disaster."

It was Wallace who broke the silence. "We cannot lead our men into worse disaster than you led us at Dunbar and Irvine, my lords." Anger appeared on the noble's faces, but James Stewart held out his hands for calm. Moray replied, "Perhaps as you entered our camp you noticed that we fly the standard of Scotland and it is for Scotland that we fight." A messenger came and Wallace was called away for a while. Lennox said, "Think, Andrew, your father is still a prisoner in the

Tower at London. If you persist with your actions it will go badly for him and for your estates."

"We are free men in Moray, my lord, and owe our allegiance directly to our lord King John. Edward is not my liege and those who follow me pay homage to King John." Wallace was seen to be returning and they fell silent.

It was Wallace who ended the meeting saying, "My lords, we have said all that can be said and only action will prove the day." They prepared to leave, but Wallace and Moray took James Stewart to one side and Wallace said, "My lord, we would remind you that in the quiet of your chamber you encouraged us to resist the English, yet on the brink of success you ask us to give in."

The Steward looking embarrassed, mounted and without a backward glance rode back to the Earl of Surrey who was thunderstruck when he was told that Wallace and Moray could not be persuaded to disband. He was doubly infuriated when he heard that the Scots demanded that he withdrew, along with the garrison of Stirling Castle, and return across the border into England. "What impudence!" he bellowed, but the Scottish nobles told him that they intended to withdraw their following because they had no wish to take up arms against their own. The earl turned angrily, "Go now, the English have never needed others to fight their battles for them."

The Scottish lords took themselves and all their followers to nearby woods. Their pennants were fluttering bravely, but they were at some distance across the River Forth from Moray and Wallace's camp, with whom they did not wish to associate.

Surrey held council with his captains that evening, "We will cross the river in the morning," he said. "Let us hope that they will see the futility of fighting us and surrender. Goodnight gentlemen."

On the opposite side of the Forth the two young commanders of Scotland's army spent the evening walking around their camp and talking to the men to inspire and give courage where that was necessary.

When the first light came both armies began preparing for battle. The English gave extra bran to their horses, while the Scottish archers from the Selkirk forest tested their bow strings and arranged their best arrows handily in their quivers. From both sides of the river could be heard the final sharpening of swords, battleaxes and pikes, commands and trumpet calls. Then silence fell on the waiting men.

The English captains were in a quandary. The earl was well known for his rigid chain of command, yet here they were ready, men and horses nervous with expectation of battle and their commander, the

Earl of Surrey, was still in bed. His steward said his master had had a restless night and he would not hear of waking him. "The men cannot be kept in readiness for long. It's bad for morale," blustered Sir William Fitzwarenne. Hugh Cressingham, the hated Treasurer, like the others sat on his mount impatiently waiting for the battle to begin. The previous evening the earl had said they would attack in the morning and attack they would. He assumed command and gave the order to advance.

The war horn sounded. Two abreast, as the width of the causeway and bridge would permit no more, the English cavalry began its advance. On the Scottish side Wallace also gave an order and his pikemen formed their schiltrons and archers took their positions on both flanks. His small force of cavalry, one hundred and fifty lightly armed men, were in readiness out of sight among the trees. All stood quietly watching their enemy while John Blair walked among them giving absolution.

The English cavalry formed up along the bank of the Forth on the Scottish side, the bridge and marshes behind them. Five thousand had crossed before their commander woke from his fitful sleep and flew into a rage when he heard that Cressingham had dared to assume command. He gave the order for his cavalry to return immediately. The Scots took turns at watching the enemy and warming themselves at their campfires. They remained silent but alert.

The earl, anxious that his men should believe he had recalled them for a purpose, not a whim, created fifty new knights then gave the order to advance. As they began to cross again a bugle called from the camp of the Scottish nobles, separate as they were from Wallace and Moray. From the woods galloped the Earl of Lennox and other Scots of importance.

Wallace, watching with his drawn claymore ready for battle, slowly lowered it with a look of disdain on his face. Moray took a few angry steps forward grinding his teeth with passion and calling out loudly for all to hear. "Aye, go to those who'll give the greatest reward," his anger being the more intense for they were of his own kind.

Surrey ordered his army to return again although he could see that the Scottish army had not stood down. Perhaps the Earl of Lennox would bring news of a change of heart in the renegades on the hillside, but this did not happen. Lennox had come to plead that Surrey would give his countrymen one last chance before he attacked. It was a surprise and exasperated Moray and Wallace, who received two Dominican friars demanding once again that they should surrender. "Seek King

Edward's peace and you will receive pardon for past offences," was the friar's message. Andrew Moray was silent but Wallace said, "Tell your commander that we're not here to make peace, but to do battle. Aye, to defend ourselves and liberate our kingdom. Let them come on and we'll prove this to their beards."

There was no answer that could be given to his direct reply and they returned to their camp. The Scots still in battle formation sat down and prepared for a long wait while the English angry and confused grumbled among themselves.

Sir Richard Lundie had deserted the squabbling Scots at Irvine and was with the English army. He had been among the mounted knights who had already crossed over the river Forth twice and he went back to the Earl of Surrey. "My lord, if we cross the bridge now we are dead men. We can only cross two abreast and the enemy have already taken up positions from which they can charge at will." Cressingham interrupted him, "Perhaps your heart is not truly with us, sir. If this is so, you should leave now." Lundie snorted, but gave no reply to Cressingham continuing to direct his objections at the earl.

"My lord, the land is boggy on the other side. Mounted men cannot fight on such ground. The river loops in such a way that we can only go forward with the river at our backs and on both flanks." He needed to make his point before Cressingham could intervene. "I know the country in these parts. Upstream there is a ford where at least fifty or sixty men may cross at one time. Give me command of five hundred and we can outflank the enemy and attack from the rear, then ...," but he was unable to pursue his plan further for Hugh Cressingham, anxious that this day would bring him glory, interrupted him, "What kind of fools do you think we are? Take a goodly part of our men away so that the enemy may have less to fight. My lord," he turned to Surrey, "let us get on with the important business now. We lose the king's money with time wasting and vain manoeuvring. To our duties now, my lord." The earl could find no excuse with Cressingham's words and ordered the advance.

Wallace was busy with plans of his own. He had sent Hal the carpenter with two good men to the river. Using cover of bushes and tall reeds that grew along the bank of the Forth they had hidden under the bridge. "Wait until you hear our bugle call and we begin the attack, then complete your task and the bridge will collapse under the weight of the English." Hal made a toothless grin, wiped his nose on the back of his hand and with mallet inside his jerkin, saw strapped to his back and a coil of rope wrapped around his shoulder made his way to the bridge.

Cressingham, red in the face with the physical effort of wearing heavy chain mail and the excitement of the forthcoming battle, rode at the head of the English vanguard. Among the troops there was grumbling and premonition of doom. The veterans of many campaigns in France sensed the mismanagement and poor command. They understood the dangers of the superior position which the Scots occupied, but their superb discipline held and to a man they obeyed orders grumbling as they went. On the northern bank they formed up as best they could in the narrow strip of firm land. Welsh archers, whose hearts were not with the English, congregated in groups along the river bank behind the mounted men. They talked to each other in Welsh, casting fearful looks at the deep waters of the Forth. They saw the danger they were in and gradually moved to the right and left flanks in the marshy land, but still close to the river bank. The remainder of the English army lined up on the other side waiting to cross.

Andrew Moray and William Wallace, both mounted, watched from Abbey Craig. Their men were expectantly tense and ready, but none moved. Moray turned, looked at Wallace who gave an agreeing nod and Moray raised his hand. The English heard the blast of the horn even above the clatter of their own arms. Then a great roar arose from the rocky crags above them as if all the kelpies, hobgoblins, imps and evil spirits of Scotland screamed from the rocks and crevices, "Vengeance, on them." The schiltrons moved forward and downwards with revenge for Berwick, Dunbar and other countless murders and indignities in their hearts.

Cressingham was corrupt, corpulent and greedy, but he did not lack courage and bellowed to the sergeant-at-arms to move forward. He gave his mount the spur and other knights and squires tried gallantly to rally their dazed men before the Scots could fall upon them. A few tried to group on the marshy land that they might charge, but their heavy horses floundered in the soft ground. Men who had just completed the crossing found they could not move forward turned and tried to return across the bridge, but men still trying to cross blocked their way. The shouted commands and the whirr of the first flight of arrows frightened the horses.

The schiltrons, pikes bristling outwards, crashed down into the English horses impaling some and scattering the others. The Welsh archers saw the weakness of their own position and fled wherever they could across the marsh or jumped into the river and struck out for the opposite bank. Not encumbered by armour some reached safety. One or two caught hold of the tail of a swimming horse and continued down stream. On the far bank the rest of the English army was forced to watch the horrifying sight. Cressingham was one of the first to be dragged from his horse and the life was pounded from him by many Scottish spears. Wallace and Andrew Moray fought on foot with their men.

Hal and his carpenters hidden in the reeds under the first pier of the bridge had attached their ropes to the weakened section. They pulled and under the weight of the English above the creaking bridge gave way, throwing armoured men and horses into the water.

With the bridge gone, the battle turned into a massacre and the tears of mothers and widows in England were to flow as sadly as they had from the women folk of Scotland after Dunbar.

The English commander had seen enough. The Earl of Surrey turned his mount and his army followed in disorder. He paused at Stirling ordering Sir Marmaduke Tweng to hold the castle at all costs, then abandoning his men to their fate, galloped for the safety of England with a small escort of picked men.

In the evening Wallace walked around the battlefield with John his brother. "It's a terrible sight, Will. So many good men gone." Continuing their walk they came across a group of men having fun with the obese body of Cressingham. His clothes and armour had been divided and his head, which had been hacked off, was impaled upon a spear. Its sightless eyes were staring at the English dead. With dirks they were busy flaying the skin from his body. John turned his gaze away saying, "Will, in God's name put a stop to that," but Wallace shrugged, "They have fought hard for this victory, John, I must allow them some amusement."

The bodies of the English were being picked over by their victors, old crones and other scavengers. The monks of Cambuskenneth Abbey had taken the Scottish wounded from the field. The fallen English were left naked and grotesque for the crows, rats and dogs. The following day John Blair persuaded Wallace that his Christian duty was to give them proper burial. He ordered a pit to be dug near the trees under the crags and when the task had been done, Blair said a blessing for their eternal souls, while Wallace stood at some distance watching, detached, without compassion. He felt that he had done his Christian duty.

Andrew Moray had fought fiercely but towards the end of the battle he received an arrow wound just under his right arm. They carried him to the abbey where the monks removed the arrowhead and splinters of bone which were deeply embedded in his flesh. They cleaned the wound applying a soothing salve and said he would make a good recovery. Then they gave him some of the precious syrup made from poppy seeds, which sent him into a deep sleep. A period of rest would help the healing process. He had spoken with Wallace and Pilche before they bore him away. "See to the mopping up, Will. As soon as these Godly men release me from their grip, we'll discuss the defence of the kingdom from further attacks". He grinned then obediently lay back as they asked him to do, but as an afterthought, added, "Watch our noble lords, Will. They'll return to us now with full speed."

Wallace sent for Henry Halyburton. "Harry, take your men and pursue the English. See they remove themselves from Berwick. It's important that Berwick is once more in our hands." Halyburton's mounted men had remained hidden and took no part in the battle. They were fresh and keen for action. With them rode Alexander Pilche who wanted to see Berwick liberated.

Andrew Moray was right about the Scottish lords and their loyalty. They watched the massacre of the English army from their vantage point and saw the rearguard flee in disorder. The knights and mounted men put as much distance between themselves and Stirling as possible, leaving behind baggage, pack animals, wagons and camp followers to struggle home as best they could. They took the road to Falkirk and received no mercy from the Scots as they passed. The weak and wounded were left behind. They streamed along the track by the side of the merrily sparkling River Pows. The Earl of Lennox led his force from the shelter of the trees, killing and seizing booty at will.

In Stirling Castle Sir Marmaduke was preparing to hang on and defy the Scots until his king could send another army north, but the only news allowed through to them by the besieging Scots was demoralising, and he saw the hopelessness of their situation. Enough true men had died. He wanted to live to fight another day. Within a week of the battle, when Wallace had given his word to show mercy, Sir Marmaduke surrendered Stirling Castle to its rightful owners.

A few days after the battle, on a golden day in autumn when the trees rustled with bronze and gold, and the crimson rowan berries hung in heavy clusters, William Wallace rode to Cambuskenneth Abbey to visit Andrew Moray. John Blair came out to greet his friend and Wallace and his followers spent time visiting wounded in the hospice before going to the cell where Moray was resting. Moray was in a restless mood. His mind darted from one topic to the next. He was anxious not to forget any points that his enfeebled state had given him time to consider.

"We must press on with the advantage, Will. We mustn't let them rest." This he said in reply to Wallace's intention to take a mounted force to harry the English who had not surrendered in and around Cupar. Wallace told him that Dundee Castle was now theirs and Alexander Scrymgeour had been given the post of Governor. "Aye, he's a loyal man and a fine soldier. He'll do a good job." He lay back on his pillows. The pain in his right side had returned with the effort of talking, and beads of perspiration formed at his temples. Wallace, noticing Moray's pallor, arose, "I shall depart in the morning, Andrew. I wish you well."

Andrew Moray grinned, "Good hunting, my friend." He lay with his eyes closed. He liked Wallace, but the man was aloof and, although their difference in rank did not spoil their partnership, Lennox and the other nobles would find it difficult to accept Wallace's popularity with the army.

Wallace swept through Fife like a snowstorm in winter. The English were fleeing before him. Fields, farms and cottages were burnt along with the newly harvested crops. Livestock had been driven off by the English as they went, or lay dead, rotting and maggot infested. Graham rode with Wallace and together they watched the smouldering ruins of a mill. The miller and men from the village were busy trying to save what they could from the ruins, while a group of women and children attempted to glean any precious barley and rye which may have escaped the flames. "What will we eat when winter comes, Master Wallace. The English have devastated our land. We have nothing to eat or sow."

There would be famine and much hardship for the people during the coming months. Whenever he made contact with the enemy, Wallace showed no mercy and hardened his heart even against the women and children, making no attempt to check the excesses of his men. Yet in spite of all their sorrows, he was welcomed as a hero by the people, who looked to him for deliverance from their enemy.

He received a message that the nobles had called a Council to meet at the Abbey of Scone. Andrew Moray had already been taken there and the Earl of Lennox commanded that Wallace should present himself. The main army was still camped at Stirling, living in some style on the captured English stores. He checked that all was well, leaving his brother and Tom in charge, then turned north for Scone.

South of Scone Wallace's party met an escort from the Council. "Master Wallace, we have been sent to escort you to the abbey where the Council awaits you." Wallace had reigned in his mount, "Thank my lords, but there is one whom I must see before I present myself. I'm sure they will discuss affairs well enough without my presence," and he took the road which led towards Kilspindie.

Lady Margaret Wallace sat in the small, walled herb garden. It was a beautiful day and the air was heavy with the sweet smell from the plants. She was watching her granddaughter who was sitting at her feet playing with some stones and flower petals. The little maid put them into a small pot, clambered to her feet and tried to pick some more leaves and flowers to add to her collection. The door leading into the house opened and Edith, her serving woman, came running through, smiling and excited.

"Oh, my lady. He's just arrived, your son, the Wallace." In the doorway stood her second son, tall and bonnie beyond words. The big man strolled over, bending to kiss his mother while the little maid, startled by the stranger, came to her grandmother holding out her arms to be picked up. Wallace sat down on the bench, "Well Meg, do you ken your father?" She smiled shyly then buried her head in her grandmother's lap. Wallace smiled and stroked the child's soft curls.

"All Scotland speaks of my son. Your father would have been so proud." He smiled putting his arm around his mother's shaking shoulders, for her joy at seeing him had made her cry. Then he picked up his daughter and carried her shoulder high into the house. As they sat over their meal he spoke earnestly to his uncle, "I am worried about Meg's safety, uncle, perhaps even by coming here I am placing you all in danger, but I am at a loss to know where she would be safe in these troubled times." "They are both as safe here as anywhere, Will." "My mother looks tired and pale. Does she ail?" "She has not been herself since your father's death and – like us all – she grows old."

Margaret Wallace had been poorly for sometime. She was an old woman. Her body no longer responded to the moons waxing and waning and her abdomen was swollen as were her ankles, which made walking any distance painful. It saddened her. She was not fearful for herself if it was God's will that he should call her to his presence, but she was anxious about her granddaughter's future. Perhaps He would spare her long enough to see the child grow somewhat. She had been working on a new kirtle for William. That night with the help of her women it was finally finished. It was made from a rich, rust-brown woollen material and she had embroidered the hem and armholes with a pattern in yellow and orange silks.

In the morning, when the time came for the men to leave for the Council, Wallace wore his chain mail with the new kirtle over. There were tears in Margaret's eyes as he kissed her farewell. Each of his young followers bowed courteously to Lady Wallace as she murmured, "A mother's blessing on you". Then her brother blessed the party and the work that they did. As they rode through the gate, Wallace looked back over his shoulder and waved. His daughter held high by a servant waved back. "They are a fine sight, Margaret, the flower of Scotland" said Lady Wallace's brother. She said nothing, but wiped her cheek with the hem of her linen coif and hurried inside.

Scone bustled with earls, lords and knights of the realm. As danger had passed everyone had regained their patriotic zeal and needed to be seen with the young heroes of Stirling, but they watched each other, careful of their own interests and suspicious of others. Wallace met with Wishart, Stewart, Lennox, Comyn and Andrew Moray in the bishop's quarters. He noticed that Moray's condition had not improved since their previous meeting. The young man was weak and unable to walk without assistance. His skin was hot and dry with fever and when he spoke his voice was weary. He sat back in a heavy chair made more comfortable with many cushions, listening to the conversation around him, but plainly he was in pain.

The nobles took charge of the meeting while Wallace listened. Then Stewart turned to him, "Well, Will, what say you as commander of our army?" "My lords, our victory at Stirling does not mean it is the last we shall see of the English. When the New Year comes they'll be back. Our army must be trained and disciplined. The English have ravaged our land and the people will be in misery this coming winter. We must feed them, but keep order in the kingdom or there will be strife among us." He looked sharply at each man in turn, "I have observed how well you nobles love one another." At any other time they would have been affronted by such impertinence, but they remained silent and respectful, for Wallace had the ability to silence men of less character with his truthfulness. He continued, "We must regain the trade which we have lost and we must feed the people. Since it was the English who devastated our land, it will be the English who will supply the food. I shall take the army across the border and will find food sufficient for the winter." He turned to Andrew Moray, "What say you?"

Moray coughed painfully, catching hold of his side to ease the pain. "Absolutely, Will, we must continue pressing the English and regain the trade through Berwick and Aberdeen which we have lost. God willing, I will be fit to campaign in a month or so."

Bishop Wishart sat watching the two. Who would have thought it possible in so short a time that the two young men could have achieved so much – and how Wallace had changed. He had been an unambitious, easy-going farmer, but his misfortunes had transformed him into a shrewd and calculating soldier. A pity he was not of higher rank. Lack of influence could bring problems.

Later that day another meeting was held which all attended. "All talk and no do," Wallace had said quietly to Graham. They stood near the back, listening and watching and being ignored by those who thought they had more right to be there than master William Wallace. Almost every earl and lord in the land had had their say, but Lennox now held up his hand for silence.

"My lords, it is necessary for the safety of our realm that today we come to some decisions. Therefore I put it to you that we appoint as commanders of our army Andrew Moray and William Wallace in the name of our liege lord John, who is by God's grace our king. They have gained this title by virtue of their success at Stirling and by the respect which the army has for them."

All present understood the hidden meaning in the latter statement. They would defy, at their peril, the army so close at hand. There were shouts of approval from around the room sufficient for Lennox to take his proposal as passed, but a loud voice from the body of the hall called out, "How can we give command to such a man as William Wallace without even a noble title?"

Lennox reddened hesitating. Robert the Bruce, Earl of Carrick, was standing by his side and said, "If that's all that worries you, my lords, William Wallace, come forward." Surprised Wallace stepped from his humble position by the door and walked to the dais where Bruce stood. "It would seem there are those present who would try to deny you your position, even though you have earned it," said the earl. Drawing his sword he said "Kneel, William Wallace." Whatever was in his mind, Wallace's face was expressionless as he knelt before the Earl of Carrick. "In the name of the illustrious Prince John, King of Scots." He tapped Wallace on each shoulder, although it must have been painful for a Bruce to have acknowledged John Balliol as king. "Rise, Sir William Wallace."

Wallace rose and Robert the Bruce took his arm and holding it high he led Wallace from the dais. "I give you Sir William Wallace, joint commander of our army." There were cheers around the chamber and any voices of dissent remained silent. Andrew Moray rose unsteadily to his feet taking Wallace's hand. "I congratulate you, none deserves it more," then he slumped back into his chair.

On the following day Wallace returned to Stirling. The army had grown as new recruits were arriving daily, but if Scotland was to remain safe from English attack, the goodwill of the people was not enough. Wallace sent orders to all parts of the kingdom that men between the ages of sixteen and sixty should report for training with pike and claymore. He sent a message to Harry Halyburton to meet him at Haddington at the beginning of October, when they would march on England. Then he turned his attention to reorganising the army and training his men. Andrew Moray was brought back to the care of the monks at Cambuskenneth, but by the end of September, as Wallace prepared to leave on his campaign, it was plain that Andrew's wound was not healing and he could not be expected to join Wallace that winter.

On the final day of September Wallace addressed his men. He stood on a large rock where all could see and hear him. "Soldiers of Scotland. You've earned the people's trust and respect by delivering them from the English. We have been left devastated and the people you have saved now face famine this coming winter. We must take from the English what our people need until the harvest comes again." There was a stir of excitement and general banter from his listeners. "We'll pee on the walls of London itself if you ask us, Sir William," called one. Wallace held up his hand and his powerful voice reached all in the gathering, "From where I stand you look as if you could bring down the walls of London stone by stone if it were asked of you, for you are a terrifying sight." They all roared and cheered, excited and confident as they were. "Go see your loved ones and muster at Roslin Moor in the second week of October, for on St Luke's Day we shall march on England." Again a great roar went up.

Wallace accompanied by fifty of his closest friends, with John Blair as his chaplain, rode to Haddington. The banner of Scotland was held in front of him. He had said farewell to Andrew Moray whose young wife and mother had arrived to help care for him, and as they rode past the abbey Moray was carried out into the golden sunshine to watch them pass by.

At Haddington more work awaited him. Scouts were sent out along the borders. Reports had also to be despatched back to Moray and the Council. He had many visitors eager to seek his favour, but never would he indulge in fruitless conversation. He was brisk and did not seek rewards for his services. One morning two merchants arrived asking help with their trade in the towns of Hamburg and Lubeck. He sent letters with them to the Mayors of those towns assuring them that their merchants would have safe access to all corners of the kingdom of Scots, now that the land was delivered from the English. He asked that they would help Scots who sought honest trade. "When the letter is copied, John, let it be signed Andrew Moray and William Wallace, generals of the army of the realm of Scotland and make a copy for our records in case any should ask questions."

Then he bid the merchant's farewell, asking them to visit him again on their return. He watched as they left the courtyard. These men were peaceful traders, perhaps somewhat crafty, but steady and shrewd, the kind of men the realm would need if wealth was to flow again into Scotland.

A few days before he left for Roslin an unexpected visitor arrived, James Stewart was shown in. "My lord, this is a surprise. I trust nothing is amiss," but the High Steward of Scotland reassured him. "I regret that I cannot come south with you William but, if you are willing, I will assist with the storage and distribution of all provisions which are sent from England and I will see that the people benefit from the supplies during the winter." Wallace was surprised that such a wily man as James Stewart should openly associate with him but said nothing.

"Before I leave there is one other thing which requires your attention. As commander of the army none other has the authority and before you go south you must make official the election of Master William Lamberton as Bishop of St Andrews." The former Bishop of St Andrews, William Fraser, had been Scotland's ambassador. A patriot who had worked tirelessly to seek support for Scotland's cause from the French king. Now he was dead and the kingdom needed another strong man to take his place. Lamberton, former Chancellor of Glasgow, had been a good friend to the Wallace kindred and Wallace gave his whole-hearted approval for his appointment as bishop.

James Stewart left, taking with him an order from Wallace making William Lamberton Bishop of St Andrews. At the beginning of November Lamberton left for Rome, carrying with him messages for His Holiness the Pope from Sir William Wallace, asking for his

Holiness's aid against the king of England and begging for his intervention in gaining the freedom of King John.

On St Luke's Day 1297 the Scottish army of many thousand mounted and foot-soldiers, began their invasion of England. As they moved south, English settlers fled carrying with them the news that the Scots were coming. The little town of Alnwick was razed to the ground and its population slaughtered, although the castle held out. From Alnwick they marched to Rothbury, north of Newcastle, and there set up their headquarters. Scots ranged across the rich county of Northumberland, indulging in many evil and ungodly acts. Livestock, food and fodder was taken from township, manor and farm, then sent home to Scotland. As news of the Scottish advance spread the northern English fled west to Carlisle or south to Durham. Wallace himself led his men into Cumberland and laid siege to Carlisle were he called on the townspeople to surrender. From the safety of their thick walls they called back defiantly and pointed to their siege engines along the walls. Adam Wallace watched their bravado saying to his cousin, "Let's try a night attack, Will, they need to be taught a lesson." "Nay, I'm not interested in laying siege. Just keeping them holed up here while we make free in the countryside will be good enough." He turned and walked away leaving no opportunity for further discussion.

Wallace left a small force around Carlisle and continued plundering the countryside. When they had taken all that they could, they turned east towards Durham, travelling through the harsh wild country of Stainmoor. The winter descended early and it snowed in November. Frost froze the water hard and biting winds swept across the land. Many men died from the effects of the weather and rumours began to spread. It was a warning from God because the Scots were plundering the County of Durham that He had placed under the protection of Saint Cuthbert. They must return to their own land before worse befell them. By the middle of November scouts told Wallace that they had seen a large army of Durham men heading their way. Wallace sat listening to the arguments of his kinsmen. Except for their bravado at Carlisle, this was the first time the English had shown any fighting spirit. He weighed everything up and decided not to be caught in the enemy land in winter. If His Holiness in Rome heard that they had continued to fight on English soil, he would be less likely to give them his support. Better to return now.

When Wallace gave the order to turn for home there was relief in almost every heart. They crossed back into Scotland in the third week of Advent. They were tired but exhilarated and heavy with booty. As they passed through Scottish villages, the people came out to greet them and to cheer Wallace, offering him small gifts, honey cakes, flagons of ale and good ripe cheeses. Wallace was touched, especially as all the signs were that it would be a hard winter and they would need these things for themselves. Those who came to cheer him were the common people, not men of wealth and position.

The booty was divided amicably enough among the army, but he was pleased to see the back of some, particularly the men of Galloway. They were wild, undisciplined, cruel men, useful to spread fear in the enemy territory, but difficult to control now that they were back in their own land. With three thousand of his original army and his closest friends and kinsmen, they marched back to Stirling. It was a blow, if not unexpected, when he heard of the death of Andrew Moray. When they arrived at Cambuskenneth Abbey, he gave alms that they should say Mass for the soul of Moray and of all who had departed in Scotland's service. "Andrew Moray and those who fell with him were true champions of the land. We must all hope to be like them," he told the abbot. On the following day a messenger came from the Council. They were meeting at Scone and requested that Sir William Wallace present himself.

While Wallace was absent in England, there had been many furious and bitter arguments between the nobles of Scotland. The problem was a simple one. Scotland had a king who was a prisoner of the English and the kingdom did not have an effective leader. Robert the Bruce had a strong claim to Scotland's throne, but so did Comyn and to give Guardianship of the kingdom to one would bring the other around their ears. A further problem was that almost all the earls and barons had pledged allegiance to Edward of England. If they took the guardianship of the land all knew what his reaction to such treachery would be. No one wanted to see another put in power over them, but none would take up the reins, not as long as Edward lived.

For Bishop Wishart and, to a lesser extent, James Stewart the answer was a simple one. The Guardianship of Scotland should be offered to one who had no such allegiance, no lands in England and was no threat to any Scottish noble. Such a person was William Wallace. At a special meeting of the Council, Bishop Wishart, backed by Stewart, proposed that the Guardianship of Scotland be offered to Sir William Wallace. The commotion was not as great as they had expected. Each Council member was secretly relieved that the burden of Scotland would pass from him. They could not be accused of treachery when Edward of England once more reared his head.

Sir William Wallace entered the council chamber at the Abbey of Scone and all men stood to acknowledge him. Wishart smiled inwardly. The transformation of Wallace – the farmer, the rebel and the army commander – was complete. Sir William Wallace, Guardian of Scotland, stood before them and accepted the burden of high office with the dignity and confidence of a statesman.

# Scotland's Champion

Edward of England was in Ghent when he received the news of the defeat of his army at Stirling. His anger was directed towards Cressingham and Warenne, Earl of Surrey, for having allowed themselves to be fooled by a rabble. The defeat was nothing more than a mishap. Next time he would do the job himself and sweep the oafs from the field of battle. He sent couriers back to England. The levies must be called out; horses and stores procured; ships and siege engines built and the bishops of Canterbury and York would raise the money for his new invasion of Scotland. He had always found that careful planning would win the day.

He returned to England in March and made a pious pilgrimage to the holy shrine at Walsingham, where he asked the Lord for divine intervention against the Scots. By Whitsuntide he had progressed to York to meet his Parliament. Accompanied by the Archbishop, he went in humble supplication to the shrine of St John of Beverley. As a sign that God's special favour would be with England when he embarked on his campaign, he carried before him the sacred banner of that saint. Everyone knew that St John was a powerful protector of soldiers. It would look well, held aloft with the banner of St Cuthbert, a saint who had already protected them against the Scots by sending such a hard and early winter.

One evening in early spring the king sat with the Archbishop of Durham. "What are the people saying, Beck?" "They grumble, my lord. They grumble about the increase in taxes." "We both know that the people always grumble, but whom do they blame?" "The Scots, my lord. They reason that if the Scots had not rebelled against you they would not be asked to raise money and men for your army." The king smiled and went to bed a happier man.

Far away in Scotland, Wallace was also busy planning. His people's hatred for the English was no less determined and fierce than English contempt for the Scots. He was at the Templar's Preceptory at Torphichen during Lent. It was an excellent central base, guarding the approaches from the eastern marches into the heart of the kingdom. His friends and kinsmen were with him. Blair, his brother John, Graham, Sir John Stewart and many other supporters whose advice he valued. "They refuse to obey, Will." John Wallace had returned after trying to enforce the Guardian's command that landowners provide men and arms for the army. Most obeyed, but here and there some thought Wallace's actions high-handed and refused to cooperate – even though he was the elected Guardian. "Then we will have to make them," he said turning to Blair. "John, have gibbets built in the parishes and warn all by proclamation that refusal of service will result in dancing a merry jig. Make sure it is clearly sealed - Sir William Wallace, Guardian of Scotland. The people must be in no doubt that I mean what I say. John, tomorrow I ride north."

As they travelled north, the people came out to greet them. Many had lost sons and husbands to the people's army yet they showed no sign of hatred nor discontent: that they reserved for the English. It was, Wallace said to his friends, men who had little that gave the most. The great men of property were frightened of their own shadows.

They arrived in Aberdeen in the late afternoon on a bitter day with a cold north-easterly wind and icy rain driving into their faces. Even the horses were in low spirits and stood dejected, heads lowered, legs and bellies covered in mud. As his own animal was led away by a stable boy Wallace said, "Rub him down well, lad, with handfuls of good straw and give him warm bran. He has carried me well and safely."

The boy had a clubfoot and had been delighted when he was given work in the castle stables. It was warm and dry with the animals – which were better housed than he had been in all his life. He looked up at the big man, the Guardian, with awe. He must be very important yet he had spoken so kindly about his horse. The boy looked at the animal. It was quite an ordinary nag. He had seen lesser men with much finer horses and equipment. The boy decided he liked this man.

Men of consequence in the city and surrounding countryside who had refused service were summoned to the castle. The following morning in the great hall Wallace addressed the gathering. Landowners and merchants whose names appeared on the muster rolls were present. Many grumbled. Leaving their businesses would be disastrous and their profits would drop. Landowners said that to lose men during the spring sowing would continue the famine into the next year. Wallace listened to their complaints. Finally he raised his hand for silence. His voice was quiet but most determined when he spoke. "Fellow Scots, I understand your fears, but do you think your profits and crops will be safer under an English yoke. On each tower," he pointed outside, "you will see carpenters hard at work. You have until tomorrow at noon to obey my instructions."

Turning his back on the uproar he left the hall, leaving his followers with drawn swords to force the angry men from the hall and placing them under guard while they pondered over their situation. Some felt that Wallace would not carry out his threat. One merchant had known William Wallace during their days at the Monastery School in Dundee. He had not been of Wallace's circle. He had never thought him to be a hard man, but equally he had never considered him so skilful as to become the Guardian. Wallace must have hidden powers and could not be judged as he judged other men. He decided that in the morning it would be prudent to obey, which was fortunate for him.

On the following day at noon Wallace stood on the raised platform where the high seat was usually placed. A tapestry embroidered in rich browns, reds and greens, depicting a hunting scene, hung the full length of the wall behind him. Otherwise the chamber was empty of all furniture or finery. He stood, large and formidable, with his right hand resting casually on the hilt of his claymore which he held point downwards in front of him. Nine men stood before him, four merchants and five lesser landowners. Earlier in the day John Blair had tried to persuade Wallace to order the castle governor to pass sentence. He would not listen, since the responsibility for defending the realm was his and therefore all must fear him.

They stood truculent and defiant while Wallace listened to their pleas and the Chaplain's petition for mercy, but his face remained grim. When all was said he roused himself. "I have listened to your excuses, but if you are not prepared to resist the English then you are supporting them."

There were loud protests from the prisoners, but Wallace nodded towards his brother, who was in charge of the guard. Before they fully understood their situation, they were hustled out into the yard. The commotion outside grew louder as they were dragged to gibbets surrounded by a crowd of jeering people. Wallace walked into the yard where he could see and be seen and when all was ready, he gave the signal. Only when the bodies had ceased their dance of death and swung slowly round and round in the cold grey day did Wallace turn to the castle governor, "Make sure they remain there. I shall have no more defiance of my orders."

News that the Guardian had ordered the execution of leading men of Aberdeen spread rapidly. A few who had considered him to be a man of little consequence decided to tread with more care and heed his orders, at least for the time being.

Scotland prepared to defend herself again. They had failed at Dunbar not through lack of valour but because of their contempt for discipline. Wallace knew that the English army behaved in an orderly and disciplined way, obeying idiotic commands given by an incompetent leader. He knew that when they met again they would be under the command of the English king, a man of proven cunning and military skill. Wallace must be equally skilled and as his people's army grew, he developed a strict chain of command and improved training in the use of arms. Men already experienced in war were put in charge of those without such skill. They must be dependent upon each other. "If a comrade falls, close ranks," said the Guardian. Back at Torphichen he began his day among the men, guiding and advising, until he knew each man by name and they knew him. Wherever he went he inspired confidence and they trusted his judgement in all matters.

At first the nobles had withdrawn to their own castles, remaining aloof from 'Wallace and his outlaws' as Sir Gartenet of Mar had described the Guardian and his following. Some, however, were anxious to promote Wallace. Stewart, Bishop Lamberton, Wishart, the Grahams – for old Sir John had relented – and men from Galloway and Moray had remained loyal. As the weeks went by, other nobles threw in their lot with Wallace, as they were anxious not to lose influence. Yet as John Blair confided to Graham, "Many would like to see him take a tumble." Graham replied, "You are right. There are few I would trust with my life."

Wallace appeared unconcerned about his own future or safety, and continued to throw his energies into matters of state and the training of his army. His friends, anxious that he should have some relaxation, arranged for Agnes from the Blue Boar to join the army followers. She was a kindly soul and almost without his knowledge she took his care and comfort onto herself. Ready with a smile and quick lively answer, loyal and tender. Whether she was washing his clothes, lying in a grand bed in a noble castle with his warm back at her side, or lying on bracken under the stars with his arm about her, William Wallace was her man. She did not know what he thought of her. He was always preoccupied with his own matters. It was enough that she was with him.

England's second invasion became imminent as spring gave way to summer. In the third week of May 1298, Edward held his parliament at York summoning his Scottish lords to attend, but none came. Always meticulous in his planning he ordered provisions for his men and beasts to be delivered to depots along the east coast and from Ireland to Carlisle in the west.

Sir John Warenne, Earl of Surrey, still smarting from his defeat at Stirling, had crossed the border in early February at the head of a large army. Wallace's spies reported that three thousand mounted men and many thousands of foot-soldiers were heading towards Roxburgh Castle and he sent an order to evacuate the castle. Let the English come on. Commanding fifty men, he rode out to harry their rearguard. Stragglers, foragers and many pack horses disappeared and at night, as the English slept near their campfires, cries could be heard from the edges of the vast camp. Just before Kelso the huge army came to a halt, rested for a few days, then turned and followed the Tweed towards Berwick.

The English defending Berwick Castle had been under siege since the autumn struggling to keep Harry Halyburton at bay. Their food had run out and since Christmas they had kept themselves alive eating their horses, dogs and lately any rats which had been foolish enough to stay in the castle. Yet on the brink of surrender they watched from the castle walls as far below them the Scots began to withdraw. That afternoon the vanguard of Warenne's army came into view.

From Berwick the English army marched north but only found deserted, burnt-out villages and homesteads, and shells of barns emptied of livestock and grain. Foraging parties, if they returned at all, had little to show for their efforts. The retreating Scots had cleared the land of everything. At the end of February, a messenger arrived from the king ordering the army to stand down until he could personally lead them. Warenne – and all the knights who were with him – breathed a sigh of relief, and men from the northern shires returned to their homes.

Wallace realised how vulnerable the enemy was, and continued burning the towns and villages in the borderlands. The people of Berwickshire and Lothian he sent north. There would be no sowing or harvesting this year, nothing to sustain the English.

Skirmishes continued throughout the spring and at the beginning of June a large force of experienced English knights sailed from Flanders under the command of the Earl of Pembroke. They landed in eastern Fife. The earl's orders were to march on Perth, secure it and sweep down on Stirling to join his master the king, who was marching north with the main army. Pembroke met with little resistance as they travelled across Fife and by the time they reached Abernethy they had grown confident. It was heavily wooded countryside, and scouts returned with news that the ford across the Tay was low after the dry weather and was but a day's march away. The main force could skirt the stronghold of Elcho on the southern bank of the Tay, but the earl decided he would leave sufficient men camped before the castle walls to keep the defenders within.

A seasoned campaigner, Pembroke was pleased. So far things were going well, but he was a superstitious man and looked for signs and omens before embarking on any campaign. All the omens were favourable: good weather, a calm crossing and on his first night on Scottish soil he had seen a shooting star, surely a sign of favour from the Almighty. The dangerous time would be crossing the ford. After that Scotland would be open to him. "If they are going to try an ambush, the ford would be the place," he said to his lieutenant.

The forest, strangely silent for midsummer, made the earl uneasy. He glanced back at the column behind him, but the trees obscured his view. He had more foot-soldiers than he would have wished for and their progress was much slower than that of his mounted men, but horses were troublesome on long sea-crossings. The order was passed back to close ranks and he looked suspiciously around at the greenwood. The sunlight danced through the leaves and the air was heavy with the perfume of bluebells. The track allowed three men to walk abreast. Perhaps he was being unnecessarily cautious, allowing his imagination to wander. After all it was a very hot morning. No wonder the birds were silent. He would have preferred to sit by a stream than clang along in heavy armour bothered by sweat and flies. He leant forward and patted the neck of his chestnut war horse. The animal was clearly irritated by the swarm of flies buzzing around its twitching ears.

W allace was at Dunfermline Abbey when he heard of the Earl of Pembroke's landing. He was visiting his mother, who had been ailing for sometime and was now approaching her end. Lady Margaret lay back on the pillows with closed eyes, her second son sitting beside her. She had taken his large brown hand into hers, sighed and tears filled her eyes.

"William, my dear William. Your father would have been so proud of you." She lay quietly for speaking tired her. A sister came in to place fresh hot stones along the sick woman's body and by her feet. Margaret Wallace stirred and smiled at her son. He had removed the basinet from his head, but still wore his chain mail, for he had come straight to his mother's bedside. Over his chain mail, was the rust-brown surcoat which she had made for him, and she noticed that it had been carefully darned at the hem.

"I see you have someone to care for you, my son," she said, indicating the neat repair. "Is it one who will make a good stepmother for your little maid." Her son looked embarrassed, "Nay mother, she is a kindly wench, but my Margaret is safer here with the kindly women." Again she closed her eyes and drifted into a light doze. She worried so about her granddaughter. Margaret, who was entering her third summer, was bright and independent of spirit, but when she had gone, she did not want her grandchild to remain within the cloister of the abbey. Lady Margaret honoured the good sisters and the lives which they led, but her grand daughter should have a fuller life: husband, children and a house of her own to rule. When she came of age, she would inherit Lamington in her own right and would make a fine match. Lady Wallace stirred when her son bent to kiss her thin cheek.

"Mother, I must leave you, but I shall return in a few days. Until then give me your blessing." He squeezed her hand as she murmured, her tears welling up and rolling silently down her cheeks. Then in a stronger voice she said, "Good bye, my son, I shall always watch over you and your work." Wallace picked up his helmet and claymore, walking quickly from the cell, but his face betrayed the intensity of his sadness for he did not know if, in this life, he would see her again.

A lay-sister entered the room as her son left and sat with the sick woman, but they did not speak. Lady Margaret lay thinking about her sons and their father. She was proud of them all, but perhaps she would have had a more peaceful mind, now that she was nearing her death, if the Wallace kindred had been like other men: accepting the easy path and leaving great decisions to others with power and influence. Once again tears brimmed from under her closed eyelids. The sister lent forward and patted her hand and a little later she knew from the quiet breathing that the sick woman had drifted into sleep.

Wallace had ridden to Elcho Castle to join Graham and his men. Duncan Balfour, the Sheriff of Fife, and his followers had swelled their numbers. Late in the afternoon they had left Elcho to prepare their ambush and wait until morning for the English when the trap would be sprung.

The Earl of Pembroke urged his horse to a canter, with the foot-soldiers running to keep up with the column. There was such a clatter and jangling of equipment as they progressed noisily through the forest that all other sounds were lost in the din. That was why they did not hear the whirr of the first arrows.

The forest was dense and in the confusion and confined space Pembroke found it impossible to order his men into sensible battle formation. There was nothing for it but to make a dash along the forest track to the open countryside beyond. As Pembroke and his knights were fleeing towards safety, arrows rained down on them from each side. The path turned sharply to the left where a rope had been tied taunt across the path, high enough that the war horses might pass under, low enough to catch the rider across the upper chest. Pembroke was the first to come down. As the dazed men staggered to their feet, a Scottish pike or claymore awaited them and the horses trampled many. By the end of the afternoon, the English dead lay throughout the forest glades. The few, who battled their way through the trees to the open country beyond, were caught by the Scottish rearguard.

These Englishmen were hardened warriors of King Edward's continental campaigns and they did not give up easily. The fighting continued into the gloaming of the short northern night. The warm air was scented by honeysuckle, a night meant for lovers. Leaves rustled, twigs snapped, but not with sighs and groans of man and maid under a full moon. Instead sharp cries were heard as men in the Earnside Forest closed their eyes for ever.

Graham fell wounded. Only John Wallace's swift intervention saved his life. He carried Graham to the camp on the banks of the Earn and placed him in the shade of an ancient oak. In the early evening Wallace came to his friend. "How goes it, Will?" Graham asked anxiously. "We are finishing off the stragglers," said Wallace. "By morning we'll have cleared them out like a nest of vipers."

Wallace looked at his friend's wound. It was a long deep gash in Graham's thigh and from his pallor Wallace knew that Graham had lost much blood. Now the bleeding had stopped and the heat of the day had dried his clothes around the wound. The usual camp-followers were not with them. They had marched at speed to meet the enemy and there were none to care for the wounded. Wallace rose, walked to the river and carried back water in his helmet. "Drink this, then I shall get more to cleanse your wound." John Graham tried to raise himself to drink, but was too weak. Scotland's Guardian knelt and cradled his friend's head to enable him to quench his thirst. When the wounded man lay back satisfied, Wallace washed and bound his leg. "Nay, Will, rest awhile. You'll have more pressing tasks when this is done," but the Guardian would not heed him.

Two days later Wallace marched south at the head of his men. He had heard that Edward Longshanks was marching north with a mighty army. He would have gone to Dunfermline Abbey once again to see his mother, but it was not possible and he asked John Blair to visit her in his stead.

As they marched a company of archers, led by Sir John Stewart, joined them and together they met the main army. Waiting for him was Sir John Comyn with a company of lightly armed horsemen. "Will, better they are here with us than swelling the ranks of the English," said John Wallace as Comyn came to greet them. "As long as we are not forced to put too much store by them," was the Guardian's tart reply. Indeed not many of the great lords joined the army of Scotland.

Sir John Graham rejoined them at the beginning of July although his leg was still stiff and tightly bandaged. Robert Boyd also brought many good fighting men from Kilmarnock. Robert the Bruce, Earl of Carrick, had recently been deprived of his estates in England by the English king and decided to throw in his lot with the Scots, but did not ride with his men to join Wallace. Instead he held Ayr Castle where he kept watch for English supply ships from Ireland sailing for Glasgow with provisions for the English army.

If Wallace cared that the earls of the kingdom had not given him their complete support, he did not voice his annoyance nor ask for their aid. The people were behind him. The nobles could only watch and envy the unity which existed between the people and their Guardian.

Edward at the head of his vast army found the border country bare of all that sustained life. What could not be moved had been burnt. His experienced eye surveyed his morose, grumbling troops. The Welsh archers were the worst and dissatisfaction and fighting between English and Welsh became a daily occurrence. As the army progressed slowly through barren land he was bothered by the thought that his large army laden with wagons overflowing with baggage had very little food. They were hungry and for a while the promise that food could be found further north kept them going, but as each new day took them further into the hostile land, sickness began to increase. Expected supplies from the eastern English ports did not get through as they were intercepted by pirates or sunk by storms. The frustrated and angry king demanded from Beck where the Scottish army could be found.

"My lord, they disappear into the mist." "Don't be ridiculous man. You can't lose an army. It takes time to move it." Beck had never seen his master in such a gloomy mood and he was alarmed when the king said, "I'll allow another week and if we haven't found them, we'll turn back." Edward noted the expression on Beck's face and said, "I've never given up as you know well, but soon the men will be too weak to fight."

That night the Earl of March sent out another scout to look for the illusive Scots and the following morning Beck received the news that two supply ships had arrived at Leith near Edinburgh. He was sure that this was a good omen. His premonition was short lived for the ships carried little food and only two hundred casks of red wine. When the king heard, he swore and ordered the wine to be given to his troops, which did little for their hunger or their tempers and many brawls broke out.

At dawn on the following day one of the scouts returned. He had seen the Scottish army camped not more than eighteen miles away, close to Falkirk. "Sire, they await only our starvation and retreat. Then they will fall on us." The king walked up and down irritably. "Then we'll save them the bother. We'll visit them instead." Turning abruptly to his commanders he said, "We march on."

The army continued to grumble not knowing where they were going. They and their horses were hungry. The experienced men walked beside their gaunt mounts allowing them to rest whenever they could. "Where's the ol' bleeder taking us now?" was the general moan.

All day they marched until late at night, when they were ordered to rest in full battle order. Even the king lay himself down on the earth with sword at his side and his black warhorse by him. The king's page stood near his master trying to calm the hungry, restless animal, but once the lad could hear the royal snores, he sat down holding the horse's reins. In the moonlight he could see the shapes of sleeping knights, hear the coughs, grunts and night sounds of an army. It had been a long day and he tried to fight his weariness, but his eyelids began to droop, his chin slipped onto his chest and the reins slipped from his hand.

The shouting and cursing of his master awoke him. The prostrate king was clutching his chest. The boy ran to his master, but was pushed violently aside by Beck. "Away boy, you have done enough for one night." The royal doctors were for once in agreement. The bruising to Edward's ribs from the horse's hooves would heal, but he must rest quietly for a week or so. Edward laughed and would not listen. He had come this far and the Scots were within his reach. If he backed off now the morale of the army would be broken. "Strap me up you fools and I shall be in the saddle before light."

The sun had not risen over the horizon when Edward, sitting stiffly in his saddle, led his army forward towards the Scottish encampment. As they approached the river Avon they caught sight of the Scots drawn up ready for battle.

S he did not suffer and passed peacefully into Our Lord's care." The Guardian, John Wallace and John Blair sat quietly on a rock near the camped army. Blair had just arrived from Dunfermline Abbey. "Before she received the last rites she sent you both her blessing, and her speech was only of her sons and your father. I wish I could have brought you better news at such a time, but she is at peace, safe in Paradise."

William Wallace said nothing, but his face showed his anguish and his friend put a comforting hand onto his shoulder. After a few moments the man roused himself, "And my little lassie, Margaret, what of her?" She is safe in the care of your uncle Crawford, but he will take her west to the manor of Sir John Shaw as you desired. She is a bonnie little maid and grows well." The Guardian made no reply, and shortly after John Blair left to attend to his pastoral duties. At times like this he had found men needed solitude.

Wallace's instincts told him to continue his retreat northwards. The English were desperate for supplies and sickness was rife among them. "If we wait a week or so they will retrace their footsteps without our help," he told Sir John Comyn, but Comyn was anxious for a glorious victory against the English. A victory would enhance his family's claim to the Scottish throne for he was a kinsman of Balliol. Surely even Wallace could see that John Balliol was king in name only. Scotland needed a strong king. A resounding defeat now would clear the English out once and for all.

Normally Wallace kept his own council on how to wage the war, but he needed the mounted troops which John Comyn commanded and when Comyn persisted with his demands to stand and fight he had to yield. He reasoned that his men were anxious to prove their worth against the English. They were well trained and if they continued withdrawing the whole kingdom would be charred and desolate. The people would have nothing left with which to face the coming winter. Surely they should stop the English in their tracks now and attack the weakened army.

The English came into view and he gave the order which they all awaited. They drove their sharpened staves into the ground and linked them together with ropes. The ground in front of the schiltron sloped downwards to the marshy land by the river – and the forest which offered sanctuary, if the need arose, was not far off.

Wallace rode around the four closely packed schiltrons joking, praising and giving words of encouragement, their twelve foot pikes bristled upwards. In the land between the schiltrons were the bowmen led by Sir John Stewart and at the rear Sir John Comyn with his light horse. The priests were walking along the ranks giving blessings and the sacrament to the troops.

Across the river the English priests did the same for it was the feast of St Mary Magdalene. King Edward piously knelt before the Bishop of Durham and was shriven with bowed bare head and eyes firmly shut. As he rose stiffly to his feet, he clenched his teeth that those around him should not see his pain. The men must not know.

Scotland's Guardian sat on his horse overlooking the army and the standard of Scotland fluttered by his side. Silence had fallen on both armies. Each man guided by his own thoughts how to inflict vengeance for the loved ones lost. For some the simple desire to plunder and to receive honours after victory was sufficient. No attempt was made to parley by either side: battle would be to the death.

Wallace rode around so that all his men might see him. "You are a fearsome sight, I have seen none more so. I've brought you to these rings, dance as best you can. God be with you all this day." A hearty cheer went up from the Scottish side.

War trumpets sounded from the English to signal their advance. Their first cavalry charge became stuck in the mire by the river and they spent some time extricating themselves from the soft, marshy ground. Gaining more stable foothold they rode west to find a more suitable approach. The second cavalry attack was led by the Bishop of Durham himself, who had removed his sacramental robes for the occasion and rode to the enemy's left flank, looking for a way to the rear.

John Wallace shook his brother's hand, then made his way to the schiltron where the men of Ayrshire and Clydesdale knelt or stood shoulder to shoulder. He went into the middle of the ring mingling with those who would replace the fallen. A priest was there. "Father, you should leave now, the English have begun their advance." "I shall remain here for this is where I will be needed," he replied as he passed on murmuring a Benediction to men who fell on their knees before him. Alexander, Laird of Faulkerton, pushed his way through the throng taking John by the arm. "It's good that you, brother to the Guardian, stand here with us John. It'll put heart into the men."

John Wallace smiled the same cheerful grin which the Wallace kinsfolk had been accustomed to see in happier days. "I've looked forward to meeting the English again." He could say no more because a cheer went up from the waiting Scots as the English cavalry were seen making their charge from the right flank. John Wallace took up his position with the standing men on the right side. "Lower your pikes on my command." Hurriedly some made the sign of the cross and whispered Hail Marys. The thunderous pounding of hooves came nearer. Everyone stood silent with eyes fixed on the approaching enemy.

The English under the command of Beck had also begun their charge on the left flank while their king in command of the third cavalry brigade was preparing a frontal attack.

"Steady, pikes ready, lower," bellowed John Wallace and Alexander Faulkerton. Together the pikemen lowered their deadly weapons. The thundering war horses with nostrils and eyes wide flew towards them. "Steady, hold."

Hearts beat faster as the men swallowed, fixing their eyes on the charging enemy, bracing their backs for the impact. The screams from the wounded and dying horses impaled on the wall of stakes and pikes, the clash of arms as bewildered mounted knights struck at the enemy, could be heard across the Avon by the waiting Welsh and Lancastrian archers. The remnants of the English cavalry galloped from the field. A shout went up from the excited pikemen. "Steady," shouted John Wallace, "hold ranks."

He saw his brother ride between the schiltrons and saw him speak to Sir John Stewart who was commanding the archers. Sir John gave a command and the whir of arrows flying after the retreating English was heard.

In spite of his pain, King Edward had taken his cavalry to the enemy schiltrons but had returned with most of his men. Grim faced he sat on his horse. With an experienced eye he watched the enemy archers as they sent arrows into his own retreating cavalry. Well, he had never lost a battle and he did not intend to lose this one. He turned to his aide and gave orders for his Lancastrian and Welsh archers to assemble. He pointed to positions on the English side of the river. The Scottish arrows would not reach his archers, but English arrows would reach the Scots because of their longer range.

Wallace, Graham and others rode around encouraging their men. Then came the first flight of English arrows. Flight after flight rained down on the crowded men. Men with shields held them over their heads for protection, but most were peasants and craftsmen with little to protect them from such an onslaught. In the outer rings they began to fall but were quickly replaced by comrades from the centre.

Sir John Stewart's archers sent volley after volley back to the English, but those who had time to watch saw that their arrows fell short of the target. The English aim was swift and deadly. MacDuff of Fife commanding the schiltron on the left flank was forced to order his kneeling front rank to step back behind their standing comrades to tighten the circle and close the growing gaps. Still the arrows rained down on them.

The Guardian and Graham saw Sir John Stewart hit by an arrow. Graham jumped from his horse and ran to the tightly packed Scottish archers. Rallying them he ordered a fresh flight to speed on its way.

Wallace watched the terrible scene and knew he had to break the hold which the enemy archers had on the battle. He must send in his horsemen. At least their approach might draw out the English cavalry again. He signalled to Comyn in charge of the mounted men at the rear to advance. Sir John gathered his mount and with sword in hand pointed the way forward, but some other nobles with him shook their heads, turned their horses and left the field. In the general melee, Comyn stood up in his stirrups shouting and cursing at their retreating backs, but either they did not hear or chose not to. The flight from the battlefield frightened Comyn's mount. Taking the bit between its teeth it followed its companions. Wallace watched grimly, then turned his attention back to the battle. The English foot-soldiers had crossed the Avon. Slowly they advanced using slings with stones and other missiles, which they hurled at the Scots.

Bishop Beck saw the withdrawal of the Scottish cavalry and immediately took advantage, hurrying his brigade around to the rear of the Scottish position intent on cutting off any organized retreat.

Of Sir John Stewart's archers not one remained on his feet able to hold a bow. Wallace saw the utter horror of the battle, the fallen men, the closely packed schiltrons and Beck's cavalry trying to encircle them from the rear. God help them. He must save what he could. Grasping the banner of Scotland he galloped around his army shouting, "Save yourselves, fall back to the forest." He drew Vengeance, his great claymore and rode towards the approaching English cavalry, attacking any who would prevent his countrymen's retreat to the cover of the trees. His claymore sang its deadly song. He allowed himself to seek safety only when all who could leave the field of battle were safe. He had a small wound in his left upper forearm, but was otherwise sound.

As the day closed and evening drew in it became plain that few had escaped the English sword. John Wallace was safe, but Graham had fallen as had MacDuff of Fife, Alexander of Faulkerton, Sir John Stewart, his old friend Tom Johnston and many other brave men. Wallace listened to the sounds of sadness after a battle and the loss of so many fine fellows pressed heavily on his mind. "Aye, the cream of the kingdom," he kept repeating to those near to him. He said nothing of Comyn and his men.

When the night was at its darkest, the Wallace brothers, accompanied by John Blair, returned to that terrible hillside to search for those they had loved. The English and Welsh robbers had already been at work. The Scottish dead lay in naked piles. The carcasses of the dead horses had been butchered on the field and the English sat around their campfires on the far side of the Avon eating their fill. Wallace could hear them laughing and singing in the soft night air.

They found Graham and John Stewart with the fallen bowmen, but of MacDuff and Tom there was no sign. They placed the bodies of the two men on their horses. They looked back once and Blair murmured a prayer for the souls of the fallen.

As dawn broke they left the bodies of their friends at Falkirk church for Christian burial. Wallace was impatient to bury his friends with his own hands, but Blair disagreed, "Take care, Will. You are the Guardian and the kingdom has sore need of you." Wallace glumly shrugged his shoulders and sadly said, "They will do well to look to another. See what I have brought them to," but he allowed them to take his arm and lead him to his horse.

The Guardian rallied the remnants of his army and marched to Stirling where he ordered the town and castle to be torched. Only the Dominican convent was spared. He could not bring himself to order the destruction of this holy building. The English army was following closely on Wallace's heels as he continued to withdraw northwards towards Perth. Nothing was to be spared which might give protection to the enemy and he ordered the clearance and firing of manors and farms as he went. In Perth the citizens were in confused flight, taking anything which could be carried, before the Guardian and his men burned their homes. The flames from the burning lit up the night sky and could be seen for many miles.

In spite of their victory morale among the English remained at a low ebb. Their horses were skin and bone, barely able to stand, the poor beasts were dejected and in such a state that all spirit had left them. Long awaited supply ships failed to appear and the land around them was charred with nothing for the animals to graze. The men were hungry, thin and wild-eyed. Their minor wounds refused to heal and many developed boils and other weeping sores. Both great and lowly men complained of watery bowels and were so weak that they were barely able to march. Their king led them across country into Ayrshire. Wallace and his men followed and dealt with the weakest left behind by the army, harrying wherever and whenever they could.

Ayr was burnt and deserted and the supply ships that were expected from Ireland failed to appear. There was nothing to give them any comfort. Edward astride his weary warhorse gazed at the surrounding hills. "The buggers are up there watching us. Damn them to Hell," he said to Beck. He was right. As the last English wagon trundled away to the south, the citizens of Ayr came down from the hills and fell upon English stragglers unfortunate enough to be left behind.

The Guardian harried the English throughout August and followed them to Ayr where he handed over his command to Robert the Bruce, Earl of Carrick. With a few close kinsmen and friends Wallace rode to Stobo, manor of Wishart, Bishop of Glasgow.

King Edward arrived back in England during the first week of September. Left behind him were the corpses of men and horses and all kinds of paraphernalia of war. He was tired and embittered. He had won a battle but had not won the war. Wallace was to blame for that. From that moment he felt a great personal hatred for Wallace.

The Stobo lands basked in the warm golden sunshine of the early afternoon. Bees and insects buzzed in the sleepy air, while doe-eyed cattle grazed contentedly in the pasture by the river. The manor was peaceful and prosperous, untouched by the calamity that had overtaken Scotland. They passed a group of peasants working in the field who stopped their work and ran to the riders. Sturdy looking men, well fed, lacking the gaunt strained faces of the peasants and townsfolk whom Wallace had so recently seen. The bishop and his folk still lived well.

"Good day to you, Sir William. Is it true then that the English won the day?" "Aye, it's true but only the battle. At this moment they march back to their own land." "God be praised for that then," said some. The Guardian, usually so at ease with the people, was in no mood to talk further and bidding them good day, rode to the manor hall.

The bishop had been waiting for him and, with James Stewart, greeted Wallace in friendly fashion. The bishop's steward showed Sir William to the best guest chamber and all was done for the comfort of Scotland's Guardian. It was a fine manor house, stone built, with thick thatch and leaded windows. There were many upstairs chambers with rich furnishings. In earlier days Wallace would have been pleased to have a dry comfortable bed with a warm fire to rest by. It would have pleased him to watch the firelight dancing on the richly coloured scenes on the wall hangings, but events of the past weeks had dulled his senses and he looked angrily at the prosperity and comfort of the hall.

The steward, followed by servants, entered carrying hot water and a goblet of wine. "For your refreshment," the steward waved his hand. "The difficulties of your journey have been such that my lord ordered I lay fresh clothes for your comfort." Shoes, hose and surcoat had been laid on the bed. Wallace looked angrily at them, but beyond nodding made no reply.

Left to himself he hesitated before drinking the wine, then sat in the high-backed chair by the window and watched the comings and goings in the yard below. Did it matter if they had laced the wine with a poisoned draught? It would be better if he joined those he had led to disaster. He closed his eyes. He was weary. The wine and warm afternoon encouraged him to doze for a few minutes and once again he relived that terrible day.

He awoke with a start. Not being a man to rest quietly for long, he washed himself, trimmed his hair and beard, then paused looking at the neatly laid clothes on the bed. He had not changed his clothes since Falkirk. They were caked with mud and grime and were not fit for such a manor as Stobo, but it grieved him to be in debt to such men. He changed and took himself down to the walled garden, at the rear of the manor, where he walked for a while enjoying the peace and scent from the lavender until the steward came to tell him that food was prepared in the great hall.

The Earl of Buchan and Bishop Lamberton had recently arrived and they and their followers were seated around the board. The Guardian was offered the place of honour to the right of Bishop Wishart, but it was not a merry meal and when all had eaten their fill, the Guardian stood up raising his hand for silence.

"My lords and my friends, I have looked to you all for support during these past months and each of you has given it according to your ability. You know that it has been my wish to liberate the kingdom from the English in the name of our sovereign lord, King John. You know better than any that I have not spared myself in his service. Since Falkirk it has become plain to me that I can no longer serve as Guardian of Scotland and lead the people to their ruin. Far better I serve with them and accept those misfortunes which they must also accept. Now that the English are being driven across the border, I must return this which has been in my keeping." He took from the pouch at his belt the Seal of Scotland and handed it to the bishop for safekeeping.

There was uproar from his followers, shouting and banging the boards. One or two jumped up to their feet and the steward, standing behind his master's chair, put his hand to his dagger, but the bishop turned and held up a warning hand. It was Wallace as always in command of his own passions, who raised his arms to silence the din. He spoke again directing his words to James Stewart and Bishop Wishart.

"There are others who have been born for leadership, my lords. You must choose a new Guardian from among your own. I thank you for your hospitality, but – with your permission – I shall withdraw from your service in the morning."

"My son, I am sorry that it should end for you like this. There are none in the land who could have acted with such honour as you, Sir William." Bishop Wishart raised his glass to him. For once the bishop had voiced sincere thoughts. There were shouts along the benches and more banging on the table boards. In an effort to keep the young men in good humour, the steward quickly began to refill their goblets.

The morning following his resignation, Sir William Wallace rose early from his bed. Wearing his own freshly laundered clothes, with basinet on his head and Vengeance strapped to his back, he went to the stables where a servant had his horse saddled. As he prepared to mount, Bishop Lamberton came out holding out his hand to the young man who had sponsored him for his post as Bishop of St Andrews. "What are your plans now, William?" "I shall spend time putting my own affairs in order." "Is Scotland to lose her champion then?" "My lord, I shall serve Scotland as before, but it is time to seek other ways to deal with the English." "Then farewell, I wish you God's blessing and a safe journey."

# In the
# Wilderness

During the feast of Christmas in the year 1298, Sir William
Wallace was at his manor of Borthwick. The old people had
died and the land, livestock and buildings were in a sorry state.
He had arrived in the late autumn with his brother, Agnes and a few
of the men who had remained with him. They spent the short daylight
hours repairing timbers and ploughing, ready for the spring sowing.
It was late for such tasks, but there was famine in the land and he had
to do whatever possible. His few remaining ewes were brought down
from the high pasture. They looked neglected and thin. Those that
could not survive the winter were slaughtered, and Agnes and her
women prepared the meat for winter. Agnes was so happy caring for
her William and caring for his house. After giving up the Guardianship,
he had returned sad, morose and silent, deep in his own thoughts.
Now that he had so much work to do he came to his bed a tired but
relaxed man, happy to accept and return her love.

When it became known that Sir William was back in his manor,
men from the forest came to visit him. They were veterans of Stirling
and Falkirk. It heartened him that they greeted him with friendship,
demanding to know when he would again lead them against the
English.

In the middle of October he had travelled westward by little used
paths through the forests, across the Clyde to the manor of Sir John
Shaw, foster father to his little maid Margaret. It was a fine manor,
nestling into a hillside by the bank of a river overlooking the isles of
the west. It was isolated and the catastrophe which had overtaken
Scotland had hardly touched its rich fields. The storehouses and barns
were full of hay, oats and barley. Sides of meat hung in the smoke-
house and cheeses lay maturing on the shelves.

Sir John was not young and his wife, buxom and jolly, was past her child-bearing days. Little Margaret had been with them for a little over three months and already she ran to Sir John's wife for comfort, calling her foster mother and hiding her head in the lady's skirts. When the strange man, who they said was her father, tried to pick her up, she felt so shy. Wallace laughed and said he could wait until she came to him.

He spent a week with his daughter, sitting in the yard watching her at play and carrying her shoulder high to the river bank with Tom Shaw, the eight-year-old son of Sir John, running at his side. They fished for the brown trout in the peaty pools, and Margaret followed the young boy, who showed much fondness and indulgence towards his little companion, unusual in so young a lad.

The evening before he was due to leave, when the children and lady Shaw had gone to bed, Wallace sat drinking with the master. When Wallace first arrived Sir John, eager to hear news of the war, had tried to ask many questions, but Wallace gave him little encouragement and instead sunk deep into his own thoughts. Eventually Sir John had left him in peace, but on this evening Wallace wanted to talk. At first of general things, the manor work, Sir John's falcons, then Falkirk and eventually he came to the subject which troubled him deeply. "You must know, sir, that I and those I love will be marked by my enemies. My life will not be fit for so tender a lassie to bide in her father's house and it is my wish that if you are willing she remains here with you as your foster-child".

Sir John shifted uneasily in his chair, putting out his hand to stroke the hunting hound sitting at his side. Foster-father to the daughter of Scotland's Guardian had held a certain prestige, but now the situation had changed. It needed careful thought. Wallace continued, "Further I have noted that your lad has a certain fondness for the child. It is my hope that you will consider a betrothal between the pair. My daughter is heiress through her mother to the manor of Lamington and as my only child she will inherit Borthwick as well." Sir John smiled and said, "Forgive me, but you are still a very young man and may remarry and beget many sons." Wallace grinned, "Perhaps, but in the life I have chosen for myself a wife and sons would rest heavily on my heart."

Sir John sat thoughtfully for a while before saying, "The Wallace kindred are an honourable family and I held your father in much esteem. I'll consider what you have said and when you return we shall again talk about the matter." When on the following day Wallace left the Shaw household his heart was at ease for his cherished daughter's future.

His return journey took him first to his brother Malcolm at Elderslie, then to Lamington. He had not been near the manor since Marion's death and he braced himself for the ghosts that would visit him. Neil was there and some of the old folk, but the young men had gone. Yet in spite of all that had happened they greeted him with tears in their eyes. He could not bear to remain there for long. He gave instructions for the management of the estate and left for Borthwick, promising to return in the spring.

That winter Wallace remained at Borthwick, but if King Edward believed Wallace had given up the struggle he was sadly mistaken. As Wallace's estate was remote and difficult to find, he was free to spy on the English and their comings and goings in the eastern marches throughout that harsh winter. Agnes hoped that her William, no longer a great and important man, would stay quietly on his manor, but as spring heralded new life she realised that it had never been his intention to give up the fight.

When he returned home late one evening from where she knew not, she chided him, crying and fearful, that she would lose him. He listened patiently until she had said all that she had to say, then he said quietly, as if he were explaining something to a fractious child, "Aggie, so many have died who trusted me. I cannot forget them. If the English king would stay in his own kingdom perhaps I could rest, but at this very moment he is making more plans to return as soon as the weather improves. Do you want to live under his yoke when so many have given their lives for freedom?" Agnes looked at him through her tears. "I only know that I want you to be safe, William Wallace, and for our lives to continue as they are."

He grinned his old winning smile, "I'll try to stay with you until I'm a toothless old man, Aggie. Then you'll be sorry you ever set your eyes on me." She smiled. It was very hard to be angry with William Wallace for long.

Malcolm Wallace had visited his brother during the winter and on one of these visits he had brought news of Bishop Lamberton, who had returned to France in the autumn. "He continues his work for Scotland at the French Court, Will." As he spoke he took a bag from around his neck and gave it to his brother. "It contains gold for your work, Will, from the bishop." Wallace weighed the bag in his hand, "I can put this to good use," he said. "Take care, Will, there are English spies everywhere. No one is to be trusted."

One bitterly cold day Wallace rode into the yard. He had been hunting with his brother John and had brought down a magnificent twelve-point stag. The horses stamped on the frozen ground, steam rising from their flanks. Dusk was falling. In the light from the torches held by the serving men, the hoarfrost shone on the beards and mantles of the hunters. John Blair came out to meet them. He had not seen Wallace looking so jovial for months.

"You have a visitor, Will." Wallace raised an eyebrow. "Who's it this time? Many are seeking me out who paid me little attention before." "The warden of Selkirk Forest, none other, Will." Wallace looked startled. Sir Simon Fraser, staunch ally of the English king, seeking out Wallace, the king's enemy, was indeed something unusual. "Surely this is some trick?" John Blair shook his head. "Listen to him, Will. He comes without supporters".

The fire had been built up in the hall and the flames were casting their wild, dancing patterns on the timber walls and hanging tapestries. Sir Simon Fraser sat by the fire warming himself. He had brought two serving men with him and they had hung their shields and weapons by the door as the rules of hospitality demanded. As Wallace entered, Sir Simon stood up. "My lord, I am honoured," said Wallace.

Agnes appeared with tankards of mulled ale and, after Wallace had seated himself in the master's chair, she left the hall taking his damp cloak with her. Wallace started the conversation by saying, "You are very bold to enter the wolves' lair in this manner." Fraser shrugged his shoulders. "All know that you are a man of honour, Sir William. I have come to speak with you. You have my word that your presence here will not reach the ears of your enemies." Wallace laughed and those who knew him recognised the bitterness of his laugh. "I have learnt during the past few months not to trust the word of men who have much to lose." Simon Fraser reddened but said nothing. "You are here and for now we will eat and talk," continued Wallace. Agnes had appeared with her women carrying wine and meat.

Simon Fraser stayed with Wallace until noon of the following day and when he left they parted on friendly terms. Once again he promised he would not reveal Wallace's hideout and promised his aid for Scotland's cause. As he departed Wallace said to Blair, "There rides a confused man, John. He wants to do the right thing while keeping his feet in both camps." During the following weeks, Fraser sent messages and warnings to Wallace enabling him to move freely in the lands controlled by the English.

One morning towards the end of March Wallace sought out Agnes. At that time of the morning she could always be found at work in the bake house, wearing her wadmal dress, a kerchief wrapped around her head, her hair in one long plait and her arms covered in flour. As he entered she turned, stopped her kneading and smiled. Wallace seated himself on a barrel and they talked for a while about the new bull-calf born that night and about the ewes and their lambs, but Agnes knew he had not come to her to talk about such homely things. Usually she would have led him gently towards whatever troubled him, but today instinct told her to fear what he wanted to say, and so she was quiet. Finally rather irritably he said, "Agnes, now that the weather improves I must leave on campaign," he broke off a piece from a freshly baked loaf and began munching it waiting for her to make some protest, but after pausing briefly with her work she continued kneading and said nothing. Wallace took heart from this. At least she was not crying.

"I can't leave you here Aggie. It would be dangerous for you, but I have a small farmstead up by Glasgow. There you will be safe and it is no great distance from your sister." She turned and looked at him. Her eyes were full of brimming tears, but still she said nothing. He went to her and gave her a hug before leaving, pleased to have got away without a noisy scene – but left alone Agnes began to sob. Finally she wiped her tears away. What was the point of crying? She was a lucky woman to have the protection of such a man as William Wallace. There were few of her kind who had such good fortune. If she did not accept what he could give, perhaps she would lose him altogether and that she could not bear.

He escorted her himself as far as the hills by Lanark and then bid her farewell promising to come to her later in the year. With two of his serving men to protect her, she went to his farmstead a little to the north of Glasgow.

Wallace and his tough veterans of Falkirk camped in the wild country to the north-west of Dumfries. It touched him that they still had such faith in his leadership. He knew them all by name and their fellowship appeared extraordinary to any who saw them.

Robert the Bruce, Earl of Carrick, was now joint Guardian of Scotland with John Comyn. They met at Wallace's camp and together planned the campaign for the coming season. The English were to be harried and permitted no rest. Their messengers were to be intercepted and their supplies captured. Other earls and barons were preparing to do the same along the eastern seaboard of Scotland.

Throughout spring and early summer no official of King Edward was safe. The bailiffs of the district of Cunningham were seized and Wallace demanded ransom for their safe return. The monks of Sweetheart Abbey were affronted by Wallace's audacity when they awoke to find him and his men outside the abbey gates, demanding ransom for their safety. The English might have won at Falkirk, but they were to be in no doubt that the kingdom of Scots was still brave and free – and the war had not yet been won.

King Edward had arrived back in Carlisle from his victory at Falkirk in the autumn of 1298, consumed by the idea of reorganising his army and returning to subdue the Scots as quickly as possible. "Once you have the wolf by the tail, don't let go," he said to Edward, Prince of Wales. Almost immediately he began planning and sending dispatches to his earls with commands to prepare for a spring offensive. He gave endowments, lands and titles to Scottish estates to many of his followers from his recent Scottish campaign. "That'll encourage them to fight," he told the Bishop of Durham. He wrote to the Earl Marshall of England, "We must press forward upon our Scottish business against the enemies of England. Their disobedience and malice is against this realm. They wish to bend us to their will." The Earl Marshall, alone but for his wife, reread the dispatches then flung them irritably to the floor. "I believe he thinks if he says it enough times we'll all believe it."

In December sheriffs throughout England received orders from their king to send provisions to Berwick, which were to arrive not later than the first week of June. The Sheriff of Lincolnshire groaned when he received the royal command for wheat, oats and bran. His warehouses would be completely empty if the king continued making such demands each and every year.

As winter changed into a gentle English spring, Edward became uneasy about the news which he received from France. Scotland's envoys to King Phillip's court were busy seeking the French king's aid. Phillip, anxious to embarrass the king of England, loudly proclaimed his admiration for the constancy and valour of the subjects of his dear brother the king of Scots. They struggled to defend their land against injustice from a cruel English king and he, Phillip, was seriously thinking of ways of helping them.

"Your majesty, the French king will not go to war against you. Scotland can give France nothing," said Beck at a council meeting in April. "No doubt, but while I deal with their rebellion in the north he could try to extend his territories at my expense in the south," was Edward's sharp reply. He could have added, "For that is what I would do," but he was in a bad mood and said nothing.

"Lamberton is at the back of this. I would feel happier if he were under lock and key in one of my castles. See to it and cancel the invasion until we have more news of Phillip's intentions."

Beck's many spies had been busy during the early months of 1299. No Scot could belch in France without Edward knowing. A Scottish messenger had been captured attempting to cross from France. At that very moment he was being stretched on the rack at the Tower. He had been carrying letters to the Guardians and Wallace. No doubt he knew more, which he would certainly divulge before the day was out.

Two weeks after the capture of Scotland's messenger Edward sent urgent orders to the masters of ships in the ports of Rye and Winchelsea to search and capture the Bishop of St Andrews, Scottish clerics and nobles on their way home from the French Court. A reward of one hundred marks was offered. All summer they kept watch, but in spite of their vigilance and greed, Bishop Lamberton landed safely in his homeland and quickly went to Stobo, Bishop Wishart's estate. Awaiting him were Wallace and the Guardian Robert the Bruce, Earl of Carrick.

Wallace had been in and around Galloway and Dumfries since the spring but intended to spend the summer in Stirlingshire. The English garrisons were still very active there and he had a mind to clip their wings. Bishop Lamberton noted how friendly all the Wallace kinsmen were towards the Earl of Carrick, for Sir Malcolm and John Wallace were also present. That evening they talked about the bishop's work to gain help for Scotland's cause from Phillip of France. Towards the end of the evening, the bishop turned to Wallace, "I have done all that I can and it has bought us time, but I believe he may listen to someone he holds in high regard for his loyalty and valour. That man is you, William."

Wallace sat in silence for a few moments, then laughed, "Nay, my lord. I am powerless. Besides I am no diplomat," but the bishop continued, "Scotland does not need a diplomat, Will. King Phillip has seen any number of them. An honest man who understands our problems must persuade him. There is none more qualified than you." The Bruce, Wishart and others joined in the debate and eventually Wallace, rather irritably, said, "Many are loud with their opinions, yet few are prepared to act on them." His bitter comment brought the discussion to an abrupt halt and Wallace – who was normally so good-humoured – glared at each man in turn and then said, "I'll think carefully and give you my decision in the morning."

Wallace spent a restless night. He had tried – and indeed was still trying – to free his country by force of arms, but the English continued their relentless destruction of the kingdom. Perhaps diplomacy could succeed where warfare had failed. After all it was because of Edward's suspicion and distrust of the French king that he had not invaded Scotland in 1299.

When Wallace met the bishop the next morning, he said he would go to France for the sake of the realm. It was agreed he would leave towards the end of the campaigning season before the autumn weather brought in the gales. The decision to send Wallace on a diplomatic mission was to be kept secret for fear that the English king would hunt him at sea.

Wallace and his followers went to Stirling for the summer. The English were very busy collecting taxes and moving troops and provisions. Once Wallace arrived none were safe from his ambushes. On St Bartholomew's day the supplies for the garrison at Stirling disappeared. The garrison soldiers were already eating their horses, and with Wallace back in the area only God knew when they would get relief.

Early morning mist clung softly and caressingly to the land like the soft folds of a woman's shift around her naked body. The hull of the vessel could not be seen through the grey swirling vapour, but its mast and prow rose through to greet the late summer sun. Wallace and his companions had boarded under cover of darkness and were lying hidden from view by bales of fleece, hides and barrels of salted herring. As the outgoing tide lapped at the hull, trying to drag the ship from the safety of the land, the crew loosened the ropes which held her steady and sixteen oars pulled her gently away from her moorings.

A few fishing boats had put out from Arbroath harbour but they clung to the coast. If anyone had been watching, they would have seen that the crew of the merchantman rowed strongly away from the shoreline until they caught the offshore breeze, hoisted their sail and began to make rapid progress into the North Sea. Wallace kept low but when they were well out he went to the starboard side to watch his homeland disappear. Edward of Leitholm joined him but they said little to each other. There was a heavy swell and as Sir Edward had never been happy at sea, he quickly left Wallace's side, briefly visited the stern before retiring to the safety of the cargo hold, where he lay covered by a blanket and with his eyes tightly closed. Richard Fraser took Sir Edward's place at Wallace's side, watching the sea birds flying overhead, but as neither man knew one another well, few words passed between them. Fraser was a short-legged, portly man with an open and cheerful face, and Wallace thought that with time they would work well together.

The captain came to greet them, "We're heading eastwards across the North Sea, Sir William," he said. "Once we're out of sight of land we'll turn south. That way we may slip past the English."

Wallace continued watching the dim coastline. His mind was mulling over their quest and his own triumphs and failures. How many times had he dwelt on Falkirk? It was easy to blame Comyn and his horsemen, but it had been his decision to stand and fight instead of continuing to withdraw. It was the English archers who had defeated them and he had no answer to their range and accuracy.

In the confined space of the ship he had little to do but think and he turned his mind to more pleasant memories. Before leaving he had seen his little daughter Margaret. She was bonnie beyond words, happy and carefree. She had placed her small soft hand in his and together they had walked by the seashore collecting small shells. Wallace still had them for they had told him that silversmiths in France were very skilled, fashioning necklaces and other trinkets. It made his work easier knowing she was safe. He had visited Agnes and realised how important she had become to his life. Surely the Lord Jesus Christ, who had forgiven Mary Magdalene, would also forgive Agnes for her previous trade for she was a good and loyal soul, Wallace thought. He had had another barn built at the farmstead. Agnes had three goats for milk and cheese and for her comfort he had the farmhouse improved. She had cried and clung to him as he led his horse from the stable and stooping he kissed her goodbye. Before departing he promised he would return. He looked back once before the bend in the track blocked his view. She stood still as he had left her and he waved in reply to her raised hand.

Well, the lords of Scotland were rid of him now. Scotland was in their hands. He roused himself looking around at the craft and her crew, then he and Richard Fraser walked to the prow chatting about trivial things.

Agnes was indeed a loyal and loving servant of her dear lord William Wallace and though she had known many men before him, since she had come under his protection she had remained faithful to him. The farmstead was isolated but she had a serving man, a veteran of Dunbar, Stirling and Falkirk, where a wound had left his right arm wasted and John Clubfoot, who had followed the Guardian from Aberdeen Castle and of whom Wallace had grown fond. Glasgow was not so far away and on market days it was her delight to walk to see her sister who was married to a blacksmith in the town. They chatted and Agnes played with her sister's baby, talking to and cuddling the boy and wistfully imagining that he was her own child. Her sister had a large brood. All were healthy and well-formed and in the late autumn her second daughter Mary, a child of nine, went to live with her aunt at the farmstead to keep her company and to help with the work.

In such a place it could not be secret for long that the leman of Sir William Wallace lived close by. Short, landlord of the Ship Inn overlooking the harbour, knew about Agnes, but it was not until the second week of September that he heard of Wallace's journey from Arbroath and by that time it was too late for the Bishop of Durham to act. He sent a message to Short ordering him to keep vigil, watch Agnes, and inform him of any comings and goings.

Two years previously Short had acquired a wife. She was a comely young woman from Ayr whose father, knowing nothing of Short's reputation, thought his daughter fortunate to catch the eye of a prosperous landlord. Her happiness had been short-lived. Short was brutal and impatient because she was slow to give him a son. Now at last she was big with her first child and Short showed her a degree of respect unknown since the first days of their marriage. When he suggested she should make friends with the smith's wife, that the woman might give her support and advice when her time came, she thought perhaps she had misjudged her husband. It was through this friendship that Short learnt a great deal about Agnes and her household.

The bells of Tournai Cathedral rang the *Angelus* across the French countryside when Wallace and his companions rode through the north gate. They knew France well and were men of substance, allied to King John and Scotland's cause. Richard Fraser had managed the king's finances when he had first been elected to the Scottish throne, Edward of Leitholm had been the king's chief councillor while Hugh Fotheringhay, the oldest among them, had been the Queen Mother's attorney for many years. To a man they were their lord's loyal servants.

In an antechamber of the abbot's palace they awaited an audience. Refreshment of wine and honey cakes were served. "Well, if the weather holds fine we'll be at Cambrai within two days," said Edward Leitholm. Hugh Fotheringhay groaned and carefully seated himself, pulling the cushions behind his back. "You're pushing an old man too hard, Leitholm," he said. Wallace poured a beaker of wine which he passed to Sir Hugh. The elderly knight was good-natured, but his face was tired and his body stiff from the long ride through the flat, fen country and France. He accepted the wine gratefully.

Wallace was to remain at Tournai while the other knights continued to see King John who now lived under the protection of Phillip of France at Malmasion near Cambrai. It was still unclear if the king would receive Wallace because of his fear of English spies. The following morning the knights left, but Hugh Fotheringhay needed to rest and stayed behind with Wallace. Wallace was restless and walked into the prosperous town. The market offered fine woollen cloth and leather goods and the people were well fed and noisy. The women washing in the market square watched the tall and handsome stranger, laughing and nudging one another, but Wallace was engrossed in his own thoughts and ignored them.

On the east side of the square was a wine merchant's booth. There were benches outside and upturned barrels served as tables. Men sat drinking in the warm autumn sunshine watching a troop of jugglers. Wallace wandered over and sat for a while, drinking some of the ruby wine, but his mind drifted back to his visit to Berwick with Marion. Berwick had been like this French town, exciting and busy. In his mind's eye he saw Isabella's happy face as she prattled to Marion about her babes. Wallace arose and walked hurriedly back to the cloister of the abbey. He wandered around the abbey herb garden. The perfume in the warm sunshine calmed him and he chatted to a lay brother about the plants before he walked back to his lodging.

A few days later Richard Fraser returned, accompanied by a servant of the king and two men-at-arms. "The king will not receive you at his residence," he told Wallace, "but he will hunt in the forest south of Tournai in two days and will come to the cathedral to receive mass, then he will see you."

On a blustery day Wallace waited in an antechamber to be called before his king, John Balliol, King of Scots: the man for whom he had risked so much and so many had been sacrificed and lost. The heavy oak door opened and Hugh Fotheringay nodded. Wallace entered and knelt before his monarch.

"You must rise, Sir William, for we have heard how much Scotland and her king owes to our champion." Wallace coloured slightly as he stood. John Balliol was a small man with receding sandy-coloured hair. He had a kindly look and smiled as he held out his jewelled hand for his subject to kiss. "We have read the letter from our servant, the Bishop of St Andrews. There is – we fear – little that we can do for King Edward's spies constantly watch us, but we will write an introduction for you to King Phillip. Your fame is known even here and curiosity, if no other reason, will gain you access to him. The French king has many disputes with the king of England. Assist him with these as you have helped us and he will be in your debt."

Afterwards, Wallace sat and thought about the audience with his king. It had been so short. The king did not question him about Scotland, nor did he seek Wallace's opinions as if he had washed his hands of his troublesome kingdom and no longer cared that it was leaderless and prey to wolves. Instead the king had spoken about the hunt that he had so recently enjoyed. Then there was a long and embarrassing silence. King John looked angrily at the tall warrior standing in front of him. Then, casting his eyes to the floor, he dismissed William Wallace. Of course, his advisors would have kept the king informed of Scotland's fortunes, but Wallace could have told him so much more, straight from the heart, if only Balliol had shown an interest.

Wallace arrived in Paris, accompanied by Richard Fraser, with the letter of introduction from his king in his pouch. The hustle and bustle of the French capital fascinated him as they rode towards the royal castle. Wallace was excited. He had high hopes for his interview with Phillip of France. They were shown into an anteroom. Wallace was prowling around the small room, looking at the hunting scenes on the wall hangings. Fraser, used to such waiting, stretched out on a bench and dozed, as he was weary after the long ride. Eventually he drowsily said, "For God's sake, sit down man. Take the weight off your feet. You can be sure that they'll keep us waiting."

Wallace grunted but eventually sat down. Fraser was right. It was well past noon before the door opened and a court official entered. The French, which Wallace had learnt as a schoolboy had returned to him, but the courtier spoke in clear, precise Latin. Wallace was also conversant with that language. Courteously he asked after their health, comfort and their journey. Fraser, happy to abide by these formalities, accepted hospitality for himself and Wallace, trying hard to ignore Wallace's scowling face. When they were alone Wallace demanded, "Why didn't you tell him of our reasons for coming." "He knows, man. You must be patient. They have their ways. Take it slowly and enjoy yourself. French food is magnificent – and so are their women!"

By evening Wallace agreed that this was true. The long, carved tables groaned with the weight of roast fowl, swan, venison, boar, pies, fruits and many other dishes with which he was not familiar. He did not see the king and enquired of his neighbour where Phillip was. He was told that his majesty had left to hunt near Pierrepont. Wallace was angry for he had been told that the king would not leave his capital for another week. He asked Fraser if it was true. With his face flushed with wine and good food, Fraser laughed, "Will, I told you to enjoy yourself. Diplomacy takes time. We'll have to wait and you must be patient."

During the weeks leading up to Christmas, Wallace whiled away the days perfecting his French, teaching the lads who lived around the castle to use the bow and in the evenings, as Fraser had said, the French women were very pretty. During the last week of Advent, the French king returned to court and Wallace went to Fraser, anxious that he might conclude his mission. "Will, be patient. He'll not grant you an audience to talk of such matters until after twelfth night. Enjoy yourself."

On the first day before the celebrations of Christ's birth, Wallace caught his first sight of King Phillip of France as he walked around the tables while they feasted in the vaulted hall. He greeted each wishing them God's peace and when he came to Wallace he extended his hand to be kissed, "We have heard much of you, sir. It is our wish that we shall speak together when Christmas comes to an end." That promise had to satisfy Wallace for the time being and he settled more comfortably to the enjoyment of the festival.

On Christmas morning he attended mass at Notre Dame Cathedral. There he gazed at the great dome, painted ceilings, and the carved images of saints and angels looking down. He marvelled, not for the first time since his arrival in France, that a stranger could enter God's House and feel at home understanding the Mass. Church and Latin unified all. Around him stood the courtiers and citizens of Paris, celebrating Christmas like men and women throughout Christendom. His mind wandered back to his days in the monastic school at Dundee. How different his life would have been if he had entered the church. Immediately after Falkirk, in the depths of black despair, he had thought that the church might offer sanctuary from his torment, but he had taken up the challenge as Scotland's champion and there could be no turning back. The congregation fell to their knees as the chalice was raised at the altar and Wallace said a prayer for the souls of those he had loved: Marion, his parents and friends, Graham, John Stewart – and all who had died for Scotland.

Christmas was also a time to celebrate and indulge the senses with boisterous dancing, singing and the ladies of court who were very wanton. Once he overcame his shyness he delighted in the company of pretty women and spent many pleasant nights with one or another, but in the grey dawn one morning was shocked when a dark-haired young woman brazenly told him that of all men, including her lord husband, William Wallace had been the best. A married woman! What depths of depravity had his inactivity brought him to lay with another man's wife. By the end of the Christmas festival he was pleased that the self-indulgent frolics at court were coming to an end.

Towards the end of January Wallace was finally ushered into the king's private chambers. If he had been told that it would take so long to gain an audience with the French king, he would not have believed it, but he fell humbly to his knees as he would have done for his own liege lord, King John. The act of submission from so famous a warrior seemed to please the French monarch who ordered his steward to bring a chair for Sir William close to the fire. Wallace told him of Scotland's troubles, of the English army with their deadly archers and the jealousy and treachery of Scotland's lords. When he reflected later he wondered whether he was lacking in caution, but Phillip already seemed to know everything anyway. The wine, heat from the fire and Phillip's apparent interest had lowered Wallace's guard.

He came to the end of his story and the king said, "We wish that we had among our own a champion to whom we could entrust our affairs, Sir William." "I fear, your majesty, that I have been too loose with my tongue," said Wallace. "A king rarely hears the truth and there are times when the truth should be told. We will do what we can to move your mission forward, but since you have been honest with us we must tell you this. In matters of state a king cannot always do what is his wish, but what is expedient. It is my belief that for as long as Edward lives he will not give up his claim on your homeland. All that you can do is to divert his attention to more pressing matters. Meanwhile stay here with us. King Edward knows that you are at my court and he watches carefully what I do. Perhaps I can find you work which will distract the English king. It is all I can offer you at the moment." "Thank you, sire. While I am in your kingdom I shall do my best to serve you honestly."

Wallace had come from Scotland with few belongings: they fitted into a small pouch strapped behind his saddle. He wore his chain mail when travelling and a short brown surcoat. At court he was conspicuous for his simple dress and bore the brunt of many jokes. A few days after his meeting with King Phillip, a young lad of about fourteen came to the small garret room that had been allocated to him. The boy was short for his age with a pale face and dark curly hair. In his arms he carried some clothing. "Sir, I have been sent by his majesty to be your page and to give you this gift."

Wallace was taken aback. To have a page he found slightly amusing, but costly presents made him feel uneasy, although he knew that many accepted gifts for favours. There was a long blue kirtle, reaching to the ankles, with side slits and elaborately embroidered across the breast and around the hems and a fine pair of red embossed leather boots with a matching belt. These were truly gifts fit for a noble lord. "Well, lad, they're fine gifts. I suppose gifts from a king cannot be returned can they?" "No sir," the pale face looked shocked. "And you, what do they call you?" "Guillaume Lebeck, I am called, sir." Wallace laughed, "Well, we can't both be called William boy and I've been William longer than you have. We'll call you Curly."

The boy tried to say the unaccustomed word 'C-er-lee' which Wallace had named him. "You'll get used to it, meanwhile make yourself useful by finding faggots for the fire." The boy was excellent at foraging. The pile of logs for the fire never appeared to dwindle, however large the fire, there was always a tallow candle in the wall niche, and flagons of freshly drawn water and wine ready for his lord.

One crisp February evening when Wallace had returned after a day's hunting in the king's company in the forests south of Paris, he found the boy had acquired a wooden tub of sufficient size for a man to sit in with his knees bent. It was half-filled with hot water standing near the fire. "My lord, it is so cold that your cloak is stiff with frost and stands by itself."

Wallace had seen Frenchmen bathing, had smelt the costly, sweet-smelling oils, which they rubbed on themselves afterwards and had not been impressed. But he was cold and wet and the boy had worked so hard carrying the hot water up the many stairs that he could not disappoint him. So he climbed into the warm water and afterwards dressed himself in the long blue kirtle, red boots and belt before going to the great hall for his evening meal.

As the winter drew to a close the court began to prepare itself to flee into the countryside, away from the smells and dirt of a city in summer. Wallace fretful at the inactivity and lack of progress for his cause began to think about returning to Scotland. The Holy Father in Rome had written to Edward of England ordering him to quit Scotland and his claims on Scotland, but as far as Wallace knew Edward had not yet received that letter. Scotland needed Phillip to act with more determination against the English and this it seemed he could not bring himself to do. Recently King Edward had married Phillip's sister and as brothers-in-law they tried to ease the tensions between their two kingdoms. Yet still they argued over Gascony and Guienne and King Edward had sent his forces to attack Bordeaux and the coastal area of western France that he claimed for England.

On a blustery day in March, Wallace was commanded to attend his majesty in his private chambers for an audience. Phillip spoke of hunting, his falcons, his favourite deer-hound bitch that had just whelped before coming to the true reason for their meeting. "We see that you tire of life at court, Sir William." "I have affairs close to my heart, which are still unresolved, sire. Soon the English king will again invade and lay waste my homeland while I fill my belly at your table and lie with your women." "You are very blunt, sir. May we suggest a small diversion which will give concern to the Edward when he hears of it. You know that England and France have disagreed over the lordship of Guienne for some years. We have many Scottish men fighting for France. Lead them. Secure that territory for France and I shall give you my support for Scotland in return."

After Wallace had left, Phillip said to his steward, "There goes an honest fellow, but his honesty will bring him down. Give him whatever help he needs in his task." Then he dismissed Wallace from his mind.

Wallace began his preparations immediately, in secret, for there were many English spies at court. Curly helped running messages and arranging meetings. His master was in a hurry to muster his forces, and the king's warrant opened doors to equipment and stores even in the dead of night.

That year Easter came early and on the day before Good Friday, Curly came running excitedly to Wallace who was in the smithy, a huge, vaulted building some distance from other dwellings because of the noise. Here the king's master smiths and their apprentices worked. The atmosphere was hot and smoky from the many forges. It was still cold outside, but the men worked with bare chests, perspiration on their foreheads and shoulders. The clatter and banging of iron on iron made speech in a normal voice impossible. Wallace had ordered a new chain mail tunic and was watching as the final links were being attached when a breathless Curly appeared. "Sir, you have visitors who have come from your own land. One of them is your brother." "This is good news, lad. Watch for me and when it is ready bring it to my quarters." Wallace dashed off to greet his guests.

John Wallace, John Blair and Robert Boyd were waiting in his small chamber. They carried with them many letters and greetings. One letter was from Bishop Lamberton, imploring Wallace to continue with his efforts to please King Phillip and gain time for Scotland. Finally he wrote, 'if Scottish claims cannot be successfully promoted in France, take yourself to the Holy Father in Rome for there is none other in Christendom whom Edward of England will heed'. Letters saying much the same came from Bishop Wishart, the High Steward and the Guardian, Robert the Bruce, Earl of Carrick. Lamberton also sent some gold for his use in Scotland's cause.

That night they drank and talked late into the night. In the morning, after he had taken Communion, Wallace walked with his brother. They were sheltered from the March wind, their backs resting against a stout, lichen-covered wall. They were warm in the sunshine. A quiver of arrow shafts lay beside them which they were busy feathering. John laughed when he saw what his brother was doing. "Will, why not get freshly made arrows from the fletchers? You have better things to do." Wallace smiled and asked him if he remembered their father who had always warned them against relying too much on other men. Besides he enjoyed doing such work. They sat together, fixing feathers to shafts, and Wallace listened to his brother telling of the intrigues and jealousies at home.

"Comyn and his men picked a quarrel with brother Malcolm at a meeting of the Council. John Comyn said that you ran away and left Scotland to the mercy of the English. He demanded that the Guardians confiscate your lands and goods. There were many that spoke for you, but such an argument broke out that knives were drawn. Bruce said that you had gone at his command and he was very angry with Comyn." "I see that nothing changes at home," replied Wallace.

They finished the full quiver and Wallace took his bow, placed one of the new arrows against the taut bowstring and aimed it at a gnarled yew tree in a far corner. The arrow flew straight to its target. "Not bad, but I wish we had the bows the English used at Falkirk."

They could hear the bells of Chartres Cathedral ringing *Angelus* long before the town came into view. The party of foreign knights had not passed through the countryside unnoticed.

So large a body of mounted men caused a commotion as they passed, but the people were busy with the spring sowing and had no time to question what was a common sight at that time of the year.

Wallace mounted on a fine chestnut destierer, a gift from the French king, led the party. Beside him was Curly, proud to be out on campaign. John Wallace held Scotland's banner, while John Blair rode in their midst as their chaplain.

Early the following day Wallace visited the cathedral to receive the sacrament. The cathedral of the assumption of Our Lady was magnificent and before entering the iron-bound door he looked up at the window shaped like a rose, with twin spires on either side rising towards heaven. "Vene creatus spiritus," the monks chanted their devotions and their voices rose to the vaulted roof. Wallace stood listening before falling to his knees. Later he walked around looking at the brightly stained windows showing pictures of the merchant guilds in Chartres: blacksmiths, butchers, wheelwrights and farriers shoeing horses. "Wonderful," he murmured as he gazed at the window depicting the tree of life. It would be easy to spend all day feasting his eyes on the stories and scenes depicted in the cathedral windows, but he had work to do. God willing, one day he would allow himself the luxury of a pilgrimage to this place.

As each new dawn awoke the French countryside was bathed with spring garlands. Riding south-west, they were joined by many Scottish knights ready to accept King Phillip's gold and fight against the English. At Tours Sir William Vieuxpont, with a large company of men-at-arms, joined them so that Wallace's force numbered nine hundred men equipped with wagons, pack beasts, provisions and arms. They camped south of Tours. The English were at Chinon only ten miles away. They prepared themselves for battle and Wallace sent out his scouts.

Young Curly had begged to be allowed to spy out the land. "Sir, they will ignore me. I look what I am: a Breton of little consequence." Wallace laughed, "Maybe you did once lad, but now you swagger and are too fat and bright-eyed for a lad from the countryside." "Nay, master, I will appear to them as a peasant, have no fear." So persistent was he that Wallace gave in. It was true that a young lad would be less noticeable than a grown man.

There had been spring showers throughout the day. Pathways were muddy with many large puddles and streams, swollen by rain, flooded pastures and meadows. Towards evening it promised to be a clear night with the sky strewn with stars and a full moon. Curly had already travelled part of the route earlier in the day on his pony, but in the evening he left on foot and did not return until late the following afternoon. They had been worried that the English had caught him.

The boy was tired, hungry and excited, eager to prove himself to Wallace and the other men. To Wallace's questions he replied, "The English had the drawbridge lowered. There are many stalls and booths outside along by the moat with people coming and going. I followed some women who took cheeses for sale. That way I was not noticed. The castle is strong, built of stone, and on the battlements I saw cauldrons for oil and pitch." As he spoke he drew the outline of the castle in the dirt at his feet. "The guards looked cheerful and leaned against the walls so I do not think they have heard of our presence." "Don't be fooled by a happy countenance, lad."

While the boy refreshed himself, Wallace held council with Vieuxpont, his brother and other leading knights. "When the boy left Chinon they had not had news of us, but we cannot hope to have the best of them for long. We should strike now. The moon is high and with Curly to guide us we can attack just before dawn when the guards will be sleepy."

Richard Fraser was a cautious man and preferred to delay the assault until they were sure of the numbers of fighting men who opposed them. Eventually, however, he saw it Wallace's way and they agreed that a large force would engage the enemy just before dawn while the remaining men would travel with the slow-moving baggage wagons and pack animals.

Wallace could see the dark outline of Chinon Chateau. Torches spluttered at the entrance and two guards sheltered from the chill breeze. The drawbridge was raised and the main gate firmly shut. The small side door, however, was open and there was no portcullis that he could see. He sat sheltered by an oak, patiently watching the scene. Curly was with him but the rest of his force remained at some distance for fear of noise and disturbance.

He could smell wood smoke. Somebody was astir. It was most likely one of the peasants in the small community nestling by the river bank. He made up his mind, grunted a command to Curly, left the boy to watch and returned to his waiting men.

He divided his force. One hundred were to follow Sir William Vieuxpont, including the best archers, and make their way to the rear of the castle. When Wallace began the attack they were to cause as much disturbance as they could.

Wallace, with fifty hand-picked men, left on foot. Sheltered by alder trees at the bend of the river, he waited quietly. Here and there the birds were beginning to stir. An otter, frightened by the men, slid from the river bank into the water. Ducks nesting in the tall reeds became alarmed by the intrusion and a disturbed drake flew low along the river, quacking irritably to draw the men away from his nesting mate, but the men remained silent and still, and soon all was quiet again.

The grinding and clanging of chains proceeded the lowering of the drawbridge. The main gate opened and three horsemen trotted noisily across calling out farewells to the guards. They took the track leading away from the waiting Scots. Wallace gave the signal to advance by raising his arm. They moved forward to the open ground with peasant cottages to their left and the still-lowered drawbridge beckoning them to charge straight ahead.

Wallace turned to his brother, "Mark the guard on the left, John. Can you take him with a single arrow?" "Aye, he looks an idle fellow." "I'll take the other before they have time to shut the gates." He could see through into the courtyard where the English were beginning to stir.

The two guards wandered inside and returned carrying a small brazier. They stood enjoying its warmth as the Scots once again began to move forward. John Wallace took careful aim. It was not an easy shot. The man fell across the brazier knocking it over and spilling the bright charcoal across the cobbles. A guard sitting at the head of the steps leading on to the battlements sprang up, running to the wall, shouting a warning as he went, but the leading Scots were already on the drawbridge. "Merciful Mother," murmured the guard crossing himself. Drawing his sword he clattered down the steps to challenge the invaders. John Wallace's second arrow caught him in the throat. It protruded to the other side and the guard fell headlong.

Sir William Vieuxpont heard the shouts, gave the command and his burning arrows lit up the morning sky, falling onto the damp thatch of the dwellings, sizzling and spitting with the breeze fanning the flames. Adding to the noise of arrows, flames and fighting men, was the sound of the main force as it rode at full gallop towards the castle. They also heard the shouts and screams of the peasants seeking shelter where they could, and the clanging of the chapel bell which someone had began to toll. Everywhere there was panic and confusion.

The English garrison fought hard and bravely but when they recognised the Scottish voices and saw the cross of St Andrew on their shields they fought even harder. The enmity between the two kingdoms was such that they could not hope for quarter. The defenders numbered only two hundred and as the Scots poured through the gates the English were quickly overwhelmed but the mopping up took some time. By midmorning the survivors stood in the courtyard, five women, four children, two babes in arms and fifteen men, one who was seriously wounded.

Wallace looked at the group. It had never been his way to make war on women and children but he ordered that the men should be hanged. "The women may take what they can carry." There was a commotion among the prisoners. The men were shouting oaths and the most foul language. The women were screaming and the children crying loudly. Wallace impatiently turned his back on the scene and strode off.

The peasants from the settlement were not French. They were English settlers promised land by their lord. They were not fighting men and had taken to the forest when the Scots attacked. Wallace ordered their homes burnt and what livestock they could not take with them was slaughtered.

He stood on the battlement in the evening sunshine watching the smoke from the burnt village drifting lazily upwards. His brother carrying two beakers of red wine joined him. They drank together toasting the sun as it dipped behind the trees.

Wallace held Chinon Chateau, putting it into good order, until the middle of the following month, when a force of French knights and men at arms arrived to claim it for Phillip of France.

Wallace and his men rode south-west to Poitiers and to Angoulême. The countryside was changing. The brown cattle of the northern provinces were replaced by herds of inquisitive nibbling goats herded by brown-legged boys. The hillsides were closely planted with green vines. Sunny valleys were humming with lazy bees and the air was heavy with the perfume of herbs and flowers. "I wish I was a lazy fellow, John, in such a place as this." Wallace waved his hand at the languid scene before them and took a deep breath of the scented air.

The following week they saw for the first time the Gironde sparkling in the sunshine. In the distance were the ramparts of Bordeaux Chateau and the city walls with King Phillip's besieging army camped around it.

The Scottish brigade was ordered to camp on the western flank where the ground sloped downwards to the river. Its banks were filthy with much evil-smelling rubbish and the hulls of burnt-out boats. The bloated body of a dead donkey floated near the shore and in contrast to the sweet-smelling countryside the atmosphere was foul and noisy with the angry buzzing of flies which fed on the animal dung, human excrement and other waste. It was impossible to walk without stepping on maggot-infested rubbish.

Wallace flew into a rage when he viewed their station. Without dismounting he returned to the tent of the French commander. Sir Raoul de Gaucourt sat in the shade of a walnut tree with a flagon of wine at his side. When the angry Scot arrived, raising dust from his horse's hooves, Gaucourt rose to his feet, and shouted, "Take care you fool." Irritably he began to brush the dust from his clothes. Wallace made no apology.

"Are you trying to save the English their arrows, sir, for sure we will die of disease and pestilence if we remain in the dung heap to which you have sent us." Sir Raoul glared at the tall, impressive Scot. Never a man of easy temper but the heat and inactivity of the siege had put him into a particularly evil mood. "If you think your success at Chinon gives you special favours you're mistaken. The west is where I have need of you. Do you Scots want silken sheets and bouquets of flowers before you're capable of fighting?" He turned and went into his tent with his page scurrying behind him.

Wallace rode angrily back to his men. This was a bad start, but there was little point arguing with such a man. As he rode he noted the disorderly tents and the lazy, inactive men lying in the shade in the French camp. Nowhere could he see them training. On his return the Scottish brigade were as he had left them. Some were still astride their mounts ready to move on.

"It seems we have no choice but to remain here." He turned to his brother and other captains, "Get the men to make rakes and clear this mess. Start bonfires and burn all rubbish. And don't forget the river. Clear all that can be cleared and search for another source of water. No man should drink from this," he indicated the river.

Laying siege had never been an aspect of war that appealed to Wallace and as May gave way to June the heat and inactivity caused arguments and brawls among his men. There was much sickness among both French and Scots. Regularly a herald called upon the English garrison to surrender but they stubbornly refused: although it was plain that their condition would become serious as the summer progressed. At councils of war there were as many views on how the siege should be conducted as there were captains present. De Gaucourt was of the opinion they should wait and starve the English into submission.

Towards the end of June the Scots were ordered to take their turn guarding the sea approaches. If the English king tried to break the siege and send a large force, it would surely come from the seaward side. Wallace rode to their outposts whenever possible, filling his lungs with the fresh sea air. The marshes had been rich with waterfowl, but these had already been taken and eaten. Eels and fresh- and salt-water fish were plentiful and their comrades in the besieging force welcomed the steady trickle of food from the coast. Yet the marshes were treacherous and unhealthy. Black clouds of insects rose from the water, irritating both men and beasts and many men caught fever. The reed beds also gave cover to the enemy who slipped out from Bordeaux each night to harass the besieging army.

Wallace arrived back late one afternoon. John Blair sat writing on a piece of parchment sheltered from English arrows by a rocky outcrop. "Are you scribbling again, John?" Ever since their arrival in France Blair had spent his spare moments writing. He smiled and continuing his task said, "All that is done to serve Scotland should be known by those yet unborn, Will. You know better than any what little use I am with a sword but what talents I have I will put to good use." As he finished speaking there was a whirr from an arrow and Wallace's horse sidestepped nervously kicking up dust and grit as a bolt from an English crossbow landed close by. Wallace calmed the animal looking intently at the battlements. "I see our English friend is on duty again," said Blair. "I fear he will not rest until he sends you to meet our maker, Will."

"Aye, I see him now." The soldier had come from behind the shelter of a buttress with his tell-tale yellow scarf tied around his neck. When he saw Wallace looking in his direction he made a crude sign to him. Wallace waved back. "I have marked you, my friend," he said to himself.

In an area controlled by the French there was a particularly large outcrop of rocks giving protection from prying eyes on the walls. There the French had begun to dig a tunnel down and around the rocks towards the city walls. The digging had been going on for some time. They had endured heat, earth falls, loss of life and by July, with barely concealed excitement, they had reached the city walls. Siege engines had also arrived and the languid atmosphere in the besieging army changed.

The English lined the battlements watching the activity around the siege engines but the main gates remained firmly closed. No herald came seeking terms. The French on their part saw no reason why they should talk to the enemy. Let them rot. They busied themselves erecting their massive engines that had been dragged to the site in many pieces. As '*les loups de guerre*' were assembled, the English kept a steady flow of arrows aimed at the French carpenters, so that they were forced to build a hinged screen to protect the men at work. Wallace stood near an engine one morning, watching progress. An apprentice, a lad of some fifteen summers, was fetching a wooden plank for his master. Wallace heard the flight of the bolt then the scream from the boy. There was no hope for him. It had entered on the lad's right side just below the ribs. The barbed arrowhead was protruding through to his left side. He whimpered in a growing pool of his own blood and his frightened eyes were begging for help. Wallace stooped and as an act of compassion slit his throat. "Haste thee to His kingdom, lad," and they all made the sign of the cross. Then Wallace searched the battlements for the English archer and recognized him by the yellow kerchief tied round his neck.

Wallace returned to '*les loups de guerre*', armed with bow and quiver full of arrows. Using his dirk he carefully cut a hole in the screen sufficient to see and aim through. The French carpenters working around said little. They knew who Wallace was and what he had been, and although he had not as yet shown himself to be any different from their own knights, his own men held him in high regard and he had a bearing that demanded respect.

At about midday the master carpenter whose lad had been killed wandered over to Wallace. "The Englishman with the yellow scarf has been here each morning, sir. He has claimed four good men and my boy. You would do us a kindness to despatch him." Wallace sat quietly watching the wall opposite, "Aye, he has a good eye and a steady hand. Better he uses his skills in another world."

The archer with the yellow scarf swaggered along the battlements looking for another victim. He was a Lancastrian, a veteran of Berwick, Dunbar and Stirling Bridge, who had developed a dislike of all Scots. He had been trying to kill the big Scotsman for days and this morning had had another near miss. He wandered back to watch the French carpenters. Perhaps another Frenchman would risk leaving cover. Patiently he waited by a buttress which was his favourite spot. He felt lucky today. His sergeant stood below, but said nothing. Bartram of Clitheroe was his best marksman and it was rare for him to waste a bolt. The sun was high. It was hot and the citizens of Bordeaux had retreated into the shade. Even the stray dogs had sought the shadows.

The French below the city walls were quiet. The banging, clatter and sounds of French voices from behind the screen had decreased as one by one the carpenters stopped work to seek shade and a bite of food. Bartram looked up at the sky. The buzzards usually gliding above the besieging army had flown for comfort to the nearest trees.

He shifted his position slightly, narrowed his eyes and scanned the ground. It was a waste of time. He would go and sleep and return later. As he turned the arrow caught his upper left arm. He staggered a few steps under its force and falling missed a further arrow which flew harmlessly above him. Gritting his teeth he plucked out the arrow and slowly and carefully raised himself to look down from the wall. The big Scotsman leant against the screen with bow in his hand. When he saw the English archer he raised his hand.

That evening captains and knights met in de Gaucourt's pavilion. The tunnellers reported that they were nearly through and were busy putting in extra supports to roof and walls. "We should make the decision now to go in before the English discover the tunnel." One of the French captains was trying desperately to prompt de Gaucourt into action.

"Illness increases among the men and the English hope that if they hang on till autumn we'll be driven away by sickness." "Do we lack heart and stamina for a fight?" said another. Wallace looked at the French speaker, a knight he knew and liked from the region near Troyes. "I agree. It is time for us to break this siege," said Wallace

The Scots sat together, John Wallace, Vieuxport, Richard Fraser and Wallace. At previous meetings their opinions had been ignored. When they had made suggestions de Gaucourt, without looking at them would say, "Hardly suitable here, I fear," and then pass briskly on to the next subject.

De Gaucourt looked down at his hands, his lips in a tight line, but Wallace said, "Sir, when we arrived I had nine hundred men, now we are just under eight hundred of whom twenty-nine died at the hands of the English, the rest from fever and water of the bowels. If we die we want to take the English with us." Still de Gaucourt did not look at the speaker and Wallace continued, "We must attack combining the tunnel and 'les loups de guerre' with an open assault. There were murmurs of agreement from his listeners. "When the moon comes to the end of her phase we should attack the barbican on the northern side with fire, 'les loups de guerre' and anything else we can throw at them. When the sky is at its darkest and we have weakened their defences, troops can go through the tunnel at night, while we begin a frontal attack." There was a chorus of agreement, but de Gaucourt looked angry and began to search for excuses finally saying, "Let me think and we will discuss this matter again tomorrow."

Wallace left walking with the knight from Troyes, but before parting from him Wallace said, "I will not watch my men dying daily from the bloody flux my friend. If de Gaucourt will not fight when there is the opportunity, the Scottish brigade will return to Paris." Later they repeated his words to de Gaucourt as Wallace knew they would. The French commander would have been pleased to be rid of the big, arrogant Scot, but Wallace was King Phillip's favourite and might spread malicious tales. He could not afford to have his honour smeared by Wallace. If the attack failed he would make sure Phillip would know whom to blame and he would make Wallace and his Scots lead the advance once the walls had been breached.

July, hot by day and night, was difficult for both attackers and defenders alike. The English sent raiding parties out from time to time. Their usual targets were the siege engines. The guards were doubled around 'les loups', the fighting was bloody but the engines remained intact and the day arrived when they were ready to begin their deadly game with the walls of the city. De Gaucourt, still anxious to avoid the consequences of an all-out attack, sent an herald to the gates demanding their surrender, but the burgesses and garrison commander refused, hoping the promised relief might yet arrive.

On the eve of the attack, Wallace sat by himself on a large rock at some distance from his men watching the river. He had received absolution and as was his way he sought a few moments of solitude. It was dark and the stars looked so close he felt he could pluck them from the sky. They would have made a necklace fit for his daughter's swan-like neck. His meditations were marred by the heavy thuds and sounds of falling masonry as the siege engines continued their destructive work. The townsfolk tried to rebuild the damage between salvoes, but their efforts showed more courage and determination than success. He looked back towards the city. Fires had been started by the French and as fast as the English put one out, more burning arrows streaked across the night sky. He found himself feeling pity for the town's people. War was a terrible master. His mind wandered back to his campaign in England after the battle of Stirling. His forces had been difficult to control, particularly the men of Galloway. He had never liked unnecessary cruelty nor the pillage of churches. Then he remembered the day of his wedding with Marion riding beside him. The manor of Lamington was lying peacefully beside the river. "Oh God, just six short years ago." He stirred and made his way back towards his pavilion. Better not to think too deeply before a battle. Memories slowed a man and clouded his judgement.

John Blair sat at his small desk, writing by the light of a tallow lamp. "Come John, will you not rest? God willing, tomorrow there will be much which you can chronicle."

Young Curly offered his master a drink of wine, but Wallace waved it aside and lay down fully clothed with his boots still laced and with Vengeance drawn beside him. He fell asleep almost immediately. John Blair took a light cover and laid it over his friend to prevent the damp river air giving him an ague. Outside another missile smashed into the city wall.

Long before the dawn light had touched the eastern sky Wallace had quietly mustered the Scots opposite the breech in the wall. Blair begged him not to lead the attack, "For certain there will be many casualties," he said, but Wallace laughed and shrugged, "John, how can I ask them to do something from which I shrink myself?" In the gloom he crouched at the front of his men, Vengeance, the dragon slayer drawn, waiting for the signal that the tunnellers were in position. There were few among the waiting French in the rearguard who envied the Scots.

Wallace signalled to his brother on his right and Richard Fraser to his left to move forward under the cover of stones which continued hurtling towards the walls. The ground sloped gently upwards and there they waited, each man huddled in his own thoughts. The earth was littered with fragments from the broken wall and the yawning gap was filled with rubble. Here and there could be seen a burning torch bobbing about with a blurred vision of its owner. Otherwise the English defenders could not be seen. Wallace rightly guessed that they were awaiting the imminent attack. Another boulder crashed into the city. Screams and cries announced casualties followed by silence. He could not hear the French reloading. It was time. Wallace jumped to his feet and with claymore held high, he ran towards the opening.

Bartram of Clitheroe positioned himself on a piece of broken buttress high enough to have a good view of the sloping ground in front of the city and the narrow alleys within. His sharp eyes caught the first shadowy movements as the Scots made their final dash, hastily preparing the bolt in his own crossbow he called a warning to others. The attackers were now easily heard by the noise of their running feet on the stony ground and the clatter of their weapons. Silence was no longer necessary and a great roar arose from seven hundred throats – 'SCOTLAND'. The rosy glow of dawn spread across the eastern sky.

The French, like moles, emerged from their tunnel and spread throughout the trembling city and by noon Bordeaux had fallen. That evening, the governor of the castle agreed to terms of surrender sparing the citizens more suffering. There were many prisoners, but Bartram of Clitheroe was not among them. His yellow scarf adorned the neck of a French man-at-arms.

Wallace and his Scots remained in Bordeaux during the remainder of August and early September. Whenever possible he escaped to the relaxation of his favourite pastime of fishing along the bank of the Gironde. The weather was warm and mellow, the women welcoming, but as September drew to its golden close he prepared himself for a return to Paris with his brother, John Blair and other leading Scottish knights. Behind them they left some freebooters who preferred to seek service with French knights and continue to campaign in the western provinces.

They dallied for a while at Chinon and arrived in Paris on a grey and damp October day. After the hardships of campaign he found the comforts and lazy life of the French court distracting. The French ladies, who once again found the silent, courteous Wallace fascinating, treated him with great respect. He also found them deliciously desirable.

After the halcyon days of his victory of Chinon and his valour at Bordeaux, he was toasted at lavish banquets but Wallace soon began to fret. Phillip made no open move to assist Scotland and Lamberton sent news that Edward of England had announced a truce for the winter that would last until Whitsun. Now was the time for diplomacy. Then bad news arrived. The Guardians, who should have been consolidating Scotland's strength, were once again busy arguing among themselves.

Towards the end of November, Wallace was again ushered into the presence of his own king. John Balliol lived comfortably on his family estate at Bailleu in Picardy. He had always been a quiet unassuming man and the hardships and uncertainties of the past ten years had left him exhausted. The squabbling Scottish lords had troubled him so that he was pleased to retire to the comforts of his own bed and the talents of his cook.

Wallace journeyed secretly to meet his king late at night. "Sir William, your fame as captain and knight is sung by troubadours throughout France." The king held out his jewelled hand, "Tell us of your exploits, sir."

Wallace spoke of his French campaign as he reached for Lamberton's letters in his pouch. King John had also received news from Scotland and said, "I received letters from the Guardians. A cleric Master Baldred Bisset has been sent to the Holy Father to speak for Scotland's cause. He is most learned and has a silken tongue."

"Sire, let us hope so, but meanwhile Scotland suffers. They say that too many cooks spoil the broth, and more than one Guardian leads to confusion and disharmony. If you, Sire, gave your backing to Soulis as your sole representative, it would bring stability and the nobles may rally behind him."

"You do not suggest my lord, the Earl of Carrick, Robert the Bruce, yet we are told that you admire him." Wallace sat for a few moments considering his reply before saying, "Sire, Robert the Bruce is a fine soldier. In that I cannot fault him, but he finds it difficult deciding who is his lord, and his own claim to your throne and his hatred for the Comyns will always set him apart from others."

They continued speaking for some time until King John called for his clerk to dictate letters to him. When Wallace left the king's presence in the early morning he carried letters for Lamberton, Soulis, Wishart and others. Later he gave them into the custody of a Norwegian trader Haakon Audensen who was returning to Kirkwall in Orkney. The Norwegian had married a Scottish woman whose parents lived in Moray and he would take them greetings and gifts from their daughter. Perhaps these letters would be safe and arrive at their destination: many had not since Edward's spies had intercepted their messengers. On this occasion fortune smiled on the Scottish cause. Five weeks later a beaming Audensen handed over his dispatches.

Just before the festival of Christmas, Wallace was granted a private audience with King Phillip. "You have showed yourself to be a man of outstanding resourcefulness and courage, Sir William, and you would be an asset to any king in Christendom. Stay here and accept from me the lordship of Chinon and a lady of fortune, with powerful kinsmen, as your wife. Forget your warring homeland. It will be no dishonour to you. You have done all that can be expected of you."

The lordship of Chinon was a worthy gift and he begged leave to think upon Phillip's kindness. He could not dismiss it out of hand. The offer was not entirely unexpected, but as he walked back to his own chamber, along the draughty passages, he could not help but compare the French king with John Balliol who sat comfortably and left the affairs of his kingdom to others. He knew that any sensible man would accept the French king's gift but he? Perhaps he was not so sensible after all. He could not forget or betray those who had trusted him. What he had begun he must finish.

John Blair shook his head sadly when he heard Wallace intended to refuse Phillip's offer. He could see nothing but sadness for his friend, but he did not try to dissuade him. He understood that for William Wallace this was a matter of honour. Nor was Phillip surprised when Wallace rejected his favour. France's loss was Scotland's gain. He wondered what price would buy William Wallace's loyalty. One thing was certain, with Edward of England as an enemy, it would be Wallace who would be the loser.

I n the second week of Advent in the year 1300, Sir William Wallace, knight of Scotland, accompanied by his brother, John Blair his chaplain, and with other close friends set out for Rome to give his support to the Scottish ambassador. King Phillip had showered him with gifts, a warhorse with fine gear, costly clothes, a gold ring set with precious stones and a set of six golden goblets each larger than the other, engraved and studded with rubies. They were a fine sight as they rode south towards Marseilles.

Wallace was in joyful spirit and full of hope. He thought that at last Scotland's affairs might be coming to a satisfactory end. At least he was doing something again. In his pouch was the French king's letter, comending him to the Holy Father, who would for certain understand the righteousness of Scotland's cause.

Such an impressive party of knights barely needed Phillip's letter of safe conduct for their journey. Honest men saw that they were nobles of importance with powerful friends. Dishonest rogues and vagabonds – there were many in the wild hills and forests – recognised Wallace and his band as hardened soldiers unlikely to part company with anything and so their journey was uneventful. Christmas was celebrated at the Benedictine monastery near Marseilles where John Blair retreated from their company until the holy festival had ended. Gales kept them in Marseilles till the first week in February when a break in the weather allowed them to embark on a merchant ship bound for Genoa and from there they took the road south.

Although they travelled in winter the journey was pleasant with much to see. Wallace found himself remembering his journey with great uncle William Wallace, when he had slept by the side of the old Roman fort, but it was such a long time ago. How childish had he been imagining that he heard marching Roman legions.

On the second day of March they rode into Rome and went directly to the Scottish College. He could not hide his excitement on arriving in the immortal city and his expectations that his search for Scotland's freedom might be nearing its end. The following day he met Master Bisset: their last meeting had been when he himself was Guardian. The cleric was not physically impressive, being small and corpulent, but Wallace knew that he would give wise council and there were few as knowledgeable in both secular and clerical law as he was.

Bisset noted the deep lines on Wallace's brow and cheeks. It was the face of a man who had pushed himself beyond endurance and had taken his duties seriously. "Sir William," he indicated a thickly cushioned couch by an open window overlooking the square. "It is good that you have arrived safely. Your presence will give strength to our cause. I know how anxious you are to settle Scotland's affairs, but you will need patience for a little longer. Nothing happens quickly in Rome, particularly before Easter. In any case we await the arrival of the Archdeacon Master Frere." He smiled at Wallace's look of impatience. "What better place is there for a man to wait than in Rome?" He waved a hand to the scene outside.

Once again Wallace played the waiting game, but he was not idle. There were many men of influence in the city. It was necessary that he should take great care for the English would not shrink from using a murderer's dagger even though it was Lent. The Scottish envoys arrived at Easter and together they went to Saint Peter's to celebrate Christ's Resurrection. "*Vene Christus Spiritus*," the worshippers' voices rose to the dome of the great Cathedral and the sound swelled as it spiralled upwards until Wallace thought that the very dome itself would rise. He left the cathedral feeling light-headed and uplifted – and more hopeful than he had been for many years.

The English king's truce was due to end at Whitsun and Wallace's fears began to return. Surely the Pope would receive him in audience soon. Just before the beginning of the month of May he was summoned before Cardinal De Luca who was an official close to the Holy Father.

"I compliment you on your Latin, Sir William. You were, I believe, destined for a scholastic life." Wallace smiled briefly saying, "Destiny led me along another path, your eminence."

"Tell me, sir, why do you continue this fight? It is a war that I believe has cost you dear. Wouldn't it be easier to accept the lands and honours which I am told Phillip of France offered you and settle behind comfortable walls." The cardinal saw a flash of anger in the other man's eyes, but when Wallace spoke his voice was quietly moderated and his words carefully chosen.

"Your eminence, Scotland is a poor kingdom," he paused looking around at the lavish furnishings. "The climate is hard but we are, and always have been, a free people: even the Romans could not conquer us. As a child I was taught to cherish freedom above all things. Edward of England has taken under his dominion the lands of the Welsh princes. Now he claims lordship of the kingdom of Scots. In this way he will become master of all the islands of Britain and he uses the law to make his greed legal. Many I have loved and those who loved me have died in our struggle. I cannot waste their trust and sacrifice."

The cardinal said nothing. He was faced with a passionate man and mere words would not divert him from his intention. He asked Wallace about his conduct of the war and began to form a picture of the horrors of Berwick, Wallace's raid into Northumberland and the devastation of Scotland. Here and there he nodded and encouraged Wallace for he was a man skilled in getting information out of people. At the end of the audience he judged Wallace to be a sensible and thoughtful man, not a robber or an outlaw, and one who inspired trust in others.

A few days later Master Bisset sent for Wallace and showed him the draft of Scotland's reply to the English king's claim to Scotland. Wallace sat reading each statement carefully.

"I believe that the five points outlined here prove Scotland is and always was a free kingdom. God willing they will convince the Holy Father of the justice of our cause." Baldred Bisset was choosing his words with care. "Our cause is strong. I believe the Holy Father will judge in our favour, but you and I know that it is not always truth which wins the day." Wallace nodded his agreement. "Sir William, now that our work progresses well here, will you not go home and again serve Scotland until his Holiness passes judgement?"

Wallace grinned, "Am I getting in your way then, sir?" the cleric coloured, realising that he had been less then tactful, but Wallace continued. "You are right, it is time. I have done all I can. Better that I go home now and do what I am best at." "Sir William, when the church lost the young William Wallace to a private life, she lost a great champion," said Bisset.

Wallace would not have felt so hopeful for the future of his homeland if he could have been privy to King Edward's plans in the spring of 1301. While French and Scottish envoys met the representatives of England at Canterbury to discuss terms for ending the hostilities, his clerks finished writing his reply to the Pope's letter which reprimanded him for his invasion of Scotland. Secretly, and with his usual single-mindedness, he began his preparations for a new invasion of Scotland. "I will have what is justly mine," he said to Beck. If the Scots with their French and Vatican allies thought he was giving way to his rightful claims they were in for a shock. Edward of England always took what he considered to be his. Once again Edward sent orders into his eastern counties to provide provisions and ships. This time the army would not be starved into an early retreat.

As the truce ended the king of England made pilgrimage to the tomb of Thomas a' Becket who would surely protect England's interests. The Scottish business must come to a satisfactory end. Then he journeyed north to Berwick to meet with his barons and levies.

Wallace and his party returned through the sunlit southern country and went directly to the estate of King John Balliol in Picardy. This time he rode openly through the gates in full view of all and told his king of his audiences with the cardinal and his hopes for the future. It was then that he heard that the English king was once again mobilising his forces for an invasion of Scotland. The stern disapproval of the Holy Father, it seemed, did not concern him at all.

Two things did occur to lift Wallace's spirits while he attended his king. A few days after his arrival an envoy from King Phillip arrived bringing greetings and assuring his noble brother, King John, and his loyal friend William Wallace that their troubles were also his. He had heard that the king of England was preparing an invasion and as a good friend he would provide a French force of knights to assist his noble brother. He also stated that the Holy Father had graciously transferred the health and safety of John, King of Scots, into the safe keeping of Phillip of France. This surely was a sign to all of the friendship and unity between Phillip, His Holiness and Scotland. The letter continued in flowery phrases, but Wallace leaned back in his chair, breathing deeply. This was the first time Phillip had committed himself in writing to aid Scotland. He clenched his fists. "At last," he said as he brought a large fist down on the table in front of him. A well-trained force of mounted knights would be a match for anything the English had, and would remain loyal to Scotland's cause for as long as the French king wanted. Later he strolled in the rose gardens, pondering the ups and downs in Scotland's fortunes. He decided to return home without delay.

Before he could leave more letters arrived from Scotland carried by the Norwegian Audensen. His journey had been a fast one, for English ships had chased him across the North Sea. His crew was frightened and they had out-rowed the wind itself. "Heavy seas," he said, "had tossed them through the channel to the French coast." The Norwegian was a hearty man, fond of telling unlikely stories as he sat at the table drinking and eating with relish. Wallace, in mellow mood, indulged the seafarer sitting with him long into the night, drinking and listening to his stories. Audensen came from the valleys south of Oslo and amused everyone with his stories of trolls and witches who lived in the mountains and forests near his boyhood home. Just when they all thought he had exhausted his repertoire of outrageous yarns he began to relate a saga, an old tale of heathen Vikings. Once again the wine flowed around the table.

Wallace awoke late the next morning. His head was heavy and sore from drinking. Curly brought him a bitter brew to ease the throbbing. Then Wallace took his horse and young falcon given him by his king into the surrounding countryside. It was full summer now. The peasants were haymaking. He reigned in his horse and sat for a while, watching the line of men walking steadily forward and leaving behind them the fallen lush grass. It would be a good crop this year if they had some fine sunny days to dry it. A man began to sing in a strong, baritone voice and the tune fitted well with the rhythm of their scythes. The pain in his head began to ease.

Among the letters which the Norwegian brought was one from the Guardian, Sir John Soulis, ordering Wallace to return to Scotland, but cautioning him not to travel by the direct sea route as English ships patrolled everywhere, blockading Scotland. Nobody could arrive or depart and there were few captains on the continent who would risk entering Scottish waters. Wallace was too valuable to lose: he must return via the northern countries. To ease his journey, the Guardian sent a letter of safe conduct in Wallace's name from King Haakon of Norway. Audensen, anxious to leave now that he had carried out his commission, was to guide Wallace on his journey. The Norwegian had sold his ship as the English would be watching for it. Wallace and his party were to travel overland and buy a seaworthy boat in Norway.

In the evening prior to his departure, Wallace sat with his king. His feelings for John Balliol had altered since he had acquired a more intimate knowledge of the man. It saddened him and he found it hard to conceal his feelings. Here was a man, a pleasant kindly man, who listened to everyone's point of view and – because of this – was quite unsuited to controlling his greedy and violent subjects. He could not match his nobles' avarice and guile. Wallace liked him.

"Ah! Sir William, you have come to say farewell." The royal hand was held out for him to kiss. "We have more to thank you for than any other of our subjects. You have been a true champion. We wish that it was in our power to reward you adequately for your services to your king, but we want you to accept this token of our affection." He beckoned to his steward, then placed a heavy gold chain and pendant around Wallace's neck. The pendant was engraved with the royal coat of arms and on the reverse side was a raised arm holding a sword. Wine was poured and King John raised his goblet to toast Wallace. "Sir William, you have served us well. You have helped to keep King Phillip's interest in a Scottish alliance. Your successes for Phillip against the English have taken his mind away from his argument with the Holy Father in Rome and this has benefited our cause. Even in exile you have served Scotland well." He drank his toast. "Let us hope, sire, that if Phillip keeps his promises, Scotland's troubles will be at an end." The king looked down at the rings on his fingers. "Perhaps, perhaps, Wallace, but we must not place too much hope in promises. Perhaps we shall meet again in happier times when we may reward you fully for your loyalty."

As Wallace's party rode northwards, he confided in his brother that he would miss the sun, wine and good food, but when you got right down to it, a man was a man wherever he went showing courage, loyalty, greed and deceit. Better by far to live among his own kin. Audensen had been well paid to guide the former Guardian safely home and nothing would halt him in his task. They reached the Skaggerak in August, where they took a boat across the straits between the small islands off the Norwegian coast and up the fjord to Oslo.

Isabel Bruce, Dowager Queen of Norway and sister to Robert the Bruce took care that Wallace and his party were comfortably lodged and on their third day in Oslo she visited them. She was very much like her brother, and knowledgeable of all the events which had overtaken Scotland, as well as solicitous for Wallace's comfort.

"If you are to make safe landing in Scotland before the winter storms, you must leave within the week, sir," the lady said as they sat together. "I have found you a trusted captain who will take you to Orkney. From there you may cross easily, for few English ships venture so far north. I have letters for my brother which will be brought to you tomorrow." She smiled sadly playing with the heavy rings on her slender fingers. "I wish that I could make the journey with you as I would like to see my home again." Wallace guessed how lonely the young woman was and wondered if being a queen – even with all the servants, jewels and fine clothes – had been worth the sacrifices of home and kindred. Yet what choice did a woman of her noble status have in such matters? Isabel rose holding out her hand which Wallace kissed bowing gallantly.

The north-easterly wind was cold and brisk and a week later they were on the mainland of Scotland. They rode south, stopping briefly in the homes of various patriots. Among them was Alexander Pilche, who greeted Wallace as an old friend and insisted that he took the master's seat at table. They were served by Pilche's young daughter. Her flaxen hair was flowing around her like a mantle and her eyes were demurely downcast as she offered Wallace a silver goblet of fine Burgundy wine. "Will you be returning south, sir?" asked Pilche. "Aye, that I will but there is someone I must see first."

Accompanied by Curly – who had refused to leave his service – as well as his brother and John Blair he rode west to the manor of Sir John Shaw. He sat warming himself by the fire with his brother when Lady Shaw brought his little maid Margaret into the hall. She was shy of the two strangers and clung to her foster-mother, turning her face away and burying it in the folds of the lady's skirt. "Come Meg, will you not greet your father with a kiss." Margaret turned shyly, looking with sidelong glance at the big, handsome man. Wallace smiled, holding out his arms, while her foster-mother gave her a small prod whispering, "Go to your father, Margaret." Obediently the child went to him, smiling as he drew her onto his knee. He smelt of leather, perspiration and horses and she liked the feel of his big muscular arm around her. Her foster-father was kind, but he never dangled her on his knee nor did he have the same presence about him as this man they said was her father.

Wallace was just as enthralled with his daughter and could hardly take his eyes from the child. He watched her as she moved about the hall helping Lady Shaw. Meg had the looks of his mother. She was tall for her age, with clear skin and thick chestnut hair, but he noticed that – like her own dear mother – Meg had a liking for animals and wherever she went a young deerhound followed. When she sat, it sat protectively near her and when a serving maid came to take her to bed, the animal would also rise, stretch itself, yawn and follow his young mistress. When

Wallace went to sleep, for he preferred to rest with his daughter, by the foot of the bed lay the dog.

They rested at the peaceful manor for a week and on the seventh evening a messenger arrived from Lamberton and Soulis, requesting Wallace's return to the south. That evening, the Wallaces sat with Sir John. A storm was blowing outside, whistling around the eaves and blowing through the smoke vent. The raindrops sizzled on the hot embers of the fire and much smoke was blown back into the room below. The hall was full of folk as none cared to venture outside. Margaret sat at her father's feet, leaning against the dog stretched by her side. One of the house folk had taken his harp and began to sing a wild, sad Gaelic song. The words blended with the sounds of the wind and distant roaring waves. The song came to an end and John Wallace called out to Curly. "Give us a song lad." Curly flushed, but borrowing the harp he sang the song of the noble Roland. It was in French and only the Wallace brothers, John Blair and the master of the house could understand the tale. Curly had a good voice and the tune kept their feet tapping.

Then Lady Shaw ordered her servant to play that they might dance. The trestles and benches were moved away, the men took their swords and danced in mock joust, jumping and lunging at each other. There was a lot of laughter and red faces particularly when Curly, overcome by drink, tripped and fell headlong.

A little later people began to find places to rest. Wallace's little maid had fallen asleep with her head resting on the dog. Her father carried her to the big bed which they shared and removed her shoes and red kirtle. She opened her eyes smiling at him, holding out bare arms and putting them around his neck. He kissed her murmuring, "Sleep well, sweetheart." She turned onto her side and went back to sleep. Wallace stroked the waving chestnut hair and soft white cheek, covered her with a wolf skin, and went back into the hall sitting for a while talking to Sir John.

Meg awoke early, but when the servant came to take her away that her father might continue his rest, she screamed loudly, clinging to him and refusing to go. "Leave her woman. She wishes to torment her father a little longer," he said, tickling the child so that she squealed with joy. He played small games with her for a while, then she sat at his side quietly and said, "I want to go with you, father." "Nay child, the field of battle is no place for you." "I can look after you. I am able to mend clothes and milk a cow."

Her father laughed taking her hand and kissing the small fingers. "Are you not happy here, Meg?" "Oh aye, I love foster-mother and father, but you are so lonely." "Well, let us hope that soon I can take you to my manor of Borthwick and you can keep house for your father." "I think the English king is a bad man because he does not leave us in peace."

After this he sent Margaret away with the servant so that he could prepare himself for his journey. As he buckled his mail-coat he told his brother of his conversation with Meg. "The maid is so grown up, John, yet still so young in years." "It is the way with women, Will. They are ready to run a household before they have stopped suckling their mother's milk."

It was hard to say farewell to her this time, but he promised that when Edward of England left Scotland forever, he would return and take her to see her own estate of Lamington. It pacified the child somewhat and she stood bravely with Tom Shaw, her foster-parents, their servants and followers ranged behind them to wave goodbye.

As they wound their way through the glen leading east away from the manor Wallace was deep in thought. He pondered on his life and a great distaste of war came over him. Oh God, he knew he could not turn back and leave the work to others, yet how it wearied him! Whether he liked it or not, he would have to finish the job he had begun, no matter what the price to himself – but Lord keep her safe. He prayed quietly to himself, unable to look back again at the small waving figure. They rode in silence, Wallace morose with his thoughts. The others knew him well enough to leave him in peace.

While Wallace journeyed abroad, Scotland had continued to bear the burden of Edward's ambitions and there was much hardship and hunger in the lowlands. The countryside bore the scars of prolonged warfare. There were burnt out farmsteads and manors, the fields without sign of plough or harvested crops. The livestock had gone. In the autumn all should have been busy slaughtering, smoking, salting, setting aside for the coming winter, yet Wallace saw little to cheer his heart. There would be much famine in the Scotland this coming winter.

During the summer of 1301 Edward and his army had progressed leisurely through the borders and Lothians across to Glasgow, Stirling, Bothwell and Dunipace, which Wallace remembered with so much fondness. All felt the power of Edward's heel. In the south-west the Prince of Wales crossed the Solway Firth taking the Castle of Turnberry, but in that wild country the Scottish forces under the command of Soulis and Umfraville were more successful attacking the English wherever and whenever they could. The king intended that his armies should join forces and push the remnants of the Scottish army northwards, leaving him master of the rich lands south of the Forth and Clyde. The Prince of Wales was not the man his father was, and in the late autumn he withdrew to Linlithgow to join his father for the Christmas feast.

The ground was as hard as iron. Bitter winds blew from the north bringing flurries of snow. In the forests wild animals, sensitive to the coming harsh winter, had gone to earth and wolves howled. So hungry were they that during the first days of January their lean grey forms were seen among the charred ruins of farmsteads, searching for scraps. People had been there before, picking through cinders of burnt stables for any small morsel which they could find.

Edward did not conceal his anger when the Prince of Wales arrived at Linlithgow. After so much scheming and planning and so much effort 'this cursed land' as the king called Scotland had remained defiant. If only his son had shown more spirit and determination. His son was a disappointment to him and he was heard to say that the Prince had achieved nothing worthy of praise.

Wallace and his men were at Elcho Castle where his cousin Crawford was governor. News of Wallace's return had spread and many came to welcome him home. Some joined him so that his following increased to fifty. It touched Wallace's heart. In spite of everything and after an absence of two years they still put their trust in him.

Each new arrival, however keenly welcomed, needed feeding. On All Souls Day William Crawford set out for Perth to purchase supplies. His pouch was heavy with gold given to him by Wallace. Perth was full of English and their spies and although he visited only known and trusted merchants, the large quantities purchased attracted attention. Rumours that Wallace had returned were whispered in the market place and inns. All knew William Crawford to be near kin to Wallace. The sheriff, hearing the rumours, seized William Crawford and threw him into prison for questioning.

"Well, sir. What explanation have you for purchasing so many provisions long before the Christmas feast?" William Crawford sighed. "You are too suspicious. Is a man permitted to purchase only for Christmas? There are other occasions to celebrate." "Come, Sir William, I have not heard that you have either marriage feast or funeral wake in your household," said the sheriff. "True, but after three daughters I have got me a son. Surely even an Englishman can see that I have good reason to rejoice. My wife will go to her churching and half the countryside has been invited." The sheriff narrowed his eyes. The man standing before him certainly seemed relaxed but the Scots had fooled him before. Then Crawford said, "Come and celebrate with us. At a time like this I welcome all to my house."

An hour later Crawford and his servants, without undue haste, left through the southern gate of the city and were seen to take the road along the southern bank of the Tay towards Elcho. Safely out of sight a troop of eight hundred English soldiers followed. They were led by James Butler, anxious to avenge the deaths of his father and grandfather, who had been killed by Wallace four years earlier.

William Crawford arrived home in the late afternoon and ran immediately to Wallace. "Quick, cousin, the English questioned me and have followed us. Hide in the forest." For battle-hardened warriors like the Wallace brothers and their men it took but a few minutes to gather their mail and gear, and flee into the cold, clinging mist which had begun to creep up from the river.

The English clattered up to the gates demanding to be admitted. Lady Crawford came to a high window and leaning out called, "Is that you, Sir James, come early to our thanksgiving and accompanied by so many?" Butler angry and impatient to lay his hands on Wallace spat on the ground. "Open up woman. You know why we're here." "It's very late in the day, sir. With so many men you are a fearsome sight. I am not yet well enough to receive so many." "Tell your man to have the gates opened or we'll burn you out." "Oh well, just you wait a few moments then," and she withdrew, but time passed and nothing more was heard from within. Butler, beside himself with rage, ordered his men to fire the place.

Wallace, Crawford and the others had taken cover at the forest edge and watched the English carefully. When they saw the first fire arrows fly towards the thatch of the inner keep and the brushwood being thrown in front of the gate, Crawford grew restless saying he would go back to save his wife and children. "Nay man, do you think your sacrifice will save your wife and family? It's William Wallace he wants and I'll be generous." He thanked Crawford for his hospitality and told him to take his family, under the cover of darkness across the Tay, passing around Perth to the north. Crawford would have preferred to stay with Wallace, but his family would be in perilous straits without his protection. "God be with you, Will," and he was gone. Wallace mounted and rode into the open calling, "Hey, Butler, are you keen to join your kinsmen?"

Hearing the call Butler turned to see the large man on horseback within easy reach of English arrows. A troop of Wallace's horsemen were waiting nearby. An arrow fell harmlessly close to Wallace who decided that now was the time to depart with all speed. The English followed. Night was almost on them as they disappeared into the mist and darkness.

This was his first encounter with the English since returning to Scotland and for the next two days he played a game of catch me if you can. Striking when the English were vulnerable or off guard, then slipping back deep into the Methven forest, leaving behind many English dead or dying. On the second day he struck Butler a fatal blow before disappearing into the country north of Perth. The English governor sent an urgent message to his king at Linlithgow, asking for help as William Wallace was back in Scotland.

Wallace's instructions had been to join up with Soulis, who was fighting in the south-west of Scotland, but to do so he would have to cross the territories where Edward's army roamed at will. Wallace judged the risks too great. It would be much better to nip at Edward's heels whenever he could and join up with Soulis when the English retired to their winter quarters. He remained near Perth until the Prince of Wales was safely at Linlithgow for Christmas – then he went south.

Agnes's little farmstead was sacked by the marauding English, but she had had enough foresight to take to the hills with her people and livestock. They were busy rebuilding when Wallace paid her a visit. Her joy as he rode into the yard knew no bounds. He did not stay for long. It would have been too dangerous for her but their short encounter was full of joy and passion: it was as if they had never parted. Afterwards, when he rode south, he wondered why he had been so foolish as to leave her for so long, for she had become very dear to him.

He was tempted to visit Elderslie, but they told him it had been destroyed after Falkirk. What point was there in seeing the old place in ruins? Besides the people who had lived there had all gone.

Wallace met Soulis in the forest of Selkirk and was treated with great respect and friendship. The Guardian had heard of Wallace's recent exploits around Perth and said, "You do not tire of the struggle then, Will?" "Nay, I have returned, prepared to fight them to the end." Soulis stirred the fire with the toe of his boot, encouraging flames to send dark dancing shadows around the wooden walls. "Edward is seeking a truce and I am forced to give him his wish." Wallace looked sharply at the speaker. "Why let them rest? They are short of food. Surely if we press hard at their heels now we can finish the job."

"I believe you are right, but others do not agree with us and without their help ...," he shrugged. He thought that Wallace of all men would understand his problems. "If we have a truce, the time will come when they'll tire of Englishmen sitting on their lands and eating their food and they will again demand action." Wallace was clearly irritated. "We should continue to attack them now, not give them a chance to lick their wounds and get their feet under our tables."

Soulis made no reply. He knew the dangers in allowing the English to gain a foothold. He changed the subject and spoke of Phillip of France and help from that quarter. He was hopeful but Wallace said, "There was a time not so long ago when I felt as you do, but now I have come to understand that we cannot offer France anything which it does not already have. They will not risk angering the English and without proof of great reward they wish only to irritate the English. Scotland must look to her own defence." The bluntness of the statement shocked Soulis who had been led to believe differently by Bishop Lamberton. The following day they parted on terms of friendship for Soulis had a great liking for Wallace.

Wallace wintered with his men at Borthwick. At some time the English had ransacked the place. The buildings were in disorder and someone had tried to set fire to them. The roofs of the barn and brew house had gone, but otherwise the place was habitable. Food was short. There was no fodder for the horses and if they kept them through the winter they would have to forage for feed. If they raided the English outposts their presence would be known.

Two days after their arrival, when they were busy setting the buildings in order, a party of men led by John the Outlaw appeared from the forest. They said that they had come to join Wallace and it was a remark made by John which gave Wallace the idea. They were sitting in the hall, making oatcakes on a griddle when John said, "The English have rebuilt Berwick and they say once again the market has plenty of food and fleeces." Wallace sat thinking that they would not be looking for him under their noses. To steal would draw attention to themselves, but if each went to Berwick and bought some produce just before Christmas it would not rouse suspicion. It would also give him the opportunity to see the countryside in the east. Two days later Wallace and five closest to him set out using little-known paths. They saw no sign of people. Farmsteads and manors alike were burnt. The lands seemed emptied of folk and beasts.

A few miles from Berwick the party split. Each man led three pack ponies. Wallace skirted around to the south, so that he could enter by a different gate. He clattered through the alleys to the corn merchants' quarter, wearing an old wide-brimmed hat pulled well down against the chill of the winter's day and a dark brown wadmal cloak enveloped his body. Hunched against the biting easterly wind from the sea he looked just as he had intended: like the serving man from a manor. The merchant, nosy as are all merchants, questioned him and was told that his master's land had been plundered by the Scots and now that the family had returned to the farm, his master must spend good money if they were to survive through the winter. Before leaving the town Wallace went down to the harbour and purchased a small barrel of salted herring and dried fish and looked carefully at the new fortifications.

Once the gates of the town were safely behind him he quickened his horse's pace. When out of sight he turned his horse's head towards the west for the safety of the forest.

On a grey winter's day, when the wind found all loose timbers, thatch and shutters, William Wallace had a visitor. In the late afternoon as the weak light began to fade, Agnes – buffeted by the wind – appeared in the yard. "Good God, woman. What brings you here at such a time of the year." Agnes had been rehearsing what she would say to him since she had first left the Clyde, but now her speech deserted her. She ran to him and threw her arms around his neck, caring little that his men were around and about. They winked to one another and remembering urgent work left them alone. "Don't be angry, Will. I could not sit quietly at the farm knowing you were here. I'll not hinder you in anything."

When they were in the hall Wallace sat down pulling her onto his knee, "Nay, lass, how could I be angry? There are few so loyal that would battle through such weather. Even the English find the effort too great. You look frozen."

Agnes was indeed a sorry sight. Now that she had entered the warm hall her chapped cheeks glowed fiery red. Her clothes were wet and caked in mud, as were her shoes. Wallace removed her footwear, revealing cold, blood-stained feet. Large blisters covered her heels and toes.

"Why didn't you ride, sweetheart? To make such a journey on foot at this time of the year is hard even for a man." "I did not dare, Will. There was nothing to steal from a woman without horse or other possessions." "None challenged you?" he asked. "Aye, only one English patrol, but I told them my man had died and now I had a longing to go to my father's house for the Christmas feast, since I had nothing to keep me in Glasgow." That night, when she had fallen asleep at his side, he wondered how so simple a woman could find the strength to seek out one whom she loved. He had, however, noticed so many times before that those of high estate rarely had such dogged fortitude.

After her arrival, life became more comfortable for Wallace. With John Blair's and Curly's help she regularly baked and brewed, and a large cauldron of stewing meat always hung by the fire ready to warm a hungry man.

In January news came that Soulis and the other nobles had signed a truce with King Edward that had been arranged by Phillip of France. When Wallace heard the news he took his bow and strode from the manor into the forest, returning empty handed and glum when darkness fell. He sat eating and said to Blair and his brother, "It seems that our time in France was wasted." John Blair replied, "Surely, Will, nine months of peace is a good thing. At least our people will have time to sow and reap and perhaps Edward will not return."

"For sure this summer will bring a harvest but Longshanks, stronger than ever before, will come again. The only thing that will stop him will be his death. For fifteen years now our kingdom has been leaderless and I wish that like England we too had a strong king like Edward Longshanks."

The year 1302 was a frustrating one for Wallace, his kin and allies. Frustrated by inactivity, foreboding gnawed in the pit of Wallace's stomach. He was sure that the English would put the truce to better use than his own people. Then came news that Robert the Bruce, Earl of Carrick, had deserted the Scottish cause and also accepted Edward's peace.

William and John Wallace were on the hillside above the manor. Wallace had brought a few ewe lambs that spring and they had collected the small flock into an enclosure, and were busy shearing and clipping hooves ready for the autumn. As the last struggling beast gained its freedom, they saw the messenger ride from the forest into the manor below. Agnes came along the path which led up to the pasture. She waved to them and when she saw that they were coming she sat herself on a grassy mound in the warm sunshine to wait. The air was heavy with the scent of thyme. It was the kind of day when life felt so sweet.

The messenger wore the black habit of a Benedictine monk and had been sent by Bishop Lamberton. He was a man of middle years. He bowed to Wallace when he was brought before him. "Sir William, my lord the Bishop of St Andrews sends you his greetings and desires that you hear his message from my own lips for he fears that a letter might go astray." Wallace nodded.

"Sir, last month the army of Phillip of France was defeated at Courtrai, in Flanders, and now he is likely to seek an alliance with England. My lord bishop will take ship for France as soon as may be, accompanied by the Guardian Sir John Soulis, Sir James Stewart and my Lord Umfraville to try to dissuade King Phillip from this course. He also states that England is preparing once again to attack as soon as the truce expires. He asks that because of your love for him and this kingdom you assist Sir John Comyn, who will be Guardian, as he desires."

There was no need for Wallace to consider the bishop's words. "Tell your lords that Wallace is always ready to defend Scotland and if necessary to carry the war into the enemy's land. It was not I who signed a truce with the English. When the time comes they can count on my sword." The Bishop of St Andrews received Wallace's message with great relief and asked, "How does Wallace fare?" "He looks well, my lord. His manor is comfortable and well managed, but not very large."

Lamberton sat back in his chair, "Aye, the man has given much and taken little in return." Yet, he thought, if the French king withdraws his support Scotland will have need of William Wallace. "Does he not fear to put his trust in Sir John Comyn?" questioned the bishop. "He did not mention Sir John's name, my lord, nor raise any questions."

Simon Fraser was camped near Biggar when Wallace and his brother rode in. Fraser greeted them with friendship and respect. Since their secret forest meeting before Wallace's departure for France, Fraser had remained loyal to Scotland's cause. They spoke of many things but in particular of Wallace's visit to France and the possible loss of the French king's alliance. "In October the truce will end. They're already gathering provisions and horses. They'll not wait for next spring before beginning their campaign," said Fraser.

Outside they heard clattering hooves and a few moments later Sir John Comyn strode into the hall. They had not met since Falkirk. Wallace rose to his feet as was fitting. With Soulis now in France,

Comyn was sole Guardian of Scotland and commander of her army. Wallace bowed low, "We have come as we were asked to by my lord bishop to offer our services when the English attack again." Wallace stood calmly, carefully hiding his emotions. "Sir William, I need experienced soldiers. Your sword is always welcome." Later alone with Fraser, Comyn said, "The man is a good soldier and born to lead. Watch that the men don't think he's Guardian." Fraser nodded, but said nothing and found duties to occupy himself so that he need not drink nor have conversation with John Comyn of Badenoch.

Borthwick had been left in the care of Agnes and a few trusted men. She had been tearful when the time had come for William's departure. The night before she had lain by his side, sobbing, and nothing he said would calm her. "Come lass, let's have no more," he said in a despairing voice. "Oh, William Wallace, why must you go when others remain safe in their beds? You have already given so much"

What could he say to soothe her for she spoke truthfully. "Sweetheart, do you want to hear English voices in the market place offering a higher price for goods which should be yours?" But she was in no mood to listen to reasoned arguments. Eventually he got up and returned with two beakers of ale which he had heated with a poker from the embers of the fire.

"Drink this, Agnes, it will ease you" She was a good-natured woman and he knew it was her love for him which made her wail so. Just before she slept she said in a tearful voice. "Oh, Will, it's gone on for so long," and he thought, 'Aye, that's what makes it so wearisome.' It was six years now since he had charged the English at Dunbar, sixteen since the death of King Alexander – and Scotland was no nearer to ending the struggle. As Agnes slept, he lay listening to the hissing of the fire and he realised that she was very dear to him.

Edward, determined that the Scots should not gain the advantage, sent out orders in September for Sir John Seagrove and Sir Ralph Manton to strike with a large army across Scotland from Glasgow to Stirling.

News spread that Wallace was preparing for war and men began to join him. Simon Fraser marvelled at their trust and the hold which Wallace still had on their affections. He had such energy and was out and about before light only retiring to his sleeping place among his men late at night.

During the darkest time of the year with four hundred hand-picked men Wallace and Fraser attacked English garrisons, lightning attacks ending as suddenly as they had begun. Their purpose was to break the English morale. So frightened did the enemy become that they drew lots for guard duty in remote outposts. Nobody knew when or where an attack would come from. By Christmas Seagrove, worried by the difficulties his captains were reporting, wrote to Edward asking for reinforcements.

Edward received John Seagrove's dispatch with some annoyance. Matters were going his way on the continent and it was important Scotland submitted now. The rebels must accept his peace. He instructed his paymaster, Sir Ralph Fitzwilliam, to take reinforcements to Seagrove without delay.

The English army had been divided into three divisions and advanced through Lothian. Sir John Seagrove camped near Roslin awaiting the arrival of Sir Ralph Manton's brigade. Very early in late February, when only the night guards were awake, the Scots attacked.

Comyn had also divided his force into three, under the command of Simon Fraser, William Wallace and himself and carried out a three-pronged attack on Seagrove's sleeping force. He commanded the vanguard with Wallace on his left flank while Fraser led the right. They had marched through the night from Biggar. The final mile they advanced in silence without torches. The English would not expect them to come at night. Comyn saw the signal, a lighted torch. All were in place and he did not fear betrayal by his commanders. He knew that Wallace would remain firm. The sleeping enemy were routed and their seriously wounded commander was taken prisoner.

Comyn, seated in Seagrove's pavilion, had the Englishman brought before him. Seagrove was in a sorry state. So furious and unexpected had been the attack that he had not had time to dress himself in chain mail. He stood, supported by his page in hose and belted surcoat, splattered in his own blood from the wound in the right side of his chest. Comyn and Fraser 'the turncoat' he knew, but the other he had not seen before. Comyn turned to Wallace saying, "Surely you know the hero of Stirling Bridge, Sir William Wallace, my lord."

Seagrove leaned heavily on his page and looked long at Wallace. He would know him again, then he closed his eyes. Outside he could hear screams from prisoners and wounded men as their captors butchered them. He was fortunate in being too valuable to be killed. His chaplain helped by John Blair led him to his couch and began to care for his wounds.

Sir John Manton, keen to rendezvous with Seagrove as soon as possible, rallied his brigade early but the Scots – commanded jointly by Fraser and Wallace – lay in ambush and few escaped the massacre. Sir Ralph's body lay crushed by the carcass of his dead horse.

The third division of English troops, five thousand strong, had a lucky escape. Sir Ralph Fitzwilliam was a devout man, who had insisted that his men should receive the sacrament before they struck camp. He had heard that the Scots were near and he and his men would not meet their Creator unshriven. It was well on in the morning when a survivor from Seagrove's division galloped towards them desperate and exhausted. He had witnessed the annihilation of Manton's brigade and begged Fitzwilliam to flee for his life. Sir Ralph knew his duty. Ordering a wide detour they arrived at Seagrove's camp in the late afternoon, having successfully evaded Wallace and Simon Fraser. He ordered an immediate attack to recapture Seagrove and inflict whatever punishment he could. Luck smiled on his bold manoeuvre and he returned with the wounded Seagrove before Comyn had gathered his wits.

The victory at Roslin put new heart into the Scots and feelings ran high with drinking and feasting before they settled to prepare for the next attack but during the battle Wallace had received a wound to his left thigh. At first he had given it little attention. It did not appear serious, but it bled profusely. After the battle it began to rain heavily drenching him until he shivered with cold. That night try as he would, he could not rest quietly. His whole body ached with fatigue and fever and even though he moved closer to the fire he could not get warm. In the morning John Blair came to him, looked closely at the wound, tut-tutting to himself and frowning deeply.

"I'll find an ointment for this wound, Will, but you must rest." Wallace glared irritably at his oldest friend, but his head was aching and the pain in his leg grew worse by the minute. He obediently allowed himself to be taken to a nearby farmstead and put to bed. He lay ill for three days before he could stand unaided. Simon Fraser, Comyn and John Wallace had left Biggar to continue harrying the demoralised English, but Wallace, weak from fever and loss of blood, accompanied by John Blair and Curly went by forest tracks to his manor at Borthwick.

It was cold March weather. The trees dripped with water, the rocks shone with moisture and a heavy mist clung to the land. It was the kind of dampness that ate into all men's bones. Agnes greeted Wallace with tender care, insisting he should lie in bed and placed warm stones at his feet. He lay back on the pillows accepting mulled wine from Blair. "With her solicitous attention you should recover quickly, Will." "Aye, never have I rested in so comfortable a bed, John, not even the

French court could boast so snug a place." In the great hall they had thrown more logs onto the fire and their smell drifted to him. He took a deep breath, relaxed and closed his eyes.

John Blair smiled, leaving his friend to rest. The old bed, mattress and pillows that had belonged to the manor had been destroyed when the place was burnt. The bed was a makeshift affair. A straw-filled mattress and pillows were not well known for comfort and softness but Wallace's energy and optimism returned to him slowly.

Agnes had taken it upon herself to try to plough and sow the field nearest to the manor, but ploughing was late and without oxen to pull the plough she worried about the future. Wallace, his leg resting on a stall, sat looking out of the unshuttered window towards the hillside beyond the manor. He could see his flock of ewes being brought down to the safety of the barns ready for the lambing. Agnes was outside talking to two of the yardmen and trying to persuade them to pull the plough themselves, but she was having little success. The men liked Agnes. They respected her hard work and her small acts of kindness, but the ground was neglected and wet and the soil would not turn easily. They knew their lord valued Agnes, but she was his leman, not his lady. Wallace called to them asking what the matter was. "My lord, if the earth is not tilled and sown the harvest time will be with us again and there will be nothing to harvest," said the elder of the two. "Take my horse Duncan and harness him to the plough, but do not lay about him for he is not used to such treatment." "Sir William, he is a war horse, not fit for such work." "At times like this we must all work if we want to eat," was the reply.

For the next few days the startled gift of the French king, who had travelled through Europe, faced the dangers of the North Sea and carried his master on campaign in Scotland, pulled and strained, ploughing the sloping fields on the manor of Borthwick. When they led him back to his stable each evening as the light was beginning to fail, the beast could not hide his happiness.

The year blossomed into a perfect spring, the loveliest Wallace could ever remember. The air was so soft and clear. After each shower the sun sparkled on lochan and stream. Primroses and violets raised their pretty faces to greet the sun.

On a late April afternoon, the lad posted as a lookout came running into the yard. "Horsemen are riding this way, Master." he said breathlessly and in answer to Wallace's questioning look he added, "Your brother rides with them." Simon Fraser and John Wallace accompanied by ten mounted knights and a hundred or so pikemen with a string of packhorses came clattering into the yard. The following day a sorrowful Agnes waved her love farewell. Would this be their final parting? Using secret paths through the forest they marched into the eastern marches, watching for Edward and his army which they expected to meet at any time.

W hen King Edward heard how his forces had been humiliated at Roslin no one was safe from his anger. This business with Scotland should have been finished long ago yet still they defied him and that upstart Wallace was stirring the people to rebellion against him and conniving with the French. Edward knew that he was the rightful overlord of Scotland. His council and servants kept out of their king's way and if they had duties which demanded constant attendance on his person, they remained tactfully quiet agreeing with whatever he said as his temper was so violent and unpredictable.

At the beginning of April Edward issued writs for a levy of ten thousand men from his English counties and sent an order to Robert the Bruce to bring a thousand men from south-west Galloway and Carrick. He also commanded Sir Richard Siward to attend with three hundred men from Nithsdale. Royal orders were sent to Wales, Ireland, Gascony and Savoy to supply men. This time the Scottish rebels would have to submit. A collective groan could be heard from the English nobles when they received their orders to march north again. The only happy men were the craftsmen and ship masters of the English eastern counties who were ordered to build and transport siege engines and prefabricated bridges to Scotland, where by May Edward had proceeded himself. As his army progressed northwards he ordered that the land should be laid waste. Livestock was killed and crops, farms and manors burnt. The fires could be seen from afar. None were safe. Not even the monasteries and churches. He would leave no sanctuary for man or beast.

W allace and Fraser watched the army of England as it wound its way northwards. They had followed the English for the past two days, stopping when they stopped, eating and sleeping when they did, never losing sight of them, but unseen by them. Curly, at Wallace's side, said, "Sir, will you not order an attack?" But Wallace laughed. "You mustn't be so impatient lad. You can't fight just because you see the enemy."

The day following the celebration of Ascension Edward arrived at Roxburgh. Wallace, Fraser and their men were camped in the hills south west of Melrose Abbey watching. The king rode to the abbey, for he had a mind to take the communion. It was easy to see him among his company for he sat on his war horse, head and shoulders above other men, and he was surrounded by many nobles with at least five hundred mounted men–at–arms and as many again marching. The odds were too great for an attack to succeed and as Wallace watched, he wondered if after taking the sacrament and confessing his sins Edward would order the destruction of this abbey. He turned his horse's head south west towards his own forest sanctuary.

"*Corpus Cristi*," murmured the abbot. He offered the bread to the bowed head of the English king. Edward solemnly took it saying loudly, "Amen." Crossing himself he rose, bowed towards the altar and strode purposefully from the abbey. Outside his page returned his sword, which even a king must remove before entering God's house. The Earl of Carrick stood nearby with his men and Edward hailed him. "Sir Robert, burn all except the church which I will spare. Leave nothing". Robert the Bruce bowed low and gave the necessary order, but when all was done as he rode away, he could not bring himself to look back at the raging flames. He passed the abbot and monks, mutely watching the destruction of their home and turned his face away.

When Wallace heard the news the anger seethed within him, not so much against Robert the Bruce, for he had learned to expect anything from Scotland's nobles, but with the English king, who had corrupted them with his gifts and promises. The English continued their unhindered progress through Scotland. At the Forth they halted long enough for the bridges ferried from Kings Lynn to be erected. Then they spread out northwards through the heart of the kingdom. At Perth Edward dallied long enough to deal with various matters of state, particularly a treaty with France, then moved onwards to settle the still defiant Urquhart Castle. Once its sombre walls had protected the English from the besieging Andrew Moray, but when King Edward arrived the Scottish defenders surrendered. He was heard to say of them, "They're as irritating as fleas on a dog, but a good scratch has rid me of them."

At the end of May Wallace heard of the signing of a peace treaty between England and France: Scotland was not included. He sat on a hilltop, which was his favourite spot south of Peebles, giving him a bird's eye view of the hills and forest. So Scotland's only ally was the

Pope in Rome and recently even he had wavered. Melancholia dampened Wallace's spirits and for the first time doubts and fears confused his thoughts. Not even after Falkirk had he believed Scotland's cause to be doomed and without hope for its future. He sat withdrawn and despondent. Even the beauty and tranquillity of the land before him could not rouse his natural optimism. Curly climbed up the path towards his master. He had grown into manhood during his time in Wallace's service and was now a fine-looking young man. Wallace had noted that the young man's curling black hair and cheerful face made him attractive to the womenfolk.

He greeted his squire. "How goes it with you? I thought nothing would drag you away from the skirts of young Mary." The young man grinned. Having reached the top he turned to gaze around at the scene which his master so cherished. "Nay, my lord, nor would I, but the Lord Comyn commands you to attend him."

For a while Wallace made no reply then said, "Ah well, I will go because it is Scotland who commands, not the man." Curly looked sharply at his master's face which was so stern and drawn. He had never seen Wallace looking so sad and despairing.

They walked down towards the camp together. Curly sensed that his master did not seek a conversation and strolled silently behind. After a while the greenwood and the sounds of the birds' singing appeared to revive Wallace's spirits and he said, "Curly, this fight is not yours. I give you permission to go back to your own kindred, for I fear, lad, you'll not make your way in the world at my side." Curly was taken aback, "Are you not pleased with my service, lord?" "Nay, there are few who I value above you, but we must think of your future, which I cannot see at my side fighting Scotland's cause." "My lord, unlike you I obey the man not the call. While you have need of my service I am happy to stay," then he added, "Even though it is grey and damp". At this Wallace laughed for he knew Curly's dislike of the Scottish climate. "Ah well, it will be as you wish, but if there comes a time when you change your mind you have my word that we will part as friends."

It was Wallace's frank speech which gave Curly courage to say something which had been on his mind for some weeks. "Sir, if I returned to France, would you come with me, for I can see no future for you here either. Between the English king and Scottish lords there is no room for a man of honour like yourself."

Wallace turned with a surprised look on his face. Curly rarely said anything of a profound or serious nature. "Nay, lad, I was taught to value freedom above all things and a man cannot run away from his past: his past is his present and future, but thanks for your concern" They walked the rest of the way in silence, each with his own thoughts. Curly wondered how life could be so perverse. His master was so honourable and courageous, a leader and warrior, yet God had put others above him. Shortly after that they arrived at John Comyn's camp and Wallace got on with the business in hand.

Comyn led his small army along forest paths into south-west Scotland, to the lands held by the Earl of Carrick. There they pillaged, burnt, killed and maimed, but Robert the Bruce did not leave Edward's army to ride to his own lands. Wallace was not sure whether the destruction was revenge for Bruce's betrayal or because of Comyn's dislike for the man.

In the long days of summer they crossed the Solway Firth into England and throughout Cumberland the cry, "The Scots are coming," rang out as villages, farms and manors were plundered and burnt. Edward did not turn aside from his resolve to subdue Scotland and refused to give help to his own kingdom. Instead he retired to Linlithgow for the winter to administer and settle those lands of Scotland which now lay under his control. He ordered others to deal with Comyn and his force. He could wait. Everything and everybody would come to him in the end. His people in Cumberland must look after themselves and he remained in Scotland throughout the autumn and winter of the following year.

# Freedom is the Finest Thing

When Comyn and his men returned from their raid into England autumn had already stretched her golden fingers across the land and the rowans were graceful with heavy clusters of crimson berries. Comyn's men were glum and the banter usually heard around the camp fires was gone.

Two weeks later Comyn called a council meeting of his captains and said, "Edward sits at Dunfermline and will not budge and in the towns the English hold the power while we sit here like foxes imprisoned in our own land. I and other lords will seek terms from King Edward. Will you do likewise?" Many listening said that they had followed him thus far and would continue to do so, but Wallace and Fraser angrily called him a traitor, saying that they would not yield and the meeting ended with harsh words from both sides. Comyn and his followers left the camp and retired to their own lands. He left no orders for Wallace and Fraser although he was still the Guardian of Scotland. Gradually the other men started leaving as they were anxious about their own kin, until only a few who held allegiance to Wallace and Fraser remained.

Shortly after Wallace's return, Agnes arrived in the camp and in the winter cold she became a great strength to Wallace with her constancy. They sat together one evening in the small, wooden cot which he had taken as his own. It was bitterly cold outside. A heavy frost had gripped the ground, but they had a good fire burning in the hearth and Agnes sat rubbing goose fat into her hands which were red and swollen with chilblains. She gasped a little from the pain, noticed that Wallace was watching her, and laughed nervously, for on this evening she felt very tired and ugly. She put the dish with the goose fat to one side, pulled down her sleeves and folded her red and unsightly hands in her lap so he would not see them and said, "Have you heard that the Lords Comyn, Lennox and others are seeking terms of peace from the English king?" "Aye, I've heard lass."

"William, won't you seek peace for yourself? Must you and I grow old living as outlaws?" He looked at her sharply saying, "If you don't care for your life here, you're free to go your own way." She began to weep, although she was not a woman to use tears to her advantage. Until she had come to William Wallace, crying had been a luxury which she had not allowed herself. Wallace came to her and, putting his arms around her shaking body, said, "Nay, nay, I meant it not Agnes. You are very dear to me, but I cannot bow to Edward of England." Angrily she snapped, "Your pride will be your undoing, William Wallace." He did not reply, continuing to hold her close, but inside it hurt him a little that those closest to him should think that it was pride alone which kept him from submitting to the English. Surely they understood that to seek peace for himself would be an act of betrayal.

That year Christmas was a sad affair. The Wallaces, and those who remained firm with them, retired to Borthwick for the feast. There they heard that Comyn, Menteith and even Soulis, who had admired Wallace so much when he was Guardian, had accepted the English king's proposals for peace. The treaty was already on its way to King John Balliol in France for his seal. None asked why and for what reason had so many good men died? Each man was concerned only with his own affairs.

Late on a cold afternoon, John Wallace saw Blair going into the brew house and hurried to him. They exchanged a few pleasantries but John Wallace had never been a man to indulge in small talk when important matters pressed on his mind. "Edward has many whom he can call friends. I fear for Will. If he doesn't seek the king's peace soon it will be too late for him." "You know Will as well as I do John. He will never submit to the English," replied John Blair. "That's as may be, but if we obtained terms for him perhaps he will agree when he understands the value of peace. John, will you go to Lamberton and ask him to intercede on Will's behalf?" John Blair thought the task hopeless, but because of his love for William, he agreed to go after the twelfth night had passed.

Lamberton was hiding from the English at Stobo, but when Blair arrived he greeted him with warmth, asked after their mutual friend and agreed to give all assistance to Wallace's peaceful acceptance by Edward of England. "Take this message back to him. There are many who seek the English king's pleasure and leave Scotland without hope. The people are tired after eight years of fighting and Wallace must not think of himself as a traitor to the kingdom if he – like the others – seeks respite from strife. If he bends his knee they will not see what is still in his heart and war can be resumed once the people have regained their strength and the nobles new heart. He must not think the worst if former friends weaken." Blair answered, "I will give him your message, my lord," but shaking his head he added, "I fear he will turn away from compromise."

When John Blair made his weary way back to Borthwick, Wallace was preparing to leave for the country around Stirling. That castle had not fallen to the English and Wallace was sure Edward would attack it with full force in spring. He received Lamberton's message in silence, saw his friend's expectant face and said, "You know my feelings, John. I have not altered."

Blair promised to stay with Agnes at Borthwick until the lambing when he would escort her to her holding by Glasgow. The woman was distressed by Wallace's departure, but he was adamant that she could not go with him. Wallace met up with Fraser and together they rode to Stirling and began harrying English patrols. It was good to be back striking at the enemy again. In February news came that all men of importance had finally signed Edward's surrender terms and all over Scotland lesser men also paid homage to the English king.

E dward spent the winter sheltering beneath the sacred roof of Dunfermline Abbey, but in March he withdrew and carried out yet another act of ungodly barbarity which was confirmed by Wallace, when he saw the column of black smoke rising from the direction of the abbey. Edward showed his scorn for Scotland and her people. Dunfermline Abbey would not give sanctuary to any other. After the sacrilege at Dunfermline, Wallace's friends lost all hope that he would seek Edward's peace, for Margaret Wallace had been buried in the abbey grounds.

Edward sat watching the flames for a while, then turned his back on the hissing, spitting inferno and with his nobles behind him rode to Stirling Castle which had been under siege for a long time. He would supervise its fall himself. That was yet another piece of unfinished work which he must complete. He would have the head of the outlaw William Wallace within the year and there were now many who would willingly assist him. "Sir John," he directed his words to Seagrove, "deliver Wallace to me. How you do it is your affair, but get him."

John Seagrove made good use of Archbishop Beck's network of spies and paid informers. During the past six months the number of men in his pay had grown. They were men anxious to ingratiate themselves with the English king and his commanders. The farms and manors that had once offered shelter and comfort to Wallace turned their backs on him and often he was forced to sleep wherever he could find shelter from the wind and rain. Caves, bothies and crude shelters constructed from branches and moss became his home for the night. He never stayed long in any place for the English and their spies were everywhere.

On a cold and blustery day, when heavy grey clouds threatened rain, Wallace and Fraser met south-east of Peebles. They sat together talking on a hillside where Wallace often watched the beautiful countryside spread out before him. Fraser was glum and in sombre mood. "Come, Simon, how can we give up now when Stirling still stands defiant? Let's go north again to harass them." "I tell you it's impossible man. I'll not fear to die for a just cause but to throw everything away when we cannot win is a fool's errand." Wallace flashed an angry look at Fraser but before he could make a hasty reply the sounds of hooves and shouts were heard. A man came uphill towards them and even at that distance they could see his horse was breathing heavily and was bathed in sweat. He drew near and Wallace recognized him as one of Bishop Lamberton's men.

"Sir William, make haste. The English are behind me and they know of your meeting place." Wallace and Fraser, anger forgotten in the urgency of their plight, ran to their horses. Everywhere was noise and confusion. They rode from the camp as the first whirr of arrows and shouts announced the arrival of a large company of English men-at-arms. Two or three men who had refused to abandon their possessions fell.

The Scots sped south and the English followed. Although they did not gain ground, Wallace could not lose them. In a desperate attempt to shake off the enemy he turned west, then north following a deep gorge through which the river, swollen with the winter rain, was rushing and drowning the noise of the fleeing and pursuing men. Another river joined the flood and the frothing white foam splashed its way over the slippery boulders. Ahead he could see the ford where they could cross in safety and ride westward. It would be easier to spread out then. He urged the men and horses on, pausing only to send an arrow towards the leading Englishman. It hit the man's horse sending the rider sprawling. The confusion among the English, as they stumbled over the wounded animal, caused only momentary delay.

218

Most however circled round the fallen horse and rider and continued the chase.

The Scots galloped out of the gorge turning west, but there Sir Robert Clifford and more English men-at-arms were waiting in ambush. They let loose a flight of arrows but only a few found their mark and they did not check the Scots' flight. Clifford emerged from cover to join in the pursuit. They drew close to Happrew, country Wallace knew well, but sheltering among the trees was Sir John Seagrove who fell upon the fleeing Scots.

With the English on all sides Wallace, Fraser and all their company urged on their tired mounts, but the English were gaining ground. They must fight. "God be with us," Wallace roared. With his sword held high, the dragon's red eyes winking wickedly and clearly seen above his fist, he brought the weapon down with full force on the helmeted head of an English knight.

Outnumbered some of his oldest friends fell in the encounter. John Wallace's horse fell from under him with blood gushing from a deep wound in the animal's neck. Wallace saw his brother throw himself clear as the beast fell, legs thrashing in its agony of death. Fraser yelled to Wallace, "Pull back man." Wallace took in the scene around him: Fraser was right. "Pull back!" he yelled.

Each man looked for an opening to withdraw, but many, particularly those in the centre, could do nothing but fight until the bitter end. John Wallace fought on foot, hacking at the legs of men and beasts. His brother caught the bridle of a riderless horse yelling to him, "Come John," then with a final desperate glance at the scene he galloped away. John Wallace, Curly, Robert Boyd and a few other hardy men followed. Seagrove and a dozen of his knights gave chase, but the day was drawing in and they were forced to halt. Sir Robert Clifford was eager to camp and continue the hunt in the morning, but Seagrove said that in such a remote place they would be ambushed. "There'll be time to track down Wallace and there are plenty who'll aid us," remarked Seagrove, nodding in the direction of the two Scots, Short and Musselburgh, who had assisted them on this occasion. When Short had been ordered to help in the ambush of Wallace, he had taken to the idea with relish, remembering his father's death at the hands of Wallace's father.

A few days after the ambush Short and Musselburgh bowed low before the English king at St Andrews. They received their reward from his own hand and Short rode home, the reward for his treachery hidden within his jerkin with the promise of more if he assisted in capturing Wallace. Short was in such good humour that for a few days he left his wife and young children in peace.

After the encounter at Happrew, Simon Fraser and William Wallace gathered those who still held firm to the cause and by stealth, travelling only at night, they rode northwards towards Stirling.

A warm breeze from the south-west brought a mild spring. The English were so strong and confident that they billeted troops in all villages and farms, and that made attacks by Wallace and Fraser impossible. The frustration and isolation of his situation began to irritate Simon Fraser. He could see no future for Scotland's cause unless there were some dramatic changes. Wallace remained adamant, particularly since the burning of Dunfermline Abbey, that he would not surrender. "Then let's go abroad, Will. Edward cannot last forever. He is already old. They say he is a sick man and his son cares more for bed and buggery than the battlefield. We've only to wait." But Wallace replied, "Then I prefer to wait here in my own land until the time is right."

In May came news which John Blair had been dreading. Bishop Lamberton had asked for and been granted Edward's peace. He spent sometime considering how he could tell Wallace and went to John Wallace to seek his advice. "He already knows," was the blunt reply. "But have you heard anything of Will's situation? Did Lamberton speak for my brother?" "Aye, he did that, but Edward would not hear of granting either full pardon or banishment to William and he has offered three hundred marks for his capture." John Wallace sat down with a look of despair on his face. "Now everyone will be against him and he will find shelter hard to find. The worst of it is that Will is right. If the embers of a fire are not kept alive, they would be difficult to rekindle with new wood." For a while neither man spoke before Blair said, "Let's await events. Stirling must fall soon. Perhaps then we can persuade Will to go abroad."

Stirling Castle was indeed in dire straits. Each morning Edward rode around the walls looking for weak points. He had in position no less than thirteen siege engines and other machines to pound walls and defenders alike. The noise from crashing masonry and screams of crushed men left the citizens of Stirling terrified – but each time the English launched a new attack, boiling oil and pitch poured down on their heads. By the middle of the summer both defenders and attackers found conditions desperate. Edward sent messengers to Berwick, demanding that all stores be sent in haste to Stirling for there was not even meal for the horses, but towards the end of July Stirling's defenders surrendered. Edward sat seething in his pavilion. At last the final obstacle was overcome and Scotland was his. He should have felt elated after so many years of warfare, but the sense of power which normally came upon him was lacking.

His newest machine of war, 'Warwolf', was at last ready for action although he had had many problems with it. Now that the garrison had surrendered, it would not be used. He had been looking forward to seeing it work. "By God no, they shall not escape," and he called Seagrove, ordering him to bombard the castle with Warwolf. "Let's see how it handles, Seagrove. When you're finished, then they can come out. Not before." Sir William Oliphant, constable of Stirling Castle, sheltered from the flying masonry. He was tired of waiting for his ordeal to come to an end.

When Wallace heard of the surrender of Stirling, he remained silent, for it had been expected. Apart from his brother, John Blair, Curly and twenty men loyal to him he was quite alone. After the news of Bishop Lamberton's surrender, Simon Fraser and his followers had left to seek the Edward's peace.

During the long summer days, they moved around the country, mostly in the wild hills north of Glasgow. They never stayed in one place longer than a night or two, sleeping in the open in the lee of rocks: always alert, never resting – not even with loyal friends for the English, always close at hand, dealt harshly with any who gave them aid. Once or twice during the short night he slipped down to see Agnes, but by first light he would be gone taking with him what provisions he could carry.

In September they came down from the hills looking for a way south, but the roads and tracks were well patrolled by the English. Near Earnside they were ambushed by Aymer Valance with three hundred archers. They could not withdraw for their retreat was also barred. He was not anxious for another battle with so many and would outrun them if he could only turn eastwards.

The chase was hard as the English had better-fed horses and Valance was not a man who gave up easily. For three days they followed Wallace, never allowing him to rest or stop for food. Horses and men were tired to the bone. Between him and the wild hills and forests of Selkirk lay the Forth, wider and more unfriendly the further east he was forced to ride. Valance was confident that Wallace would have to stand and fight: if not today then tomorrow. For he would have nowhere else to run.

On a dark and moonless night Wallace chose to break out from the trap which the English were trying to spring. There were many sheltered bays along the north side of the Forth and, with help of local fishermen, he slipped away leaving everything except weapons and a little food.

His horse left on the shore whined gently and its bridle rattled as it shook its head. He had given the animal a final pat and it had put its soft muzzle into its master's hand. He had grown fond of the beast during the past three years. Some Englishman would no doubt find him. Wallace hoped he would be a kind master for the animal had served him well.

Without the moon to light their way they tried to steer a course due south. As the grey dawn broke they found that they had drifted eastwards and the southern coast line of the Forth could barely be distinguished. About a league on the port side lay the Isle of May, the priory buildings hazy in the early morning light. Their oars dipped into the green rolling waves and the wake from their bows was creamy white as they sped forwards to the isle with the sanctuary of its church, now showing clearly on the horizon.

The English prior, outraged by Wallace's intrusion, indignantly demanded he should leave immediately. Wallace cold and exhausted by his wanderings impatiently dismissed his demands, but the prior continued to insist loudly that Wallace and his men should depart. Then in quieter tones he said, "The war is ended. Why do you continue? Seek the king's peace while you may." "Nay, John, keep him from me for I cannot keep my peace with such a man," Wallace said turning to his brother.

Gales blew in from the east and boats could neither land nor depart. They sheltered within the thick stone walls and dozed in front of the sweet-smelling peat fire burning in the hearth. Outside the wind whistled around the walls.

Wallace sat in the abbot's finely carved chair with legs stretched before him and allowed the warmth from the fire to creep through the soles of his boots. He closed his eyes and, drifting gently into a light sleep, he dreamt that he was again in France. It was a fine summer's day and the air was heavy with the smell of lavender. By the banks of a river stood a woman with her back towards him, but he knew her even before she turned to smile at him. Her corn-coloured hair hung loosely around her shoulders as it had before she became his wife, and she wore the blue linen kirtle made for their wedding. She held out a hand to him and he began to run towards her, yet no matter how fast he ran, she never seemed to get nearer. Marion ...

He jerked into wakefulness. His brother sat on a bench close by with his back resting against a buttress. His face was flushed from the warmth of the fire and the ale he was drinking. "Here, Will, have a drink, it'll ease your dreams." He offered the flagon and Wallace drank deeply.

"Will, isn't it time you thought of your own future? Where can we go to? The English hold Scotland and the people are weak from famine and sickness. They have no more to give, Will. There's no dishonour in seeking sanctuary abroad until they tire of the English king's peace."

Wallace sat quietly with eyes closed and head resting on the back of the chair. His brother had tried on other occasions to persuade him to seek refuge. "Have you forgotten our father, John? He died because he refused to submit to the English." "Aye, but then there was still hope. Our nobles and people held similar views. We are alone, Will. There's none left who will follow the cause." William replied, "Because the situation has changed, it doesn't mean that the cause is wrong. In time those who submit because they can see no future for themselves will return to the old loyalties."

In his heart John Wallace knew that his brother was right: that was what was so frustrating. William shamed others, but he persevered with his argument, "Why not take the easy route yourself until others rise. Let's go abroad now while we have the chance. We can sail for Norway. Better face the sea than be hounded like outlaws throughout Scotland."

"Nay, I will not let them forget, John. The English will not sleep easily while I can hold my sword. Even the Holy Father listens to the clamour from the English and Phillip of France has other problems on his mind. Robert the Bruce marches with the English. Do you think his sister in Norway will greet us with smiles a second time? The longer we are at large, the more likely it is others will remember their duty."

As John Wallace had a look of despair on his face, his brother said, "Come, John, you and I have sprung from the same root. Surely I need not explain myself to you. I grew here and this is where I hope to die." John made no reply. The only sounds came from the wind in the rafters and a gentle hiss as a flame found damp peat in the hearth. Then William said, "John, it worries me that we don't have a leader whom all will obey when the time comes for us to challenge the English. This is our weakness."

"There are none who have not accepted gifts and promises from Edward." William said, "Because the English offer more than leading Scotland to victory. To challenge the English the victor must be sure of gaining the ultimate prize." John Wallace looked enquiringly at his brother. "The throne, John. We must have a king who will challenge Longshanks, who will risk losing not only his estates in England, but his kingdom of Scotland." "You have always stood firmly by King John, Will. Do you mean another should be crowned even though King John is still alive?" "Aye, there is no alternative and it must be one who is not of his ilk, but of equal claim."

John Wallace said, "Then the only man who can lay claim to the throne is Robert the Bruce, Earl of Carrick, but his father-in-law is one of Longshanks strongest and most loyal earls and Bruce rides with them. How can he be trusted?" "I've told you John, that the prize must be the throne of Scotland."

They sat in silence for a while before William Wallace continued, "I've done all I can, but I failed at Falkirk, Paris and Rome. As soon as possible I will find a way to contact Bruce and offer him my support if he will come forward to claim the crown." "It's a mad scheme, Will. Bruce has never shown himself loyal to Scotland. He'll turn you over to the English." But Wallace said, "We'll see," then closed his eyes leaving his brother to think about their conversation. Shortly afterwards he heard from his brother's breathing that he had drifted into sleep. John got up, stretched and left the warmth of the room. It would be dark in an hour or so. He would check the lookouts and scan the horizon before nightfall.

W allace stood watching the roofless shell that had been the manor of Lamington. He was sheltered from the rain and wind at the forest edge. He had arrived well before the appointed time, hidden and vigilant. Curly and John Wallace had searched the surrounding land for men-at-arms laying in ambush, but they reported that the earl had come to the meeting with only his closest friends, among them Sir Malcolm Wallace and Robert Boyd.

Wallace left the cover of the trees. He rode his shaggy fell pony across the meadow where he and Marion – with their people – had sat to rest and eat their midday meal during harvest time so long ago. He paused near the oak, naked in its winter sleep. Well, if they took him here and now by this blessed spot of sweet memories he would be content. He spurred on his mount towards the meeting place.

It had been over four years since Wallace had met with Robert the Bruce, Earl of Carrick. Good fortune had blessed the earl. He was warmly and richly clad. The favoured follower of his lord, the king of England, and cherished husband as well as respected son-in-law to the

Earl of Ulster. It surprised him that he had agreed to meet with William Wallace. Bishop Lamberton and Malcolm Wallace had begged him to do so and for old times sake he had agreed.

Wallace had lost none of his imposing looks and vigour, but his appearance was neglected. His hair and beard were matted while his face was gaunt and drawn. His clothes were caked in mud, threadbare and worn. Since leaving the Isle of May nearly six weeks before, Wallace had not slept in one place more than once and never within four walls.

Malcolm Wallace stepped forward embracing his brothers. A fire had been lit in the only roofed building, the old byre, where once Marion had kept her milking cows. Coming in from the cold, damp drizzle into the warmth was welcoming and when the courtesies were over Wallace sat down heavily on a log placed close to the blaze.

Neither Wallace nor Bruce spoke. There was an awkward silence before Malcolm Wallace began the conversation, "My lord, my brother asked for this meeting because of the love which he has for this kingdom and the respect he has for yourself." Bruce smiled. He doubted whether Wallace respected him, but he would let it pass. Sir Malcolm was about to continue but William Wallace intervened, "Sir, you know I have fought for freedom from English rule for the past eight years. Yet still they are the masters and we call their king our lord. I pledged my sword to King John and never have I sworn allegiance to Longshanks. I have failed in my pledge but I do not believe this is the end of the matter. Where I and those who supported me have failed another can succeed. I believe that man is you."

Bruce looked startled. It was rare to come across such plain speaking, particularly now when all men looked both ways. Wallace continued, "King John will not return and his son will never challenge the English king. You must take the throne." For a few moments Bruce said nothing, then he answered, "You know that I have sworn fealty to Edward and yet you think I should take the throne of Scotland?" "You will succeed because you will have too much to lose. Edward Longshanks grows old and his son is not the man his father is. It is your own lords that you will have to bend to your will." Then Bruce laughed: this man sitting before him made it sound so simple.

Wallace ignored Bruce's reaction and continued, "I failed because after Stirling Bridge I tried to lead Scotland towards freedom. Without right of birth the nobles were jealous of my position and Edward claimed loyalty from them through land and possessions. I failed in France and Rome for the same reason. They all look to their own interests." "And what of our anointed King John, Wallace? What of him for he still lives?" "He is a pleasant man, but he cares only for his French estates and a comfortable bed. He will never lead this kingdom or challenge you." All sat quietly, each absorbed with their thoughts. The flames cast a dancing red glow around the stone walls. Boyd broke the silence, "You are right, Will. The crown must be placed on a strong head and only then can the English be forced back across the border."

Once again Bruce laughed, "You think I am that man and that the mighty Lord Comyn will let me take all from under his nose? Tell me Wallace, why don't you go to Comyn? Has he not fought bravely and consistently for Scotland's freedom?" "There you have me, Sir. You are both good fighting men, born to lead, but the Lord Comyn gave me his support at Falkirk and then whether through design or deceit left the people on the field of battle to the mercy of the English. I cannot forget his fecklessness and I doubt whether the people have. There will be those nobles who you must force to your will, but many will be relieved when you give them a firm lead," said Wallace.

He stood up, "I must be away for the English seek me constantly. Consider, my lord, what alternatives there are and if you wish to speak with me again let my brother know."

He nodded to Malcolm Wallace and Robert Boyd, collected his shaggy little mount and rode without a backward glance towards the forest. Just before he reached the cover of the trees he heard a shout and turned. Malcolm Wallace rode towards him. When they drew abreast Malcolm said, "Where are you going, Will?" "Best you don't know, Malcolm, but anyone in the forest will get a message to me." Malcolm Wallace flashed in anger, "You're an arrogant fool. You never would ask for help, not even now when your need is great. Yet help you should accept. If you can get to the spit north of Ayr where once we fished as boys, I will have a boat waiting to take you to Arran. Uncle Richard has been sheltering there for the past year." "Nay Malcolm, the coast will be watched and how do I know that Bruce will not have me picked up?" "You don't," came the sharp reply. It was the first time Malcolm Wallace had heard doubt in William's voice and he felt guilty.

Seven nights later a small boat slipped quietly away from the mainland and made landfall at Drumadoon Bay on the west of the isle of Arran. The boatman was the Earl of Carrick's trusted man. The earl knew exactly where Wallace hid during the months of winter and early spring and it was he who ordered food to be taken to him. Time hung heavily on Wallace's hands. Curly and John his brother remained with him, but they had little to do. Malcolm Wallace came once to see him, bearing gifts from Bruce and messages of goodwill from Bishop Lamberton.

Wallace had thought often about his daughter Margaret. She was eight winters now and was growing up without knowledge of her own kin or her inheritance and this worried her father. True, she was settled with her foster-parents and young Tom Shaw would make a fine husband, but the child needed to know her own family.

The Wallace brothers sat together, drinking Burgundy wine, a gift from Lamberton, and William brought up the topic of his daughter's future. "Malcolm, she needs to know her kin. For her safety I cannot go to her, but you may. Tell Sir John that my mind is still set on a union between Margaret and his son, but I should like her to visit her own family for a while. Besides Tom Shaw is now a youth. He can claim Margaret when she is fit for marriage. Her mother would have wanted her to have a carefree childhood, away from her intended husband." He drew from his pouch some gold coins, a gift from Lamberton, and gave them to his brother. "See that she wants for nothing. Use what is left to put Lamington into some order for the manor is hers and, God willing, her son will inherit the place."

Lady Shaw cried when Malcolm Wallace came to take his niece to visit her kin. She would miss the child. She wiped tears from her face with the hem of her coif as she waved farewell. The little girl sat in front of her uncle, chatting happily to the large and handsome man. Tom Shaw stood glumly by his mother's side for Margaret had been part of his life for as long as he could remember.

During Easter of 1305 Sir Malcolm Wallace, accompanied by his lady, family and followers visited the head of the Wallace kindred in Arran. Sir Richard greeted them with dignity. He was an old man now and had been ailing for some time.

After Bishop Lamberton had accepted the English king's peace, the abbot of Dunfermline had commanded John Blair to return to his religious house. He had been unwilling to leave Wallace, but his vows of obedience had to be observed. In February he was told that Robert the Bruce had requested that he should be attached to his household and when Malcolm Wallace travelled to Arran, John Blair went with him.

There were showers on Easter Sunday. The air was fresh and sweet. Wallace walked slowly to his uncle's house, enjoying the warm spring sunshine. He was excited that he would be seeing old friends and kinsfolk. He had recovered some of his former composure. His clothes were simple but clean and tidy and he did not have the neglected appearance of last autumn.

He could hardly bring himself to allow his daughter to leave his side so winsome were her ways. When he took the Easter sacrament from John Blair, a lump came into his throat as he remembered how loyal this gentle man had been to him. He got to know his young nephews whom he had not seen since their infancy and spent the afternoon at the butts teaching them archery, while Margaret sat among the women and girls watching her father, uncles and cousins.

Jack Short kept his eyes and ears open but his customers around the harbour and in the market place never mentioned Wallace. Agnes was a regular visitor to his wife on market days when the two women sat and talked. Short never forced his wife to 'move her lazy bones and get on with her work' when she talked to Agnes as he did if she dared to talk to other women. When Short's mother tried to chase Agnes away, Short spoke sharply to her and said to Agnes, "Nay, lassie, just you sit and warm yourself and have a bite to eat", but as yet Agnes had not said anything worth hearing.

There had been months of silence as if William Wallace had ceased to exist but just after Easter a drunken boatman in Glasgow, on an errand for his lord, boasted of his secret journeys to Arran with supplies for one of King Edward's enemies. The name Wallace was not mentioned, but Short was sure that it was his quarry. Who else could it be?

Short sought an audience with Sir John Menteith who was known to be searching for Wallace. Menteith listened to the innkeeper, gave him some silver coins and told him to search along the coast for news. Old Sir Malcolm Wallace had often brought his sons to the Stewart castle. Menteith had followed Wallace to Stirling and his nephew, Sir John Stewart, had fallen at Falkirk fighting with Wallace. It was even rumoured that William Wallace had stood as godfather to Menteith's young sons. Short knew what he was working for, but he wondered why this nobleman was betraying his own. Well, what should he care for the nobleman's motives.

Short prowled along the coast, through villages and manors, buying fleeces. This gave him a chance to talk to the people. His journey ended in Ayr where his wife's family lived.

A year earlier his father-in-law had borrowed money from Short and as yet it had not been repaid. When Jack appeared with his packhorse his father-in-law was alarmed, but Jack greeted him politely enough and made no mention of the loan. That evening Short sat with the old man and as they supped together, he brought up the subject of Wallace. But he had underestimated his father-in-law. The old man had fought at Dunbar and it was only a wound which had left him with a heavy limp that had prevented him following Wallace to Stirling and Falkirk. He had never betrayed a man and he did not intend to do so now. "Listen, old fool, you owe me money. I'll claim payment now and have you and yours thrown out if you don't see sense."

The outcome of his visit and threats was that his father-in-law, who had heard that Wallace sheltered on Arran, would seek out news for Short. Satisfied Short returned to Glasgow. Assiduously he continued to cultivate Agnes and a number of small boys who hung around the market and harbour.

The sunny primrose days of spring stirred Wallace into impatient anticipation and on a clear morning, when the sun sparkled on the sea, he stood confidently at the helm of a fishing boat. The brisk westerly wind swept her forward and foaming spray flew from the bow. The flight of the boat, the wind tugging at the rigging and sea birds wheeling in their wake exhilarated him. The fisherman was preparing nets to cast for the silver herring. They would arrive at Ayr with a full catch. As they drew nearer to the coast, the vessel put about and the net was thrown as they turned and trawled. The flashing herring shoal made the green waves bubble with excitement

Later that morning the boat landed its catch and the four men who stepped ashore smelt of the sea, salt was in their beards and their faces were red from the sun and wind. They sat for a while, gutting the fat fish, laughing and talking to girls who came down to greet them, but as people gathered to buy the fish three of the men faded quietly away, leaving fisherman and lasses to finish the work. None remarked on their disappearance.

Late in the afternoon Jack Short's young sister-in-law gave her father fine fat herrings for his meal. She had seen the tall stranger and as he left she noted the bundle taken from the boat. She was sure there was a claymore in it. She did not like Short, but knew of his threat and so she told her father about the strangers. "Aye, one was tall, strong and bonnie," she answered. The following day the news was sent to Short.

The Wallace brothers and Curly travelled secretly to the manor of their cousin Auchinleck, where they were greeted with such jubilation that Wallace was embarrassed. Auchinleck's lady would not hear of Wallace sleeping in the hay barn like a common man. He must sleep in the master's bed. The whole household made much fuss of their visitors. The tables were moved so all the household might sit and eat together to honour the master's noble cousin. Ale was passed around until many could not move from their seats and slept where they sat. Some fell onto the floor snoring among the rushes and scavenging dogs, but in the early morning before many were awake Wallace rose and bidding his hosts farewell continued eastwards into the safety of the forest.

Short heard of Wallace's visit to Auchinleck and his retreat into the forest and he passed his information to the Earl of Menteith.

Wallace stayed sheltering in the forest. He could not return to Borthwick as it had been raised to the ground by the English. It was in the forest that the Earl of Carrick met him again. This time they drank together. They talked of Wallace's campaign after Stirling and his administration of the kingdom. Then inevitably they came to the topic of Falkirk. Falkirk had rarely been from Wallace's mind during the past seven years. If only he had continued to withdraw and had not fought a pitched battle, but he had a large army, trained and eager to fight, and the nobles were always in the shadows criticising. He had had few choices.

Bruce listened quietly before asking Wallace many questions about his methods of training and positioning of the schiltrons. Then he said, "You're right. To challenge the English successfully I must first be made rightful king. Only a king can challenge a king, but I will have to come to terms with Comyn. Without the backing of church and nobles I cannot succeed. I'll need men I can trust and you are such a man." Wallace said, "If you lead the way, I'll cover your rear." Bruce smiled. "They told me that you would say that, but I know Edward. He'll not rest until he has your head on a spike. He'll offer you no mercy and I need you alive" "The angel of death has been my constant companion for many years," replied Wallace. Bruce ignored Wallace's flippancy. "You are valuable to me and I want you to seek sanctuary until the time is right."

Wallace frowned but, before he could make his reply, Bruce said, "Be reasonable man, Scotland needs men like you. Your family and friends worry about you. It's Bishop Lamberton's desire that you should seek shelter. If you will not go at my bidding, then go at his. My sister, who you have met, lives in Bergen. I will send her letters. Take these for me and stay there until I send for you." Wallace raised some excuses as was his way, but then said, "let me think and talk it over with my brother John before I give you my decision."

To leave Scotland for a second time was a hard decision for a proud man to make, but eventually he saw the sense of the argument. John Wallace said that he would join Malcolm in Bruce's following, but Curly wanted to follow his lord to Bergen. Wallace remained in hiding throughout the early summer, but in July two men slipped through a side door in the wall which surrounded the bishop's manor at Stobo.

Lamberton was pleased to see his friend for that was how he thought of William Wallace. They talked for so long that a new day was beginning before they went to their beds. Wallace waited for three days before Bruce's letters arrived then left for Glasgow. A vessel would be ready for him on the fourth day of the new month.

The bishop's servants had all been in his household for many years and were trusted men, but his cook had a small weakness, Annie. Annie was his only child left motherless as a small maid. Although he had done his very best for her lavishing her with every kind of luxury, she had such airs and graces and was wilful, particularly over the business of the English sergeant. Now there had to be a marriage and it was lucky for her that the sergeant had agreed. The cook did not intend to betray either his master or Wallace, but he told his daughter in passing that Wallace had been at the manor and she told her sergeant.

Menteith heard that Wallace had been at Stobo and told Short to keep a careful watch. Short collected his gang of urchins and told them that he would give a penny to the boy who brought him news of the outlaw. He held the money out for all to see. One or two had had fathers or elder brothers who had not returned after Falkirk and they had heard of Wallace, but most neither knew nor cared. Some ran among the fishing vessels where men sat mending nets and chatting. A quick boy could learn a lot from them.

Wallace had been thinking about Agnes for some months. He had tried to do his best for her. The little farm was a pleasant enough property. God knew that he loved the woman in his own way and she cared for him. Her faithfulness to him could not have made her life easy. As he journeyed secretly towards his rendezvous on the Clyde he made up his mind. He would ask her to come to Norway with him. They would marry. None there would know of her past and when they returned to Scotland it would not matter what others thought. There was a time when marriage to Agnes would have been unthinkable, but his wanderings had taught him to value constancy above everything else.

During the past eighteen months Agnes had often lapsed into despair wondering where he was? What was he doing? Often she told herself how foolish she was to wait for a man who cast her off so often and had time only for his cause. True, he was always kind to her and had provided for her, but time was slipping away. She was no longer young. Agnes had discussed her predicament with her friend the innkeeper's wife and it caused her such anguish to see the small children growing around the young woman while she was barren. Then William and Curly arrived and all her anger was forgotten.

It was the busy season on the farm. Agnes had a fine store full of ripening cheeses and a vat of brewing ale, but nothing would please her more than to offer her beloved some good red wine. She had risen early but Wallace was still asleep, for he had taken turns with Curly to keep watch at night. Agnes placed some freshly made crowdie cheese into a clean crock and told her boy to take it to the inn in Glasgow and beg for friendship's sake that they should give her red wine. The boy did as he was told with as much speed as he could muster. It was going to be a hot day and he did not want the crowdie to turn.

Wallace got up and went in search of Agnes. He found her working in the dairy. Her back was turned towards him and she sang to herself as she strained the whey from a basin of curds. When he came into the room she turned smiling as he put his arms around her and gently kissed her forehead. It was so different from the hungry caresses of the previous night. He took a handful of curds and began eating and then said, "Sweetheart, I shall be leaving tomorrow night for Norway." She lowered her head not wanting him to see her despair, but he lifted her face so that he could see clearly her reaction. "Come with me, Agnes, and when all is settled we will marry."

Agnes looked stunned. For years in her daydreams she had heard him say this to her. Now that in reality he had, she could not think of anything to say. "Come on lass, what do you say?" But all she could say was, "Oh Will," and throw her arms around his neck. William Wallace grinned.

Agnes spent the evening despondently looking through her few clothes. She had washed her spare shift and Wallace's surcoat and when she had finished repairing small tears she went out to shut up her geese. The fox had taken one the previous week. It was a beautiful evening, starlit and heavy with the scent of honeysuckle. Wallace and Curly were out checking around the farm that all was well. Curly said he would take the first watch.

When all was quiet and the night was at its darkest Short accompanied by Menteith and his men arrived. Wallace awoke as the door was thrown open. He was out of bed, sword in hand before the first man was across the threshold. Agnes awoke and screamed, and outside a voice he knew called out, "Come out Wallace. It's Menteith. Come out man. There's no escape for you. You will be tried here in Scotland. You have my word on this. You will save suffering to those here." "My woman, Menteith, will you spare her?" "Aye man, it's you we have come for." Crying Agnes clung to him but Menteith's men blocked the doorway. Menteith was right. There was no escape while he remained here.

They bound Wallace hand and foot to his horse and as they led him away he looked back at the burning farm. In the light from the flames he could see the bodies of Curly, Agnes and her people lying where they had been murdered after his surrender. This was Menteith's word of honour.

He tried to compose his thoughts as they rode through the darkness. His body was aching from the kicks and punches which he had received. He was now sure that Menteith's promise of a trial in Scotland was as false as his other promises.

The following day they handed him over to Sir John Seagrove and Wallace knew for sure that his life would soon be at its end. Menteith could not bring himself to look into Wallace's face as he handed him into the charge of the English. Quickly he turned his horse and rode away. Wallace's broadsword, which was a gift from his great uncle William Wallace, was strapped to Menteith's back. The red eye of the dragon winked evilly in the morning sun. "Damn you, Menteith, you traitor," Wallace yelled. "A curse on you and your kindred." The English sergeant jerked the reins of the horse and Wallace began his final journey south.

# In
# Paradisum

The court sat silent. All eyes were on the prisoner. He stood on a raised platform unkempt and dirty, a wreath of laurels on his head and his hands and feet chained. A guard stood on either side and the five commissioners were seated before him.

It had taken three weeks to bring the prisoner, William Wallace, before the judges for his trial and now, at the king's mercy, he stood humbled.

Sir Peter Malory, Lord Chief Justice of England, read out the indictment, his voice echoing around the great Palace of Westminster:

"By opposing his liege lord in war to the death ..."

Wallace, mind and body exhausted by the journey and mistreatment, tried desperately to concentrate on his sentence. Yet he knew there would be no mercy. He was near to his end and he hoped death would be allowed to come to him quickly as a friend.

"... and that for the robberies, homicides, and felonies he committed in the realm of England and in the Land of Scotland he be hanged and afterwards taken down from the gallows ...

"... and that, inasmuch as he was an outlaw, and was not afterwards restored to the peace of the lord king, he be decollated and decapitated ...

"... and that thereafter for the measureless turpitude of his deeds towards God and Holy Church in burning down churches, his heart, liver, lungs and all the internal organs of his body be cast into a fire and burned ...

Still the prisoner made no response or acknowledged that he had heard.

"... as a warning and determent to all that pass and behold."

So butchery was to be his end. His thoughts wandered away as Malory read the final clauses. Edward's justice would not grant him the honour of grave or memorial. The parts of his body were to be displayed in cities of England and Scotland until his flesh rotted, his bones picked clean by crows and whitened by sun and wind.

"... Sentence to be carried out immediately," said Malory.

The guards moved taking him roughly. His manacled hands and feet restricted his movements. As he was led from the hall into the bright August sunshine, a mighty roar arose from the throats of the waiting crowd, all in holiday mood.

In front of the people they stripped Wallace naked for all to view his manly grace. The signs of his mistreatment on his journey south showed on his white skin. They threw his clothes to the crowd who fought over them tearing them into pieces in their eagerness to own William Wallace's jerkin. His wide embossed leather belt from which his battle axe had once swung was offered to Sir John Seagrove, but he would not touch it and nodded to his squire who grabbed the belt. Cleaned up it would look as new and would raise a good sum. The sergeant took the prisoner's boots, but they were well worn with holes in the soles and so he threw them to the howling crowd.

Some of the women standing nearby sniggered when they saw Wallace's nakedness. "My, look at him. You'd know all about it with him inside ye," said one well-known prostitute of the city. "What a pity to cut that off".

She pulled her shift apart exposing her ample breasts and danced provocatively around, breasts bouncing, hoping the condemned man seeing her would humiliate himself, but the crowd was disappointed. Wallace stood impassive staring ahead facing the English as he always had with dignity and courage.

His silence irritated the crowd and some threw rubbish at him, but Wallace had only spoken once even in the courtroom. They had accused him of high treason to the English king and he had sternly and strongly denied it and his voice had vibrated passionately so that all could hear.

"Never was I, a Scot, traitor. The English king has never been my sworn liege lord." One of the guards had struck him and he was not permitted to say more in his own defence.

They bound him head pointing downwards to a hurdle. A pathway had been cleared through the crowd, men-at-arms standing on either side. Again the crowd roared as the horse began its journey through the streets of London to the gallows. Ahead of the doomed man rode his judges, behind him men-at-arms. Rubbish and filth of all kinds was thrown at the prisoner while groups of boys ran alongside the execution party beating him with sticks, laughing and calling out obscenities. Dogs, frightened by the noise, barked and nipped him as the hurdle bounced along on the dusty, dirty road.

Above the overhanging roofs he caught a glimpse of blue sky, so soft and welcoming. The same sky smiled on the hills of his homeland. Soon, if it was His pleasure, he would be there in Paradise. He licked his lips, thirsty from the dust stirred by the people's feet and closed his eyes trying to concentrate his thoughts on gentler memories. There had been other crowds, cheering, applauding, welcoming him, the people's hero to Dundee. The sun had been shining then, glinting on distant white hills.

It was a cold winter's day. The wind from the north had promised snow. His horse had tossed its head and mane at the joyful crowd which had hailed him on his return from England. Once again his mind wandered to the time when, as a youth, he had stood in the crowds watching the cavalcade of Scottish and English nobles ride out to meet the little Maid from Norway. How different his life would have been if she had arrived safely.

The howling crowd aroused him – they had arrived. Oh, merciful God, do not take my strength from me now.

They untied their victim forcing him to climb on stiff legs up to the scaffold where the executioners were waiting. The expectant crowd roared – WALLACE – WALLACE – TRAITOR – TRAITOR. His ears throbbed from the noise around him.

At the bottom of the steps to the gallows he had asked Clifford for a priest to hear his confession, but Clifford had said, "For your crimes, such a request is not permitted." "Let me at least see my Psalter, while yet I may," he said. Seagrove came forward holding Wallace's Psalter and said to Clifford, "Get a priest to hold this before him."

When Wallace reached the execution platform he was dizzy with the exertion. The executioners took hold of him roughly walking him around so that the crowd could see their king's vanquished enemy. The rope was placed carefully, the knot at the side, so that death would not cheat the crowd of the thrills to come.

The priest anxious that God should see his servant in an act of mercy said, "I shall read the Pater Noster to you". Wallace thanked him and the executioners heaved on the end of the rope. William Wallace was jerked into the air, the priest holding the open Psalter, a gift from Wallace's mother, before the doomed man.

He began to recite, "*Pater Noster qui es in coellum, sancificetur ...*"

They hung him high, body jerking, eyes bulging. Consciousness began to depart, but as the roaring in his ears increased and the Psalter faded from his vision, they released him. Still living he fell to the floor. Another roar arose from the crowd. The best was yet to come.

He was placed on a butcher's slab so that they could perform the final acts of violation. The priest still stood before him, with the open Psalter, but the condemned man remained silent. Never would he beg for mercy.

Visions of Marion and others he had loved appeared to him. Smiling they held out their hands raising him upwards away from his tormentors. Thus the spirit of William Wallace, champion and Guardian of Scotland, rose to Paradise.